Champions of Change

Champions of Change

How CEOs and Their Companies Are Mastering the Skills of Radical Change

David A. Nadler

with Mark B. Nadler

Jossey-Bass Publishers • San Francisco

Jossey-Bass books and products are available through most bookstores. To contact Jossey-Bass directly, call (888) 378-2537; Fax (800) 605-2665, or visit our website at www.josseybass.com.

Substantial discounts on bulk quantities of Jossey-Bass books are available to corporations, professional associations, and other organizations. For details and discount information, contact the special sales department at Jossey-Bass.

 Manufactured in the United States of America on Lyons Falls Turin Book. This paper is acid-free and 100 percent totally chlorine-free.

Library of Congress Cataloging-in-Publication Data

Nadler, David.
    Champions of change : how CEOs and their companies are mastering
the skills of radical change / David A. Nadler with Mark B. Nadler.
        p.   cm. — (Jossey-Bass business and management series)
    Includes bibliographical references and index.
    ISBN 0-7879-0947-5
    1. Organizational change—Management.   2. Corporate
reorganizations—Management.   3. Organizational behavior.   4. Chief
executive officers—Attitudes.   I. Nadler, Mark B.   II. Title.
III. Series: Jossey-Bass business & management series.
HD58.8.N297   1997
658.4'063—dc21   97–25973

FIRST EDITION
HB Printing 10 9 8 7 6 5 4 3 2

The Jossey-Bass
Business & Management Series

Contents

Preface   xi

The Authors   xvii

1 What It Takes: Confronting the Realities of Change   1

2 Where to Start: Understanding Organizations   21

3 From Tuning to Overhaul: The Dimensions of
   Change   44

4 Reshaping the Entire Enterprise: The Special
   Challenges of Discontinuous Change   63

5 Winning Hearts and Minds: Overcoming the
   Obstacles to Change   83

6 Setting the Stage: Recognizing the Change
   Imperative   109

7 Waging the Great Campaign: Developing a Shared
   Direction   131

8 Building a New Strategy: The Strategic Choice
   Process   151

9 Redesigning the Organizational "Hardware":
   The Keys to Strategic Design   173

10 When Worlds Collide: Aligning Strategy and
   Culture   197

11 Finding the Right People: A Guide to Strategic
   Selection   229

12 Staying the Course: Consolidating and Sustaining
   Change   249

13 Leading the Charge: The Unique Role of Senior
   Management   268

14   Learning to Lead Change: The New Principles
     for CEOs and Companies   289

     References   311
     Index   315

Preface

Several years ago I found myself consulting with the top managers at two companies. Both had asked me to help them manage their way through massive change. Their corporate headquarters were located about twenty minutes away from each other, and I've lost track of how many times I drove back and forth between the two. What I do remember is this: as time went on, that drive became more and more troublesome for me. I would leave one company feeling exhilarated; as I approached the other, I'd be overcome by a sense of dread. At one company, change was a racehorse thundering out of the gate; at the other, I was swimming through wet cement.

At first I was baffled. My approach to both assignments was similar. But the results couldn't have been more different. One company was infused with excitement: there was movement, there was momentum, things were happening. At the other—nothing. The change effort was stalled. No one believed in it or cared about it. I was reaching the conclusion that I was wasting both my time and theirs. So during those rides back and forth, I kept analyzing the two situations, trying to figure out why I seemed to be charging ahead with one company and firing blanks with the other.

And then it came to me. It was all about the two CEOs. Both were bright, capable, experienced executives. Both understood the compelling demands for change. But at one company—the one where change was succeeding—the CEO was leading the charge. Change was his top personal priority, and he seized every opportunity, both public and private, to demonstrate that nothing on his agenda was more important.

And the other CEO? He too was all for change. In fact, he supported it so much that he had turned it over to some of his most trusted subordinates. But through all the ensuing battles, the CEO himself was conspicuously absent from the front lines.

That lesson—the importance of a CEO's personal involvement in large-scale change—was one I've seen repeated over and over throughout my years of experience with dozens of organizations. What I've learned about CEOs—and more important, what I've learned from working closely *with* CEOs—helped shape the approach to change management that I've attempted to set forth in this book.

That approach is a view of change from the perspective of top leadership. It reflects a melding of research, theory, and real-life experience on the front lines of organizational change. I've drawn upon my own experiences, spanning two decades of intimate work with the top executives of leading enterprises—and at some companies relationships with successive CEOs over the course of nearly fifteen years. I've drawn upon the insights and experiences of CEOs who have personally grappled with the complexity of large-scale change. And finally, I've had the benefit of working with, and learning from, my exceptional colleagues at Delta Consulting Group, who have worked on change management at more than one hundred organizations over the past seventeen years.

Consequently, the approach to change set forth in this book is unusual in that it rests upon a practical understanding of change that is both wide and deep. It reflects the experiences of dozens of complex organizations and, more than that, the insights that can be gained only through months and years of work in close association with the ultimate decision makers.

Audience

This is a book that offers organizational leaders—CEOs, presidents, COOs, directors, and other top managers in the United States and internationally—a coherent approach that has been tested, refined, and tested yet again in the marketplace. But more than that it can provide managers at virtually any level with a whole new repertoire of concepts, ideas, tools, and techniques for understanding the dynamics of change and managing it within their own area of responsibility. As I'll show over and over, participation by top leaders is crucial—but not sufficient—to ensuring successful change. The successful leaders are those who build broad support among the managers who must convert a vision of change into a new reality. The successful managers are those who understand the vision and then move adeptly and aggressively to make it happen. Successful change starts at the top; but without active support from skilled and committed managers, it can just as easily end at the top.

The information in this book should also be of practical assistance to management consultants and both teachers and students in many areas of MBA programs and graduate-level programs in organizational development and industrial and organizational psychology.

Overview of the Contents

The material in this book falls roughly into three sections. Chapter One begins the first section with an overview of the forces that make change at once so inevitable and so difficult in modern organizations and describes the pivotal role of top leadership. In Chapter Two I present an approach our firm has been using successfully to understand how an organization works, how it needs to change, and how change in one part of the organization will affect the rest of the enterprise. Chapters Three and Four describe the four basic types of organizational change, with a special emphasis on the most difficult of all—the Overhaul, or radical discontinuous change. Chapter Five explores the inevitable resistance to change and offers some specific techniques for overcoming those barriers.

The second section, Chapters Six to Twelve, deals with the substantive tools and techniques that are required as the organization passes through the five phases of the change cycle. I describe in turn the issues that confront leaders as they go about changing each component of the organization: its strategy, its formal structures and work processes, its operating environment, and its people. In the final section, Chapters Thirteen and Fourteen, I deal specifically with the unique role of top managers in leading change, concluding with some important implications for managers throughout the organization and a general set of principles to help you guide effective change efforts.

How All This Started

The roots of this book go back to 1978, when I was a professor at Columbia University's Graduate School of Business and just beginning my research and consulting on organizational change. Two events, coming closely together, prompted me to start thinking about change in different ways.

The first concerned Citibank. I had been involved in some management development activities there, as part of Chairman and CEO Walter Wriston's efforts to transform the institution. George Vojta, then an executive vice president in charge of strategy (and later a vice chairman at Bankers Trust) was working on a new strategy for Citibank, and he asked me for my thoughts on what research in the behavioral sciences might tell him about planning and managing a major change.

After searching, I found that with the exception of Richard Beckhard and Reuben Harris's short 1977 book on transition management, there was relatively little that had been written specifically for managers of change.

At the same time I'd been contacted by a staff group at AT&T to do some research and problem solving for them. Bob Maher, a true visionary, was leading a group doing work and organizational redesign (today we'd call it reengineering) throughout the Bell System. Maher's consultants were having teams of people participate in the redesign of their own work, and the results were impressive: 15 to 20 percent gains in productivity. The problem was that few of their new designs were being implemented. So Maher asked me to look at the situation and try to figure out why.

The challenges of those two assignments resulted in my first paper on managing change and launched a journey of exploration and learning that has lasted nearly twenty years. This book conveys the observations, experiences, and insights I've accumulated during that journey.

Acknowledgments

There are a host of people I want to acknowledge for the support and contributions that made this book possible.

I begin with the clients I've worked with over the years, starting with AT&T and Citibank. Much of what I've learned has been the result of collaborative work with clients, and three companies in particular—Xerox, Corning, and AT&T (and now its spin-off, Lucent Technologies) have proven to be places where I could work with outstanding people, try new ideas, and learn. The leaders of those companies, including Jamie Houghton, Roger Ackerman, David Kearns, Paul Allaire, Robert Allen, Henry Schacht, and Richard McGinn have been wonderful supporters over the years, and they have my deepest thanks. And special thanks to Bill Buehler, who for the past eighteen years—first at AT&T and now at Xerox—has been a trusted friend and collaborator.

In addition I want to thank the other leaders who agreed to participate in this project through interviews for this book and a previous volume: Scott McNealy (Sun Microsystems), Jon Madonna (previously at KPMG Peat Marwick and now at The Travelers), Walter Shipley (Chase Manhattan), Randy Tobias (Eli Lilly), and Craig Weatherup (PepsiCo).

Though I am the author of this book, the ideas contained here reflect my participation in a remarkable community of exceptional people—namely, my colleagues, past and present, at Delta Consulting Group Inc. Each one of my Delta colleagues has contributed to this work in some form, but some of my longer-term colleagues deserve special thanks; these include Carl Hill, Terry Limpert, Chuck Raben, Jeff Heilpern, David Bliss, Kathy Morris, Rick Ketterer, Elise Walton, and Marilyn Showers. Throughout I have tried to indicate when specific consulting work was a joint effort with my colleagues.

Several other individuals merit special acknowledgment. Harry Levinson and Edward Lawler have been my mentors, contributing enormously to my own development in the field of organizational change; I will always be in their debt. This book also reflects the thinking of my good friend and colleague, Michael Tushman, Hettleman Professor at the Graduate School of Business, Columbia University. Michael and I have collaborated for more than twenty years, crossing the boundaries of practice and academia to work together and learn about organizations and change.

Finally, I want to thank my writing collaborator, my brother, Mark Nadler. Working with him has been a tremendous source of stimulation and joy. His unique combination of writing skill and business experience has enabled him to take my ideas and experiences and bring them to life on the page.

New York   DAVID A. NADLER
September 1997

The Authors

David A. Nadler is chairman of the Delta Consulting Group Inc. Since 1980 he has consulted to CEOs and other corporate leaders on organizational change, strategy, organizational architecture, and leadership. Prior to founding Delta, he served for six years on the faculty of the Graduate School of Business, Columbia University. Previous to that, he was on the staff of the Survey Research Center, Institute for Social Research, at the University of Michigan.

In addition to his consulting and leadership of Delta, David Nadler has written extensively, publishing numerous articles and authoring or editing twelve books on organizational behavior, leadership, and organizational change. He coauthored *Prophets in the Dark: How Xerox Reinvented Itself and Drove Back the Japanese* (with former Xerox CEO David Kearns, 1992) and also *Organizational Architecture* (with M. C. Gerstein, Robert B. Shaw, and Associates, 1992), *Discontinuous Change* (with R. B. Shaw, A. E. Walter, and Associates, 1995), *Competing by Design* (with Michael L. Tushman, 1997), and *Executive Teams* (with Janet Spencer, 1997).

He holds a B.A. degree from the George Washington University, an M.B.A. degree from the Harvard Business School, and M.A. and Ph.D. degrees in psychology from the University of Michigan. He has been elected a fellow of the American Psychological Association and the Society for Industrial and Organizational Psychology. In 1992 he was featured on the cover of *Business Week* as one of the four outstanding new management "gurus" in the country.

Mark B. Nadler is a director of the Delta Consulting Group Inc. and chairman of the firm's editorial board. He is a consultant to senior executives on communications strategies for large-scale organizational change.

Before joining Delta in 1995, Mark Nadler spent twenty-two years in the newspaper business as a journalist and manager. His experience included several years as an editor at the *Wall Street Journal* and, most recently, five years as vice president and executive editor of the *Chicago Sun-Times*. A graduate of the George Washington University, he is a former member of the American Society of Newspaper Editors and served twice as a juror for the Pulitzer Prizes in journalism.

Champions of Change

Chapter One

What It Takes
Confronting the Realities of Change

Just for a moment, put yourself in their shoes.

Pretend that you find yourself confronting the daunting set of circumstances that each of these chief executive officers actually faced.

Imagine that you're Henry B. Schacht and it's the fall of 1995. AT&T has stunned the business world by announcing the largest voluntary breakup in corporate history; you've just been named CEO of the massive spin-off containing AT&T's equipment and business systems units, along with the famed Bell Laboratories. This $21 billion operation, with 130,000 employees, doesn't even have a name yet—Lucent Technologies is still just one of seven hundred possibilities still under consideration. There's no clear mission or strategy. There's no organizational structure; the top managers are a team in name only.

The entire business world is watching closely as you rush head-long toward the most highly publicized public offering in Wall Street history. Down in Washington, Congress is moving swiftly to deregulate the telecommunications industry and completely re-shape the competitive landscape in ways no one can even imag-ine—but in ways that will most assuredly have a direct critical impact on your business. You have to drastically increase earnings growth, cut costs, and stem horrendous losses overseas—all in a company where it's been considered uncivil to talk openly about profits. You're Henry Schacht, and that's your challenge. So what do you do?

Or imagine you're Randall Tobias in June 1993. The board of pharmaceutical giant Eli Lilly and Company has reluctantly ousted the CEO, and you've accepted its offer to take his place. It's hard to imagine a worse time to be taking over. Political and market forces are buffeting the entire health care business; Lilly is in particularly bad shape, having lost an astounding $11 billion in market capital value in the previous eighteen months. The takeover sharks are beginning to circle.

As you show up for work that first Monday morning at Lilly's sprawling campus on the south side of Indianapolis, the financial community is screaming for results—and they're far from reassured by the appointment of a lifelong phone company executive. The good news is that your predecessor, after literally refusing to give up the job, has finally vacated the executive office on the twelfth floor of Lilly's administration building. He was immensely popular with the employees, who now are panicked by rumors of massive layoffs. And over the weekend, for the first time since anyone in the company can remember, several patients taking part in clinical trials for a promising new drug began showing signs of liver failure. (In the weeks ahead five of them will die.) That's what's waiting for you on your first day of work—so where do you start?

Or imagine you're Jon Madonna in 1992. Two years earlier, you had ascended through the ranks to become chairman and CEO of KPMG Peat Marwick, one of the Big Six accounting firms and a global powerhouse. But you quickly learned that behind the facade of strength lurked a host of smoldering problems that could ultimately cripple the privately-held firm. Both revenues and net income per partner had remained essentially flat for five years. All the major competitors were pulling ahead. The firm was saddled with the excess baggage of the go-go eighties—too many partners, too much staff, too much expensive office space.

So in 1990, you'd ordered a series of unprecedented cutbacks, laying off hundreds of partners. But as painful as that was, it was only the first step; you're now convinced that the underlying problems are much more serious. Beyond the flabby infrastructure the firm continues to operate essentially the way it has for more than ninety years. The partners group themselves by discipline—tax accounting, auditing, and consulting—and operate within jealously guarded geographic territories ruled by one hundred powerful local managing partners. But the business is changing; clients are clamoring for integrated services provided by specialists who understand their particular industry. A major restructuring is in order—but it will require the cooperation and involvement of the tradition-bound partners, who elect both the CEO and the entire board of directors.

You need to cut costs, restructure the business, change the firm's mind-set—and do all of it in a highly political democratically run organization where few people see any particular need for another round of change. Constrained by nearly one hundred years of tradition, how do you make change happen?

The Truth About Change

The past few years have brought a staggering outpouring of books, articles, lectures, and seminars touting an avalanche of ideas about managing change. Some rely heavily on theory. Some recount the superhuman achievements of a particular CEO. And some extrapolate universal concepts from isolated experiences observed somewhere in the depths of a large company. Each serves a purpose, but few have managed to capture the reality of change in large, complex contemporary organizations.

That reality is what the three opening examples are all about. There's nothing theoretical about them; this is real life. These were the actual situations faced in recent years by three CEOs, each of whom asked my colleagues and me at Delta Consulting Group to help them initiate and lead change. Each situation was unique, involving widely varying casts of characters, strategic demands, and operational issues. But together, they begin to capture the immense complexity of change that now confronts so many organizations.

The truth is that change is inherently messy. It is always complicated. It invariably involves a massive array of sharply conflicting demands. Despite the best-laid plans, things never happen in exactly the right order—and in fact, few things rarely turn out exactly right the first time around. Most important, the reality of change in the organizational trenches defies rigid academic models as well as superficial management fads.

Why? Because real change in real organizations is intensely personal and enormously political. If this book does nothing else, I hope it conveys the true human dimension of organizational change—a dimension that transcends neat theories, packaged solutions, and mechanistic notions about reengineering people and jobs. It revolves around a human dynamic described by David M. Lawrence, chairman and CEO of Kaiser Foundation Health Plan and Hospitals—the country's largest HMO, better known as Kaiser Permanente—in a paper prepared for a CEO conference in 1996:

> If leading change were nothing more than an intellectual exercise in rearranging structures and redesigning processes, our lives would be a lot simpler. But the CEO's job is to lead change, not just manage it. Leading people in a new direction means reshaping their view of the world. It means shattering their sense of stability, tossing out their old standards of success, and prying them loose from the status quo. And then it means replacing what you've wiped out with a new, coherent and energizing vision of what you believe the future can and should be.

That's really the essence of this book—how to change not only an organization's strategy, its structure, and its operations, but also the perceptions, expectations, and performance of thousands of people—and change all these elements in ways that keep them focused and consistent. That's the true challenge of change.

Think back to the opening scenes. Henry Schacht's biggest challenge wasn't preparing Lucent's IPO, or even figuring out a brand-new organizational structure. The real issue was how to change the mind-set of more than 100,000 people, many of whom had grown up in a paternalistic monopoly, assuming customers would always walk in the door and the company would always provide them with a job.

For Randy Tobias, rearranging Lilly's portfolio, restructuring the business units, and communicating the new strategy to Wall Street was the easy part; after three years he was still spending most of his time trying to reshape attitudes about personal accountability, candor in professional relationships, and tolerance of subpar performance.

Jon Madonna's challenge was at least as tough; assuming he could convince the firm of the need for radical change—an obstacle he never totally overcame—he had to turn 1,500 independent-minded partners into team players and then persuade everyone that the firm needed to be run more like a business and less like a social club.

Changes of that kind bring instability, upheaval, and uncertainty. To the individuals involved they mean the possibility of new job requirements, new bosses, new reporting structures, new performance standards, new compensation plans—any one of which is enough to keep most of us up at night. Change means new patterns of power, influence, and control—and, consequently, high-stakes office politics. That's what change entails—and that's why it's so hard.

The Champions of Change

But it can be done—and done successfully. That's what this book explains: a comprehensive approach to leading change in ways that will align people's behavior with the organization's business objectives. It is an approach based on nearly two decades of work I and my firm have done with more than 130 organizations in the United States and abroad—professional firms, educational institutions, government agencies, and most of all, public companies, including nearly fifty of the Fortune 500. It is an approach based on my personal experience and that of the many talented people I've been fortunate to have at Delta over the years, who have worked in close collaboration with nearly eighty CEOs. Consequently, it is an approach based on a blend of careful observation and personal involvement, often from a senior, inside vantage point unavailable to most academics or the business press.

My colleagues and I have employed this approach at such leading companies as AT&T, Bristol-Myers Squibb, Chase Manhattan, Citibank, Corning Inc., Lockheed Martin, Sun Microsystems, Weyerhaeuser, and Xerox Corporation, to name just a few. It is an approach that eschews easy answers while focusing on helpful concepts and practical tools. It is an approach that helps managers throughout the organization understand the nature of change at the corporate level as it also provides them with lessons in leadership and management that are equally applicable to operating units, divisions, and departments.

Above all it is an approach based on years of observing and participating in the management of change—and in the process, of learning the difference between change that works and change that doesn't. A key observation that lies at the heart of this approach—and part of what differentiates it from some of the current fads in management thinking—is this: not one of the CEOs I've seen could have accomplished successful change without help—lots of it. But never—ever—have I seen large-scale change succeed without the deep personal commitment and active involvement of the CEO.

And yet many current approaches to change seem to ignore that simple fact. A populist wave has swept through business commentary in recent years. One school of thought seems to be that the best CEOs are those who sit on the floor in a circle while someone beats a tom-tom and the group collectively gropes its way toward change. A little closer to Planet Earth, some argue that true change is driven by low-level teams. Others suggest that creative strategies emanate only from the ranks of middle managers, who are assumed to have no stake in protecting the status quo—a dubious premise, to say the least. Even reengineering represented an attempt to drive change—which was usually a euphemism for cost-cutting—through mid-and low-level exercises devoid of involvement by senior corporate managers.

Now, teams can be a powerful mechanism for change—if they're part of an overall effort, led from the top. The development of strategy should indeed involve the widest possible participation by people who really know the business—if their work is melded into a comprehensive strategic process led from the top. Even some forms of reengineering can be productive—if they're viewed as narrowly limited activities that are part of a larger change effort led from the top.

In short, these specific processes and practices are effective over the long run only if they are part of an overall agenda. Real change is an *integrated* process that unfolds over time and touches every aspect of the organization. It is a dynamic process that requires constant revision—staffing changes, reallocation of resources, strategic shifts, structural changes, refinement of mission, articulation of values—within an overarching framework of focused objectives. The vision, influence, and power required to create and drive that kind of change can come only from the top of the organization.

"The CEO personally has to take the lead," says Jon Madonna. "You've absolutely got to be the point person to make this happen, and I mean the point person in terms of design *and* implementation. Obviously, you need a whole lot of other folks to join you, but at the end of the day, you've got to own it. You can't delegate it to anybody."

That's why over the years I've come to think of many of the CEOs described here as true *champions of change.* In some cases they qualify for the title champion by being "best in class"—they are truly outstanding leaders with records of phenomenal achievement. At another level they are champions in the sense of advocates, fostering change within their organizations by providing guidance, support, and resources to subordinates in the vanguard of change. In both cases they have valuable lessons to offer us.

I wouldn't suggest for a moment that the CEOs whose work and ideas are the basis for this book constitute the definitive list of the nation's top CEOs. Nor would I argue that these CEOs have been uniformly successful; the truth is that some have accomplished a good deal more than others, and many are engaged in change efforts that are still works in progress, with the final outcome far from certain. What all the CEOs who appear in this book do have in common is that they have fully embraced the challenge of large-scale change and tackled it head on.

A final thought about the framework for this book: don't misunderstand my exposition on the importance of leaders. This is not a book about leaders of change; this is a book about leadership *and* change. There's a huge difference.

My intent here is not to provide an exhaustive chronicle of the achievements of any particular CEO or a collection of management maxims from successful executives. This is a book, first and foremost, about how to lead and manage complex organizational change. As should be clear by now, I believe that's a concept that cannot be discussed intelligently without a full appreciation of the role of CEOs and other senior executives. But the truth is that few CEOs can readily articulate how they envision their personal roles in managing change.

For one thing, most CEOs are oriented toward action and results; by nature, they tend not to be overly introspective. Once a decision has been made, they're eager to move on. In addition, the experienced CEOs aren't even aware of many of the specific things they do that make them successful leaders. By the time they've been handed the reins of a Fortune 500 company, they're at a point in their careers where much of what they do is second nature. Their concepts of leadership have become instinctive rather than explicit.

So as this book unfolds what you'll find are the concepts of change management that my colleagues and I have evolved in our work with CEOs and their companies interwoven with the specific experiences and insights of these CEOs and other senior executives. These concepts and insights can be adapted and applied by executives and managers at every level of the organization, providing immensely useful tools for initiating, leading, and managing change in every corner of the organization.

Given this basic framework, let's turn next to a look at the nature of change in today's business environment, and then to an overview of the issues to be covered.

The Demand for Change

By the middle of 1994, continuing upheaval in the telecommunications industry was pointing to a future in which AT&T, the once unassailable leader, would inevitably be torn by conflicting internal strategies and besieged by new competitors. The most obvious problem involved AT&T's systems and equipment operations; many of their major customers—and potential customers—would become AT&T's direct competitors once deregulation created a free-for-all in both the local and long distance businesses. At that point AT&T's various internal strategies would be drawn into direct conflict.

So that summer I sent a memo to AT&T chairman and CEO Robert Allen, with whom our firm had worked in the aftermath of the court-ordered Bell System breakup. In that memo I told Allen I believed a second round of radical change was inevitable if AT&T hoped to maintain its position of leadership. If you agree, I wrote, the central questions are, Do you think it can be done? Do you think you can do it? And do you want to do it?

Those were far from hypothetical questions. Allen had devoted much of the previous six years to the emotionally and physically draining work of trying to turn a century-old, domestic monopoly into an aggressive player in a highly competitive global marketplace. His legacy was assured, and not too many years ago a CEO at the age of sixty could easily have turned his thoughts to training a successor, improving his golf game, and spending more time with his grandchildren.

But leaders of major organizations no longer have that luxury. Through the 1950s, '60s, and '70s, CEOs really didn't have to worry much about managing radical change. In the 1980s, they could probably count on facing one major change episode during their tenure. By the 1990s, change had become so common that many if not most CEOs could expect to lead fundamental change efforts twice, and perhaps more.

That was the inescapable reality Bob Allen faced in 1995 when he undertook a second round of massive change that proved to be at least as grueling, and even more controversial, than his first. Allen announced the voluntary breakup of AT&T into three companies. (And it's worth noting that when he gave the top job at Lucent Technologies to Henry Schacht he was choosing not only an experienced executive and AT&T director but also someone who had already led Cummins Engine Company through a long, difficult, and ultimately successful radical change.)

The demands for organizational change have accelerated at an extraordinary pace in recent years. In the late 1970s and into the 1980s, much of the organizational change was prompted by economic downturns at home and heightened pressure from overseas competitors. Deregulation and changes in public policy forced companies in industries such as financial services and health care to radically reshape themselves in the '80s. Emerging technologies and changing market needs swept through still other industries, such as telecommunications and pharmaceuticals. The '90s brought an intensified search for competitive advantage through new corporate alignments—mergers and acquisitions, breakups, spin-offs, joint ventures, integrated supplier networks.

Indeed, change has become so common in the business world that it has become something of a cliché. That's unfortunate. Change is far too important, pervasive, and complicated a phenomenon to be taken for granted. Every manager may be aware of it; that doesn't mean he or she knows how to handle it.

Why Change Efforts Fail

The sad fact is that enormous numbers of companies confronted with the challenge of change have botched it. The business landscape is littered with the remains of enterprises that mishandled change and fell victim to takeovers, shotgun mergers, or outright failure. In one industry after another, once-powerful leaders such as Apple Computer, Control Data Corporation, B. F. Goodrich, Pan American Airways, and Continental Bank became marginal players—or vanished entirely. In the first half of the 1990s, one major corporation after another, from General Motors and IBM to Kodak and Eli Lilly, replaced its CEO in an unprecedented purge of top executives who had failed to initiate and implement fundamental change in response to internal needs and market demands.

Why does change so often go awry? These mistakes surface time and time again:

- Too many top executives abdicate their responsibility for personal commitment and involvement and try to delegate the leadership of change.
- Too many times, small numbers of people—and often the wrong ones—closet themselves in secrecy, hatch grand schemes, and then unleash them upon an unprepared and uncooperative organization.
- Too often executives rush to seize upon a particular set of strategic choices without generating full discussion of all the possible alternatives.
- Too many organizations make crucial decisions on the basis of incomplete and biased information.
- Too many organizations cling to the misguided hope that one magical concept—one silver bullet—will unlock the mysteries of organizational change.

The Good News

The good news is that many successful companies are well on their way to mastering the complexities of change and that success has helped fuel the resurgence of corporate America in the mid-1990s. Back in the late 1980s, as George Bush capped off his hapless trade mission to Tokyo by unceremoniously losing his dinner in the lap of the Japanese prime minister, there was a pervasive sense that U.S. business could do nothing right, that U.S. companies were doomed in almost any industry you could name.

That situation has turned around dramatically. Michigan's economy is booming, fueled by the resurgence of the U.S. auto-makers. Xerox, which stood on the brink of losing its copier business to Japanese competitors, is once again an immensely successful company. In computers, the United States maintains its lead in software and semiconductors.

The same story has been repeated in one industry after another; overall, U.S. companies in the mid-1990s have enjoyed strong growth and solid earnings. And productivity is up, by practically every measure. Starting in the late 1970s and continuing through most of the 1980s, our annual growth in hourly output lagged far behind Japan, Germany, and France; in the 1990s, the United States has regained the lead over the other three, according to the U.S. Bureau of Labor Statistics. It should then come as no surprise that for the past two years the Geneva-based World Economic Forum has ranked the United States as the world's most competitive economy.

What accounts for this resurgence? It's impossible to isolate a single cause in an era when interest rates, trade agreements, currency fluctuations, and the health of foreign economies have such an enormous bearing on our domestic fortunes. Certainly, countless firms were being strangled by bloated workforces, unreasonable pay scales, and archaic union work rules. But downsizing, in and of itself, has rarely been the answer; in fact, downsizing in the absence of real organizational change typically accelerates a downward spiral, as Apple Computer demonstrated in the mid-1990s. In the most successful companies, layoffs and downsizing were just one element of radical change aimed at altering every aspect of how business was done and people performed.

Rather than simply cutting costs, successful companies have succeeded by changing in ways that unleashed new sources of competitive advantage. They developed new strategies and revamped business processes. They designed new organizational architectures that infused their business units with entrepreneurial energy and extended traditional organizational boundaries to include new partnerships and strategic alliances. They devised new techniques for selecting and motivating people and for capitalizing on the skills and knowledge of their employees.

In one company after another, real competitive advantage has been achieved through a deliberate, long-term, and focused collection of efforts and activities—a process grounded in the integrated approach to change that is the underlying theme of this book.

The Concept of Integrated Change

There's plenty of disagreement over an organization's primary reason for being. Is it to enrich owners and shareholders, to provide a collective capacity to produce goods and services, or to serve society by providing people with employment and a decent livelihood? My concern here is not so much the *why* as the *how*—how do organizations operate, and how can they effect major change in ways that will heighten their odds of success, whatever their reason for being? And from that perspective, it is essential to start with the proposition that organizations are first and foremost human institutions. Each organization ought to have a strategy, specific business objectives that will enable the organization to thrive by strengthening its competitive position in the marketplace. However, at its center, each organization is also a complex social system, comprising a specific set of four tightly interrelated components. And each of these components must become congruent with the strategy before the strategy can succeed.

- *The work.* The activities performed by the organization's employees to create, produce, sell, and deliver the required goods and services.
- *The people.* All the employees who staff the organization's various operations.
- *The formal organization.* The structures, processes, and systems that organize activities and guide people in the performance of their work.
- *The informal organization.* The organization's collective values, attitudes and beliefs, unofficial channels of communication and lines of influence, and accepted standards for behavior (frequently referred to as *culture* or *operating environment*).

We'll come back to this way of looking at organizations in Chapter Two and explore it in much greater depth. For now the key concept behind *integrated change* is this: each of these four components is directly tied to all the others. Every one of them influences, and is influenced by, all the others. Think of change as a pebble tossed into a pond. You can try to throw it smack in the middle of whichever part of the pond you want to think of as *strategy*. But if the pebble is big enough—if the change is sufficiently intense— sooner or later, the ripples will spread, disturbing the calm of every portion of the pond.

That seemingly simple notion has enormous implications. Given the inherent complexity of organizations—of the complex web of relationships connecting each and every component—it's simply wishful thinking to believe there can ever be one single solution aimed at one specific aspect of the organization, that can bring about successful organizational change.

And yet rampant management faddism and its underlying obsession with one-shot solutions has been an obstacle to rational change since the days of management by objectives (MBO) and strategic planning. These fads all follow the same pattern. Someone develops an interesting theory and gets some companies to try it. A few of these companies become successful. Word gets around, and the hype machine shifts into high gear. Through books, magazine articles, professional journals, management seminars, and the lecture circuit, the new technique, whatever it is, is touted as "the next big thing" every company has to adopt or risk being left in the dust. Then, predictably, come the first instances where it doesn't work. And before long the hype turns hypercritical and everyone is ready to stampede to "the next big thing."

All the magic solutions of recent years—from MBO through quality circles and Total Quality Management and now reengineering—have followed the same cycle. And it's truly unfortunate, for several reasons. First, managers invest enormous time, energy, and money in implementing programs that almost never produce the hoped-for results. Second, each introduction of a new management program—usually accompanied by much fanfare and declarations that *this time* the problems are finally going to get fixed—generates new waves of cynicism on the part of the workforce, which automatically dismisses the program as the new "flavor of the month." And third, managers repeatedly abandon fundamentally sound ideas that could in fact be quite helpful if viewed as valuable weapons rather than the entire arsenal. But once the fad of the day inevitably fails to live up to its advanced billing as the ultimate solution, its disappointed adherents toss it aside and move on.

Just a few short years after gathering a fanatical following in the early 1990s, reengineering crashed and burned; even some of its creators have joined in publicly discrediting the movement. It's really too bad. Reengineering—which many companies had engaged in for years before a catchy name turned a useful concept into a mass movement—provided some worthwhile tools for increasing the efficiency of specific business processes. It ran into trouble when it was hyped as a universal approach to driving large-scale change—and more specifically because it was so often implemented with total disregard for how each change would cascade through the organization, affecting people and their operating environment. It was the very antithesis of integrated change, and its failure was preordained from the outset.

Let's face it: there are no simple solutions. If there were, someone would have found them by now, and we'd all be using them.

Given the complexity of modern organizations, compounded by the vagaries of human behavior that influence even the most sophisticated business strategies, it's not surprising that organizational change is more art than science. But it is an art that can be learned and mastered over time; there are basic principles, specific steps, and predictable outcomes for those willing to invest the necessary insight and effort.

The New Business Environment

The first step, then, is to understand clearly the nature of something I described generally earlier: the demand for change in the current competitive environment—what causes it, what challenges does it create for organizations, and what are its implications for developing competitive strength? Much of the change shaking organizations today arises from several very specific sources of pressure that cross all boundaries, profoundly affecting enterprises regardless of size, complexity, industry sector, or geography.

The overarching source of change of course is increased competition. In one industry after another, competition is expanding at an ever-increasing rate. There are more players than ever before. Geographic boundaries between traditional competitors are evaporating. Traditional oligarchies—think of health care for example—are collapsing, making way for new players. In the United States, regulatory changes—most recently, telecommunications reform—have spawned whole new industries with new companies appearing on the scene almost daily. Overseas, privatization of traditionally government-owned operations in sectors such as power utilities and telecommunications have had the same effect.

The globalization of markets is at the root of much of the increased competition. More than ever before, markets are truly becoming worldwide. Global suppliers, global producers, and the global availability of capital markets are rapidly diminishing the importance of national boundaries. In one industry after another—telecommunications, computers, apparel, autos, even fast food—customer needs are turning out to be more similar than they are different. In sector after sector we're seeing the emergence of global competitors, particularly the Japanese, the French, the Germans, and other Pacific Rim countries that can aggressively compete with U.S. companies on a worldwide scale.

Simultaneously, the exploding pace of technological innovation—both in products and business processes—fuels competitive pressure with an endless stream of new products, new players, new manufacturing techniques, and distribution systems. And the cumulative effect of these trends—more players, more products, new technology, global markets—means customers are quickly learning to expect more, better, quicker. As their expectations rise, so do the pressures on companies who hope to maintain and improve their position as suppliers of consumer goods and services. Coupled with a basic condition of oversupply, with capacity far outstripping demand in most industries, increasing numbers of companies in businesses as diverse as commercial airlines, hospitals, and personal computers find their traditionally specialized products and services inexorably turning into commodities.

Finally, the whole area of public policy is driving change. Government deregulation spawns new players and more competition, as in telecommunications. Shifts in government spending policy can dramatically alter the structure and economics of an industry, as in health care. Government can encourage or dissuade overseas investment and imports. Government partnerships can spur technological advances, as in Japan and France, and government policies encouraging privatization have spawned major business opportunities throughout the developing world and in Eastern Europe.

In turn, these trends in the external business environment have spawned internal pressures within companies intent on maintaining their competitive strength. So that sooner or later, most companies must ask themselves these key questions arising from the new business environment:

Given the rising tide of customer expectations, how do we increase quality and give better value to the customer?

How do we maximize our competitive innovation? How do we make sure we really get a pay-off for all the money we're spending on new products and processes?

How do we reduce our cycle time and shorten the period it takes us to respond to the market?

How do we expand our scope and enjoy the benefits of scale, moving into new markets without permanently bulking up the organization?

How do we slash the costs of internal coordination? How do we design, develop, produce, and deliver our product or service to market at a much lower cost so we can be even more competitive as we also maintain our margins?

In the face of all this uncertainty, how do we make sure our employees are motivated and capable of contributing?

In summary, how do we find true, sustainable competitive advantage—something that nobody else can do and that can't be copied or mimicked over time?

Searching for Competitive Advantage

In light of the ever-quickening pace of change, the central question comes down to this: How do you reshape an organization so that it can quickly and efficiently respond to constant shifts in the business environment in ways that sustain its competitive advantage and exploit its innate competitive strengths? How do you stay perpetually focused on tomorrow while not losing sight of what you have to get done today? How can you inculcate change into the very fabric of an organization without creating chaos, instability, and paralysis?

All these concerns ultimately boil down to the search for *true competitive advantage*—a search that's becoming more difficult all the time. The traditional sources of advantage—access to capital, exclusive technology, key employees, and proximity to important markets—all are quickly evaporating.

Most large players on the international scene have equal access to capital; in fact capital has practically become a commodity. You can get it in London, Hong Kong, Singapore, Tokyo, New York—in any number of global money centers. The same is true of technology—the half-life of proprietary technology is shrinking, and new technological developments zoom around the globe at an amazing pace. Nor can organizations view their people as unique assets; because of downsizing, mergers, takeovers, and constant corporate changes, valuable employees no longer feel bound to a particular company, or even to a particular country. And markets—U.S. markets in particular—are becoming increasingly open, weakening traditional advantages for U.S. companies. The common theme is the growing tendency toward equal access: access to capital, to technology, to people, and to markets.

Given those trends then, where can organizations turn today for truly sustainable competitive advantage? The answer lies in three closely related areas: intellectual capital, organizational capabilities, and organizational architecture.

Intellectual Capital

Intellectual capital is an organization's collective knowledge. Today, for example, Xerox is a leader in the area of quality—but only because it has the hard-earned intellectual capital, amassed during difficult years of institutional learning, to maintain that position. Similarly, Kaiser Permanente has been a major force in managed care for years, because it has decades of experience unmatched by any but a few competitors. As it scrambled to secure a dominant position on the Internet in 1996, Microsoft flexed its muscles and reassigned thousands of research specialists to Internet-specific projects in an attempt to quickly create a knowledge base that could take its smaller competitors years to match.

Organizational Capabilities

Organizational capabilities are the abilities of people to collectively accomplish established goals. Canon, the Japanese firm, is well known for its aptitude at successfully converting proven technology in one product into the basis for a host of new products; the optical know-how that went into Canon cameras and binoculars fueled the company's successful entry into photocopying. 3M's organizational capability is its unmatched record of constant and massive innovation and, more specifically, its ability to keep churning out not only brilliant discoveries but an endless stream of successful products. That success takes place at a company with an organizational chart practically impossible for outsiders to fathom. The key to 3M's unique capability can't be captured on a piece of paper; instead, it is a function of tradition, shared values, informal patterns of interaction, and perhaps most important, careful attention to recruiting and promoting the kind of people who can operate and succeed in its unusual environment.

Technology transfer and large-scale innovation aren't capabilities that a competitor can easily match. They do not reside in particular individuals or technologies, so they can't be bought. They do not rely on any particular organizational structure, so they can't be copied. Rather those strengths are an integral part of the fabric and culture of the organization; they are the culmination of the combined strengths of the entire enterprise.

Organizational Architecture

The third area of competitive advantage falls under the umbrella of *organizational architecture*. Simply put, companies have to design structures, processes, and systems that will allow them to exploit the collective knowledge and capitalize on the capabilities that will make them unique.

In countless corporations, managers are beginning to appreciate the immense resources going to waste because expertise residing in one corner of the enterprise is never shared with the other people who desperately need it. In past decades, restructuring work meant figuring out the most efficient way to move hunks of metal or pieces of paper from one group of workers to another. Today work flow largely involves information; it's moving data, knowledge, and insights from the people within the organization who have this information to those who need it but might not even know it exists. That requires different ways of designing work processes, different ways of grouping activities, different ways of linking people across functions and business units and geography, and different ways of assigning responsibilities and incentives to self-directed teams.

Organizational architecture also involves structural reorganizations that unearth the competitive value of each element of the corporation. It is reflected, for instance, in the moves toward semi-autonomous business units that become entrepreneurial profit centers, toward new forms of strategic alliances and joint ventures, and toward new partnering relationships between companies and their suppliers.

Don't misunderstand; I'm not attempting to prescribe some kind of corporate Nirvana. The innovations I'm talking about are hard-nosed attempts to improve the bottom line, all undertaken in fiercely competitive situations. I don't know of a single innovation that looks as good up close as it does on paper; not one is perfect. Nevertheless, Xerox saw its stock price more than quadruple after reorganizing into independent business units, which it went back and reorganized a few years later. Chrysler's partnership with suppliers has helped make it Detroit's fastest and most profitable new product designer. Corning's production plant in Blacksburg, Virginia, designed entirely around semiautonomous teams of workers, is the most profitable in its division and one of the most efficient in the entire corporation.

But such changes don't come easily. Unlocking new sources of competitive advantage almost always means turning the status quo on its ear—and that requires the deft management of deliberate change. It requires new styles of leadership, rather than traditional command and control and rigid hierarchies. It requires a broad range of skill and techniques, all focused on articulating a vision, setting strategic objectives, and winning the understanding—and ultimately the commitment—of the entire company to move together in a new direction.

Putting all those pieces together, building the momentum for change while keeping all the elements of the organization in relative balance—that is the key to totally integrated change. It's considerably more elegant on paper than in practice; my Delta friend and colleague David Bliss once described the reality of integrated change as "racing up and down the hallway," his shorthand for trying desperately to keep a host of change-related activities in some semblance of order.

Above all, leading and managing change is hard work. It allows no shortcuts. To quote Henry Schacht, "It means working through complexities that really are complex. That requires time, patience, a willingness to compromise, unbending commitment to your colleagues, and an understanding that you can't get there unless your colleagues are with you, agree with you, and have the same sense of zeal that you have."

But before you do any of those things, you have to size up the situation. The first step in any change effort is to figure out the lay of the land—to figure out how the organization works and how to pinpoint the trouble spots and areas of opportunity. So let me begin, in Chapter Two, by introducing you to some practical tools for mapping the organizational terrain.

Where to Start
Understanding Organizations

Your first visit to a new company can be awfully confusing.

From the outside you see the front of the headquarters building and the visitor's entrance—but not much more. Inside you see a maze of offices and work areas—but at first glance they don't seem to be arranged in any particular pattern. You see people rushing busily to and fro, but you have no idea what they're doing or what, if anything, they're actually accomplishing.

If you're to have any chance of quickly making sense of what's going on—of how the company is organized and how it really operates—you need a mental template, a systematic way to observe and understand the organization. For executives and managers intent on leading change, that kind of template, or model, is essential. Without it you haven't a clue where to start.

Lucent Technologies CEO Henry Schacht, who has led massive change at two very different companies, describes it this way: "The most fundamental issue about managing change, or creating change—whichever is required—is an assessment of where you are. . . . Understanding the topology of where you start is absolutely critical, as opposed to 'I have a set of things I do to manage change. Here's my bag of tricks.' If a doctor diagnoses a patient with X, he prescribes one kind of medicine; if he diagnoses the patient with Y, he prescribes another kind of medicine. You don't use penicillin when physical therapy is indicated."

Throughout this book I'm going to be talking about organizational change in terms of a model my colleagues and I have developed and refined over the past two decades. The purpose of this chapter is to share with you that model, that basic perspective on organizations, and to provide you with terms and concepts fundamental to diagnosing and understanding the need for change in any organization.

Dynacorp: A Case Study

I'm going to start with a case study I've used over the years with hundreds of managers (Delta Consulting Group, 1980). All the names have been changed to protect the innocent, but rest assured that the following scenario is based on a very real set of circumstances that prevailed several years ago at a leading corporation.

> The Dyna Corporation—better known as Dynacorp—is a major global player in the field of information technology. You are an executive at Dynacorp. You've done well with the company; over the past eight years, you've held a succession of increasingly responsible positions in its key European markets. Now, during a troubled and volatile period for this once-dominant organization, you've been told you're about to become executive vice president for U.S. Customer Relations.
>
> You're well aware of your company's recent history. Formed in the 1960s and transformed in the 1970s by high-tech developments, Dynacorp sped into the '80s with strong growth based on its reputation as an innovative provider of high-quality products.
>
> But the past decade has been tougher. Smaller companies and Japanese competitors have matched your innovations, and your image as a high-tech leader is slipping. Although the trend in your market was shifting heavily toward wholly integrated office "solutions"—combined offerings of networked hardware and software, professional support, and special applications—you kept trying to sell updated versions of your old reliable stand-alone machines. And customers who in the past would willingly wait up to a year for your products because they were considered the best now are turning to competitors who can give them something just as good, but faster.
>
> Faced with slowed growth and decreased earnings, Dynacorp started moving two years ago to address the new competitive realities. Management reorganized the company, moving from a functional organization to a set of end-to-end business units responsible for development, manufacturing, and

marketing. But at the same time the managers decided to retain the existing field organizations rather than create multiple salesforces, a move they saw as costly and possibly a barrier for customers who frequently dealt with Dynacorp for a whole range of products.

So, back to you. You've returned briefly to New York City, mainly to find an apartment. You figure since you have a few extra hours you'll stop in and see the man you're replacing, Carl Greystone, who's about to retire. Greystone, one of the few people aware of your still-unannounced promotion, is more than happy to meet with you in his office on the thirty-fourth floor of the Dynacorp building and give you an overview.

"Yes," he says, gazing with a satisfied smile at the landscape of midtown office towers beyond his office window, "we've made the big changes—we've reorganized into Regional and Customer Teams, and we have our people thinking about the business in new terms. I think we're beginning to see the light at the end of the tunnel."

Greystone arranges for you to chat with Ben Walker, vice president of the Northeast Region, "my most experienced general manager." Walker assures you the new strategy is headed in the right direction; the problem is that the company is trying to meld an army of free-wheeling equipment salespeople into seamless teams to help customers solve complex office and communication problems. "The skills and attitudes on many levels are mismatched with our current needs," Walker says, and estimates at least 25 percent of the staff will have to be replaced. Then he walks you down to the fourteenth floor to meet with branch manager Martha Pauley.

The details start getting a little grittier. The reorganization has been so hectic, Pauley tells you, that there hasn't been time for any of that training on how to sell solutions instead of specific products. She keeps meaning to hold off-site sessions but just can't find the time. And whenever she's about ready, someone upstairs revises the job guidelines. What's more, her people are still losing sales to competitors who offer lower prices and swifter technical support, and that new plant in Asia that was supposed to help cut prices has run into all kinds of problems.

Then she takes you down the hall to one of the meetings each account team is supposed to have every two weeks. Upon arriving, Pauley is surprised to find that half the team members are missing; they're attending the introduction of a new product line. Then come the reports—all bad. The competitors are offering better prices, better support, better integration of equipment and software.

"This situation is getting very depressing," remarks a member of the sales team.

For you too. Returning to Greystone's office, you look at your watch and see that you have only a few minutes left before you have to leave for the airport. You desperately want to talk with Greystone and figure out what's really going on in this operation you're about to inherit, but you have time to ask him only four questions.

What would you ask?

Yes, it is a test in a way—one Delta consultants have given to hundreds of managers with whom they've done the Dynacorp exercise. What's interesting is the range of different questions people want to ask Greystone:

"Show me your strategic plan."
"What do your monthly and quarterly results look like?"
"Describe to me how you implemented the reorganization plan."
"Show me your staffing records."
"Explain your plans for tactical support."

It's a fascinating exercise. Everyone who participates in it is constrained by the same knowledge—it's all contained in a twelve-minute videotape—but somehow, everyone comes away with different, and sometimes radically different, ideas of what's going wrong.

Why is that?

Let's step back into character once again and give this a little more thought. You're going to succeed Greystone, and soon. So what is it you really want to do?

You want to take action, of course. Before you can do that, you need an action plan with clearly defined and carefully staged action steps. Those steps in turn convert solutions into action—so first, you have to arrive at solutions. Clearly, you can't identify solutions unless you fully understand the problems, and that understanding is impossible until you've analyzed the available data. So the first crucial step in sizing up Dynacorp—or any new or changing situation in which you find yourself—is to collect data.

The problem is, the moment you walk in the door of Dynacorp—or virtually any organization you can think of—you are immersed in information of every imaginable kind. It's not just the hard data contained in research and reports and financials; everywhere you turn, people want to give you their version of Dynacorp reality. Years ago in a graduate program at Harvard Business School I took part in a research project headed by Harry Levinson in which five of us were assigned to perform a full-scale diagnosis of a three-hundred-bed hospital in Cambridge, Massachusetts. We each spent fifteen hours a week for eight months just doing diagnosis, and at the end of those eight months we had a pretty good idea of what was going on inside that hospital.

But you don't have that kind of time. In the business world no one does. So either consciously or subconsciously, you're going to make some discriminating decisions about what data to collect. That is, you are *always* going to pick up on some things and ignore others—just as everyone who goes through the Dynacorp exercise zeros in on some things and pays little or no attention to others. Everyone sees the gap between Greystone's glowing appraisal and the sense of despair that pervaded the team meeting; beyond that, each participant seizes on different symptoms, problems, conflicts, outcomes—different data.

Why? Because we all have prior notions of how business systems should work. Anyone stepping into Greystone's job—in fact, almost anyone with the business experience to have become a manager—has formed some deeply held ideas of how an organization should be structured and how it should operate. Though few of us would describe these notions as an organizational model, that is in fact exactly what they are—a set of *assumptions,* rarely explicit or all encompassing but very real to each of us nonetheless. This set of assumptions constitutes the ideal against which we match any unfamiliar situation in which we find ourselves.

Here's the problem. Your model—that prism through which you view every organizational situation you're likely to encounter—is the product of your own experience. Therefore the validity of that model, its capacity to help you understand and predict what's going to happen in any organizational setting, is based on the assumption that what you'll deal with in the future is what you've dealt with in the past.

Now think back to Chapter One and the notion that practically everything in the business environment is changing—and changing faster all the time. Where does that leave you if your perceptual guidebook for sizing up a new situation is obsolete the moment you walk in the door?

These aren't abstract theories. Remember how we got here: I was discussing how every manager's personal organizational model largely determines what data he or she thinks is important to collect. In fact, the model shapes not only what data managers collect but how they collect it—in what form, and from whom—and how they analyze it, what they perceive as problems, what they conceive of as solutions, and how they go about putting those solutions into action.

The Congruence Model

Given how crucial organizational models are to each manager's ability to analyze and act upon a situation involving fundamental change, my colleagues and I have devoted much of our work to refining a model that is profoundly useful. I'm not suggesting that it is the only model available or even the best one; what I can tell you is that it has been developed over nearly twenty years of hands-on work with practically every kind of organization and that it has worked for literally tens of thousands of managers who have used it. It is not heavily biased toward any particular kind of solution; it is, above all else, a helpful tool, one that performs the true function of a model—to take something complex and make it simpler.

This model guides managers to an understanding of the concept of *organizational fit*. It helps them answer the basic question, How do we understand and predict the patterns of organizational behavior and performance? Because if managers can't do that, they don't stand a chance of understanding and managing change throughout the enterprise.

When I ask people to draw an organization, the vast majority come up with a traditional table of organization, with columns of boxes connected by straight lines. To be sure, that's one organizational model; it has enjoyed great popularity for close to two thousand years, starting with armies and the Roman Catholic Church. But as a way of looking at organizations, it's terribly limited and incredibly static; it leaves you without the essential tools to figure out what's actually going on along those lines and between those boxes. You could easily draw a table of organization for Dynacorp's U.S. Customer Relations operation, but you'd still be a long way from diagnosing the problems.

Instead, as I've worked with CEOs to help them understand how their organizations have to change in order to compete successfully in a constantly changing environment, I've employed a much more dynamic way of looking at an organization and organizational fit—what my colleagues and I have come to describe as the *congruence model.*

Some History

The congruence model rests on thinking first formalized in the late 1940s when people in the physical sciences developed the concept of a *system* as a set of elements that took input from the environment, subjected it to some form of transformation, and produced an output (see Figure 2.1 later in this section). Think of this in very simple business terms: a company takes the input of capital, materials, and technology, subjects it to a transformation process, and the result is an output of products, services, earnings, and employment. Moreover, these early theorists believed a true system had the capacity to alter its input and transformation processes based on how the output was received or responded to; it produced and used feedback, in other words.

But this systems theory generated little interest. In the mid-1960s, Harvard and University of Michigan researchers looked further at the common characteristics of systems and organizations: both take input, produce output, are influenced by feedback, and are interdependent—if you change one piece, another piece changes. The work was interesting and insightful—but it still met with a collective shrug. Then in 1975, when Michael Tushman and I were both teaching at Columbia University, we came to believe it was important to develop and teach a unified theory of organizations; that is, we saw applications for systems theory in examining businesses as systems. Building upon the work of others (Katz and

Kahn, 1966; Lorsch and Sheldon, 1972; Seiler, 1967), we tried to develop a simple, pragmatic approach to the problem. Other people—in particular Harold Leavitt at Stanford and Jay Galbraith at MIT—were doing the same thing at the same time. The resulting convergence of thought helped me and my colleagues develop and refine the approach that became the congruence model.

Some Basic Organizational Components

As you'll see, the model provides a simple, straightforward way to understand not only how an organization looks as a system but also how it works—or doesn't. Let's begin by examining the elements that constitute the basic components of every organization. These are among the components we have to analyze to diagnose organizational fit.

Input

At any particular time, each organization operates with the following set of givens. Taken together, these three factors constitute the *input* component of the organizational system.

The environment. This includes all of the forces, conditions, and players operating outside the boundaries of the organization. They can be customers, labor unions, competitors, suppliers, technological developments, regulatory restrictions, communities—the list goes on. The environment exerts powerful demands that the organization must successfully respond to or die. It exerts constraints on the organization, and it provides opportunities to capitalize on organizational competencies. An important note: this model applies equally to organizations and to discrete units within larger organizations; in the latter case, the parent organization becomes a huge factor in a unit's external environment.

In terms of organizational change remember this: virtually all large-scale change originates in the external environment. It does not bubble up from within the organization through some mysterious process of spontaneous generation. Something is happening "out there" that is causing so much anxiety that change is unavoidable. A case in point: back in the early 1970s, when I was on the staff of the Institute for Social Research at the University of

Michigan, some of my colleagues and I got federal research money to investigate the relationship between quality and worker involvement. One day we headed out to One American Road in Dearborn, the worldwide headquarters of Ford Motor Company, to offer Ford executives the chance to participate in our groundbreaking project, at no cost to them. They listened incredulously to our research subject and then asked, "Why would we want to do that?"

About ten years later, Ford got interested. Why? Because the explosion in Japanese auto sales was sending shockwaves through Detroit, forcing U.S. carmakers to take a close look at Japanese management techniques—including quality and worker involvement. Faced with a threat of historic proportions, Ford launched a massive and fairly successful quality initiative of its own, captured in the ubiquitous advertising slogan, "At Ford, Quality is Job One." But quality didn't climb to the top of Ford's chart by itself; it took a lot of help from Toyota and Nissan and Honda. And that's the way major change almost always starts—from the outside.

Resources. These are the organizational assets that have potential value in light of the demands, opportunities, and constraints of the environment. Resources can be tangible assets such as capital, plant, facilities, and numbers of people, or they can be intangible ones like customer relations or the creativity of key employees. And of course there's money. Keep in mind that current assets don't necessarily hold their value. AT&T, for example, viewed The Network—its nationwide system of in-ground copper wire—as one of its most valuable assets. As fiber optics made copper wire obsolete, however, AT&T found itself forced in 1990 to write off billions of dollars for that very same network.

History. This comprises the past events, activities, and crises that continue to influence the way the organization works today. Like people, organizations are massively influenced by their experience, perhaps more than they realize. In the late 1980s, I was trying to help Xerox figure out why it was having so little success with joint ventures and alliances. As it turned out, history was a major factor. Xerox, founded as the Haloid Corporation, had initially spent nearly fifteen years developing the process it was to call xerography. When it designed its revolutionary new copier in the late 1950s and sought a larger partner to assist with production, sales, and distribution, it contacted such major corporations as IBM, GE, and RCA—all to no avail. (Tom Watson, the legendary head of IBM, later described his refusal to buy into xerography as the biggest mistake of his career.) In the end Xerox introduced the copier on its own—and the result was one of the most successful product launches in recent history. As a result, however, there is a strong sentiment running through the organization's subconscious that states, "Real men don't do joint ventures." Just think, managers will tell you, of the billions that would have been lost if Xerox had found a partner. The historical lesson was clear and resonates to this day: winning means going it alone.

As I said at the outset, these three factors—the environment, resources, and history—represent the givens in an organization's situation. In a sense they are the hand each new leader is dealt as he or she tries to decide which cards to play in the process known as strategy (Figure 2.1 illustrates these organizational components).

Strategy

More specifically, *strategy* represents the set of decisions made by the enterprise about how to configure its resources vis-à-vis the demands, opportunities, and constraints of the environment within the context of history. Those decisions involve:

- *Markets.* Who are our customers, and which of their needs are we going to meet?
- *Offerings.* What is the set of products or services we will create to meet those needs?
- *Competitive basis.* What features will persuade customers to come to us rather than our competitors? Low cost? High quality? Cutting-edge technology? Exceptional customer service?
- *Performance objectives.* By what measures will we determine how successful the other elements of the strategy have been?

Keep in mind that I'm referring here to *business strategy*, not *corporate strategy*. As I'll explain in more detail later, there's a distinct difference. Corporate strategy, as opposed to what I've just described, makes fundamental decisions about what businesses the enterprise wants to be in and typically focuses on portfolio decisions. I'm also

Figure 2.1. Organizational System Model: Input, Strategy, and Output.

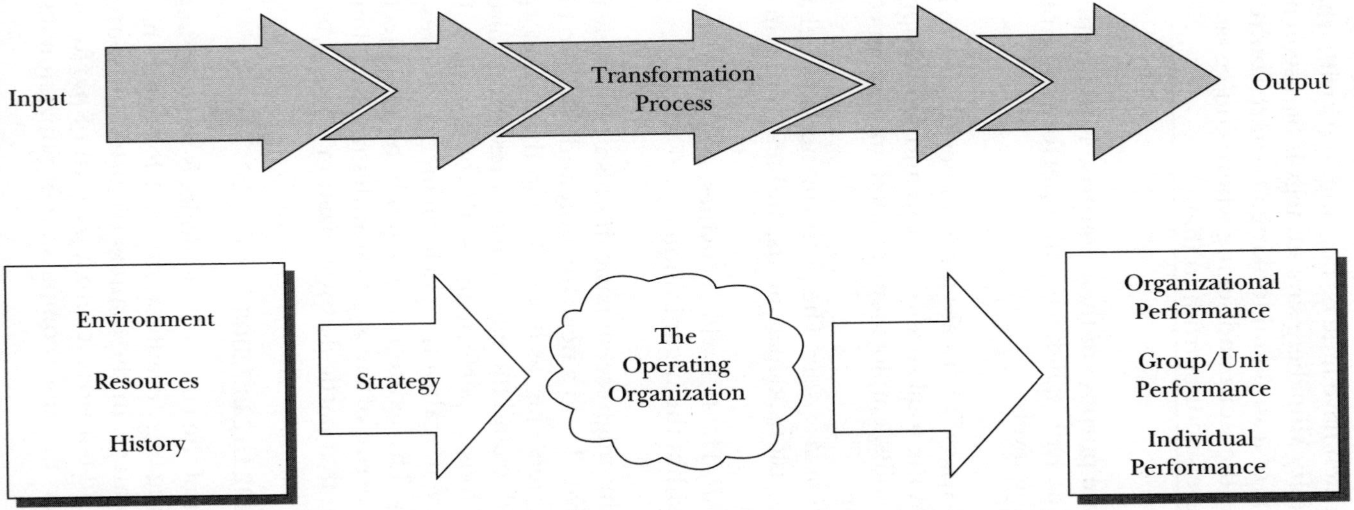

Input

Output

Transformation
Process

Environment

Resources

History

Strategy

The
Operating
Organization

Organizational
Performance

Group/Unit
Performance

Individual
Performance

talking here about enacted—not espoused—strategy. Written strategies often have little or nothing to do with what's really happening. Henry Mintzberg says strategy is best seen not by standing at the front of a ship and looking at where you're going, but by standing at the stern and seeing where you've been (Mintzberg, 1994). There's a lot of truth to that.

Output

The ultimate purpose of the enterprise is to produce *output*—the pattern of activities, behavior, and performance of the system at the following levels:

- *The total system.* There are any number of ways to look at the output of the total system—goods and services produced, revenues, profits, employment created, impact on communities, and so on.
- *Units within the system.* The performance and behavior of the various divisions, departments, and teams that make up the organization.
- *Individuals.* The behavior, activities, and performance of the people within the organization.

Although this might seem basic, it's also extremely useful. Whenever I'm invited into a new situation and asked to offer a diagnosis, my first step—just as it would be in the Dynacorp exercise—is to try to understand the environment, resources, history, and strategy. Then I look at performance—the output side of the system—and measure it against the performance objectives embodied in the strategy. The existence of a gap between objectives and output—and the size of the gap—provides my first glimpse of the dimensions of that particular organization's problems.

The Operating Organization

At the heart of the congruence model is the *operating organization.* The operating organization is the transformation mechanism that takes the strategy, in the context of history, resources, and environment, and converts it into a pattern of performance. In this model, just as the all-encompassing organizational system has its basic components, the operating organization has its major components: its work, its people, the formal organizational arrangements, and the informal organizational arrangements (Figure 2.2 offers a summary). Analyzing these components will also be part of our diagnosis of organizational congruence. Let's examine each in turn.

Work

Work is the defining activity of any enterprise—the basic and inherent tasks to be performed by the organization and its parts. Visit a company you haven't been to in five years, and the offices—even entire buildings—may well be different. You may be unfamiliar with the new equipment people are using. For that matter, you might not recognize many of the people. But the work the people are doing, in terms of creating a category of goods or providing certain types of service, will be essentially the same.

For example, Dow Jones and Company, which for decades has been publishing the *Wall Street Journal,* now offers all kinds of online services, but the core work is still the same—collecting, processing, and distributing news and information of interest to the business community.

When trying to understand the characteristics of work in any organization, there are three elements to look at:

- *Skills and knowledge demands.* What do people need to know in order to do this work?
- *Rewards.* What are the psychic rewards people derive from their work? These can differ immensely from one industry to another. Producing pine boards, for example, offers significantly different rewards than designing business software which is different again from managing investment portfolios.
- *Uncertainty.* What is the degree of uncertainty associated with the work? What are the key sources of stress and uncertainty that have to be managed?
- *Impact of strategy.* What are the constraints or demands placed upon the work within the context of strategy? For example, Wal-Mart and Nordstrom are both general retailers, but strategic decisions about the basis on which each competes result in two very different operations. Wal-Mart competes on the basis

Figure 2.2. Four Major Components of the Operating Organization.

Component	Work	People	Formal Organizational Arrangements	Informal Organizational Arrangements
Definition	The basic and inherent work to be done by the organization and its parts	The characteristics of individuals in the organizations	The various structures, processes, methods that are formally created to get individuals to perform tasks	The emerging arrangements including structures, processes, relationships
Critical features of each component	The types of skill and knowledge demands the work poses The types of rewards the work inherently can provide The degree of uncertainty associated with the work, including interdependence, routineness The constraints on performance demands inherent in the work (given a strategy)	Knowledge and skills Needs and preferences Perceptions and expectancies Background factors	Organizational design, including grouping of functions, structure, or subunits; coordination and control mechanisms Job design Work environment Human resource management systems	Leader behavior Intragroup relations Intergroup relations Informal working arrangements Communication and influence patterns

of low cost and has developed purchasing, warehousing, distribution, and sales processes all designed to lower expenses and keep prices low. Nordstrom offers its affluent customers a unique shopping experience and selects its merchandise, designs its stores, and trains its salesforce accordingly.

People

In order to diagnose any organizational system you have to analyze four characteristics of the people who work there:

- What knowledge and skills do the people bring to their work?
- What are the needs and preferences of the people in the organization in terms of the benefits they expect to flow from their work?
- What are the perceptions and expectations they develop over time?
- What are the demographics? What does the workforce look like in terms of age, gender, and ethnicity as these factors relate to the work?

The Formal Organization

If all of us were genetically programmed to get up each morning, stream from our homes in lemminglike fashion to our places of work and voluntarily—perhaps even cheerfully—perform our assigned tasks, the model could stop with work and people. Clearly, however, that's not the way the world works, and to compensate for it organizations of every kind have developed formal organizational arrangements: structures, systems, and processes that embody the patterns each organization develops for grouping people and the work they do and then coordinating their activity in ways designed to achieve the strategic objectives.

The Informal Organization

So far the operating organization on the congruence model includes the work, the people, and the formal organizational arrangements. But there's a final element that's crucial to understanding how organizations actually operate. If you put three people together for more than fifteen minutes, it becomes obvious that another powerful force is at work. Here's what I mean.

Consider the city of New York. It has an extensive and intricate system of streets that perform several functions. One, of course, is to facilitate the flow of traffic (I'm speaking theoretically). Another is to store vehicles; this is commonly referred to as parking. But people in New York, despite their many lovable traits, are not known as particularly tidy. So there's an additional work requirement: cleaning the streets. So how does the city juggle the competing demands of storage and cleaning? Alternate side of the street parking and cleaning, reinforced by street signs everywhere—"No parking this side of the street every Tuesday, Thursday, and Saturday, 8:30 to 11:30 A.M."—and a fleet of city tow trucks. In terms of our model the city has developed a formal organizational arrangement to accommodate the competing demands of two work requirements.

But that formal arrangement means that every morning, armies of New Yorkers have to move their cars to make way for the street sweepers and garbage trucks. So where do they go? To the other side of the street of course, where they double-park. But double-parking is illegal in New York City. Do these people get ticketed? No. The slips of paper you see on the windshields of these double-parked cars just carry the phone numbers where the owners can be reached in a hurry by the owners of the cars they're blocking.

Where is this arrangement written down? Nowhere. But somehow eight million New Yorkers all know about it and make it work surprisingly well. What has emerged over time is an *informal organizational arrangement* that balances the demands of the work and the needs of the people.

The informal organization, then, includes the emerging arrangements and interaction patterns that overlap the formal structures and processes. More specifically it encompasses

- The *organizational culture*—the values, beliefs, and behavioral norms
- The informal rules and work practices
- The patterns of communications and influence
- The actual behavior of leaders, rather than their prescribed roles.

Later in this book I'll describe many of these elements in terms of an organization's *operating environment*. And I'll be returning to the issue of leaders' behavior over and over again. For now it's sufficient to say that no single factor has more influence in changing an organization's operating environment than the day-to-day behavior of its leaders and managers. Several years ago, for instance, I worked on a project involving the branch banking operations of what is now called Banc One. Each branch was constructed and designed identically, each was supposed to do the same work, each had a top supervisor with the same title and job description. Yet each branch had a distinctly different feel—and the determining factor turned out to be the behavior of the branch manager.

The Concept of Fit

There's one more vital issue to discuss before leaving this central portion of the model.

Russell Ackoff, a noted systems theorist, has described it this way. Suppose for a moment that you could build your own dream car. You might take the styling of a Jaguar, the power plant of a Porsche, the suspension of a BMW, and the interior of a Rolls-Royce. Put them together and what have you got? Nothing. Why? Because they weren't designed to go together. They don't fit. You can see the concept brought to life nearly every time an all-star team of professional athletes takes the field. Inevitably, these temporary amalgams of world-class talents produce teams that are woefully less than the sum of their parts.

This concept of *fit* is crucial to understanding the organizational model I've been describing. In systems the interaction of the components is more important than the components themselves. In terms of the organization, its overall effectiveness relies on the internal congruence, or fit, of its basic components. The tighter the fit, the greater the effectiveness.

As an example, think about Sun Microsystems, one of the most successful companies in Silicon Valley. Founded in 1982, it was by 1996 experiencing an extraordinarily high degree of internal fit. CEO Scott McNealy redesigned the company in the early 1990s to create a structure he describes as "loosely coupled, tightly aligned" independent business units. Some are so independent, in fact, that some of their customers are Sun's competitors. That kind of formal structure in turn encourages independence, entrepreneurial innovation, and a heavy dose of competitiveness—all in keeping with the company's strategy.

At the same time, McNealy's own highly informal—sometimes to the point of quirky—personality has spawned a consciously anticorporate operating environment. There are no assigned parking spaces or executive dining rooms, no luxurious corporate offices. Not surprisingly, that environment attracts the creative engineers and scientists Sun needs to produce the kinds of breakthroughs—such as the Java system for creating Internet materials that can be read by any computer—that have fueled the company's success.

For now, at least, each component of Sun's organization is aligned and in reasonable congruence. The structure and the work support the strategy, and the work provides the challenges, and the operating environment provides the atmosphere to attract the highly skilled creative professionals the company's strategy requires. Somewhat remarkably, Sun maintained that degree of fit as it grew from a tiny start-up run by four twenty-seven-year-olds to a $7-billion-a-year corporation with 14,500 employees. Typically, exponential growth creates huge problems because it almost always throws some organizational component out of alignment. For instance, the demands of the work and the size of the workforce frequently result in controlling bureaucracies, which then destroy the entrepreneurial spirit that made the company successful in the first place. So far, Sun has escaped that dilemma.

Principles Implied by the Model

This, then, is the essence of the congruence model: the greater the congruence among the internal components (see Figure 2.3), the more effective organizations will be in transforming their strategies into performance. Conversely, the poorer the fit, the wider the gap between strategy and performance. For managers about to embark on change, identifying the points at which the organizational fit is breaking down is the vital first step in figuring out what has to change.

Figure 2.3. Meaning of Fit for Each Component.

Fit	Issues
Individual-organization	To what extent individual needs are met by the organizational arrangements. To what extent individuals hold clear or distorted perceptions of organizational structures; the convergence of individual and organizational goals.
Individual-task	To what extent the needs of individuals are met by the tasks; to what extend individuals have skills and abilities to meet task demands.
Individual–informal organization	To what extent individual needs are met by the informal organization. To what extent the informal organization makes use of individual resources, consistent with informal goals.
Task-organization	To what extent organizational arrangements are adequate to meet the demands of the task; to what extent organizational arrangements tend to motivate behavior consistent with task demands.
Task–informal organization	To what extent the informal organization structure facilitates task performance; to what extent it hinders or promotes meeting the demands of the task.
Organization–informal organization	To what extent the goals, rewards, and structures of the informal organization are consistent with those of the formal organization.

Let's go back to Dynacorp one more time. Think about how you would summarize what was going wrong there. The answer? Nothing fit. The Dynacorp we glimpsed was riddled with poor congruence. In a company where lone-wolf salespeople had traditionally succeeded by selling individual pieces of hardware, these same people, without any training, were being asked to operate as team members selling integrated office solutions. People were being asked to operate—and not doing it very effectively—without the technical knowledge or team skills essential to meeting the requirements of the new work. Wherever you looked in Dynacorp, nothing seemed to fit. In case after case the new requirements of work and the formal organization were running headlong into the old realities of mismatched people, obsolete skills, inadequate training, and a resistant culture.

Figure 2.4 shows the full congruence model, with the various components discussed so far. For anyone involved in planning and managing change, this model implies three general principles that can boost the odds of success. Or if ignored, they can doom the effort to failure.

1. Make sure the new strategy fits the realities of the organization's resources and environment. In the mid-1990s, Apple Computer's successive regimes stumbled from one disaster to another as they misjudged the external environment and underestimated their need to find a powerful partner to help stave off the growing dominance of Microsoft and the Windows operating system. At the same time, cost-cutting measures depleted and demoralized the ranks of first-class engineers who could provide Apple with the needed product innovations.

2. Make sure the strategy fits the formal structures, systems, and processes. Without that fit the most brilliant strategy is doomed from the start. When I first started working with Xerox, managers excitedly told me about their far-flung subsidiaries where lots of creative people were inventing new systems. The executive in charge explained that the major issue at that time was integration—how to get this array of innovative office systems to talk to each other. The company's solution was to set up each of the development groups as a separate independent operating unit. Well, if your strategic goal is integration, but your formal structure eliminates

Figure 2.4. Congruence Model.

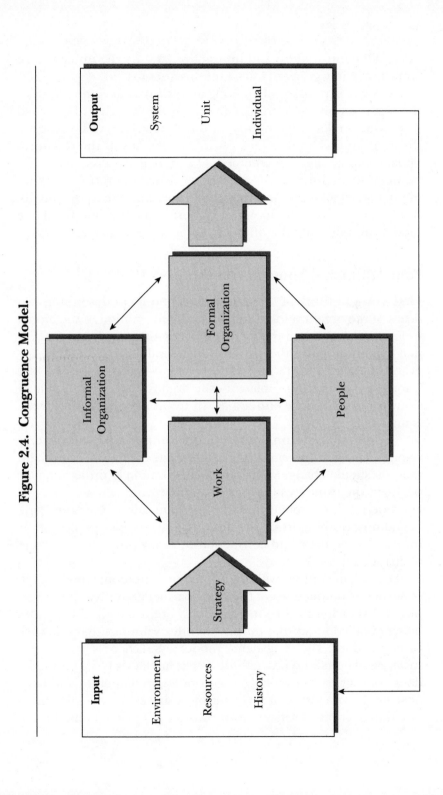

nearly all coordination and interaction among the units, you're almost certainly going to fail—and this attempt did.

3. Make sure there's fit among all the internal components of the organization—the strategy, the work, the formal and informal organizational arrangements, and the people. As I'll illustrate throughout this book, a lack of fit between any of the organizational components—between people and their work requirements, between formal structures and the informal operating environment, and so on—can produce huge problems. Whatever you do, don't assume that by changing one or two components of the model you will cause the others to fall neatly into place.

Four Additional Thoughts on the Model

First, you can think of the congruence model as describing two facets of the organization. Looking at the illustration of the model in Figure 2.4, think of the horizontal axis—the work and the formal organization—as the technical-structural dimension of the operating organization. The vertical axis—the people and the informal organization—make up the organization's social dimension. You can't ignore either axis. In terms of congruence everything has to fit.

Clearly, that was one of the major shortcomings of process reengineering in the early 1990s. Reengineering said, essentially, that you should change your formal organization in order to better perform the processes that make up your work. That's a narrow and woefully incomplete view of the organization. Reengineering had almost nothing to say about an organization's people and its informal structures, and consequently, rarely produced the scale of change it promised.

Second, in contrast with traditional organizational models, the congruence model doesn't favor any particular approach to organizing. Instead, it runs counter to many of the snake-oil bromides being peddled today that purport to offer solutions that will work in all situations. The congruence model says, "There is no one best structure. There is no best culture. What matters is fit." This model does not suggest you should try to copy your competitor's strategy or structure or culture; it says your most successful strategy will be one that accurately reflects your own set of environmental realities, no one else's. It is a contingency model of how organizations operate and as such is adaptable to any set of structural and social circumstances.

Third, this model helps you understand the dynamics of change, because it allows you to trace the ripple of change through the organizational system. As I said earlier, all major organizational change starts in the environment. It next shows up in comparisons of output to expectations, when people either see or anticipate changes. That leads to a review of strategy—what are we going to do to regain or extend our competitive advantage? Inevitably, this means changes in work and the formal organization—which is where many companies stop. Just look at Dynacorp. The environment changed; they had problems with output and saw a drop in sales and profits; they changed their strategy, realigned the work, and altered the formal structures. But they ignored their people and the informal organization. The result—huge problems of fit. Indeed, Dynacorp embodies what we have come to view as the classic change scenario.

Fourth, it's important to view the congruence model as a tool for organizing your thinking about any organizational situation, rather than as a rigid template you can use to dissect, classify, and compartmentalize what you observe. It's a way to make sense out of a constantly changing kaleidoscope of information and impressions—a way to think about organizations as movies rather than snapshots. You can't look at a complex organization as a static pattern of photos, capturing a narrow scene as it existed at one point in time, all neatly pasted in a scrapbook. Instead, it's a dynamic set of people and processes, and your challenge is to digest and interpret the constant flow of pictures—the relationships, the interactions, the feedback loops—all the elements that make an organization a living organism. In the end it is those dynamics that make change so fascinating and so challenging.

Now, keeping in mind this model for understanding organizations, it's time to take a closer look at the dynamics of change and their implications for leaders and managers.

Chapter Three

From Tuning to Overhaul
The Dimensions of Change

David Kearns's ascension to the CEO's chair at Xerox was part of a planned and orderly succession. Still, when Peter McColough retired on schedule in early 1982 and Kearns took over, he found that all his years as a senior executive hadn't fully prepared him for what was in store.

"It was a big leap from being second in command," Kearns recalled years later. "When you become CEO, the magnitude of what you have to do quickly sinks in. You find yourself thinking about the business 24 hours a day, seven days a week. You realize that everything ultimately teeters on your shoulders. If something flops, it's your fault. And so I found myself overtaken by two overriding feelings: on the one hand, a great sense of pride and accomplishment, and, on the other hand, a sense of, 'Oh, my God, I've got to make this thing work'" (Kearns and Nadler, 1992, p. 133).

Kearns had plenty to worry about. The Xerox he inherited was no longer the once-dominant industry giant, so ubiquitous that its name was swallowed whole by conversational English as both a noun and a verb. By the early '80s, more and more "xeroxes" were being run off on machines made by someone else. The company was being battered by aggressive Japanese competitors. Research and development efforts were disappointing. The quality of new products was marginal, in some cases dismal. The rift between engineering and marketing people was huge and growing. And profits, to use Kearns's word, were "cratering."

"As I thought hard about the company, I came to the conclusion that the trends affecting Xerox were so ominous that if something revolutionary weren't done the company would surely go out of business. The institution was more than threatened; it was terminally ill. We were drifting into highly dangerous waters, and it became evident that only drastic measures would work" (Kearns and Nadler, 1992, p. 133).

The kind of change Kearns undertook in the face of imminent disaster touched every facet of the huge organization—in every sense a totally integrated change that involved every component of the organizational model I discussed in Chapter Two—and reshaped the way Xerox did business in truly fundamental ways. It was difficult and often painful but in the long run a resounding success—a landmark victory by a U.S. company besieged by concerted Japanese competition. It was truly a dramatic organizational change on a grand, global scale.

Yet keep in mind that it was only one form of change. There are other forms that may be less sweeping but more appropriate for a particular organization under a given set of circumstances. The true art of managing change begins with understanding what kind of change is right for a particular organization in a given situation.

Charting Change

The first step in charting change is to dispense with any notions of change as a hazy, mysterious force swirling through the corporate universe in random, indecipherable patterns. The truth is that to a remarkable degree, change in the business world is predictable. Nor is change a steady succession of pounding waves, each following one right after the other. In every industry and business, change ebbs and flows in recurring cycles that to at least some extent can be charted and therefore anticipated and managed.

Starting in the late 1970s, Michael Tushman and his associates at Columbia University began studying evolutionary patterns—the birth, life, and death cycles—of companies within given industries, or "product classes." They charted the course of literally hundreds of companies manufacturing products as varied as wristwatches, minicomputers, airplanes, and cement. They scoured industry publications (one student, I understand, became intimately familiar with *Pit and Quarry* and *Rock Journal*), company reports, government filings—collecting mounds of information. They compiled it in massive databases, and patterns began emerging.

At the same time, my colleagues and I at Delta were working more in-depth and with a smaller group of companies—the number would grow to more than one hundred over a fifteen-year period—many of which were going through significant transformations. So while Tushman was studying change at a macro level, we were studying it on a micro level. When we put our findings together with Tushman's, what emerged was an unmistakable convergence of patterns.

First, all the industries demonstrated the same broad patterns of evolution. Initially within each industry there is experimentation and slow growth. Then comes a period of more rapid growth; the strongest competitors have survived the initial shake-out period, the product has gained wide acceptance, consumer preference has emerged for a relatively small number of dominant product designs, and producers are giving consumers what they want. Then as the industry matures, growth slows and then levels off. Eventually, the product class declines or gives birth to a new one (jet airliners replacing piston aircraft, for instance, or minivans replacing station wagons), and the pattern starts all over again.

This is a well-known pattern. Called the S-curve (see Figure 3.1), it has been established by years of research (Teece, 1987). The curve describes the pace of growth, or activity—charted along the vertical axis—as it unfolds over time—extending out to the right along the horizontal axis.

Tushman's findings went beyond the S-curve, however, by describing the patterns of change within the companies in a given industry. The concentrated periods of change within companies are represented in Figure 3.2 by the wavy lines superimposed on the S-curve. These oscillations indicate degrees of company change in strategy, structure, and people. The greater the oscillation, the more destabilizing the change.

In reality, there should be small squiggles on every portion of the S-curve, because some degree of change is going on virtually all the time. Nevertheless, the overall pattern consists of periods of industrywide equilibrium punctuated by periods of great change and instability at the company level. (Not surprisingly, this concept has come to be known as the *punctuated equilibrium theory*.)

Figure 3.1. The S-Curve.

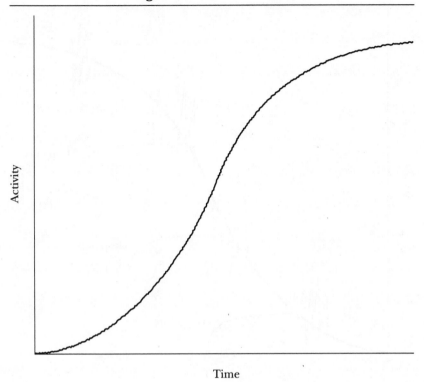

Activity

Time

Tushman found that these trends repeat themselves not only from one industry to another but among companies within each industry. The companies, by and large, tend to go through their major cycles of change at the same time, and the cycles seem fairly constant. While Tushman was studying minicomputers, for example, the change cycle was six years; the more staid cement industry, on the other end of the spectrum, seemed fixed in a thirty-year cycle.

As the wild oscillations in Figure 3.2 suggest, the periods of instability can be chaotic; in fact, the final phase of each period is littered with dropouts, companies that vanish through mergers, takeovers, or outright failure. In terms of managing change, the successful organizations are those that truly understand the change imperative. They engage in continuous or incremental change during

Figure 3.2. Patterns of Industry Change.

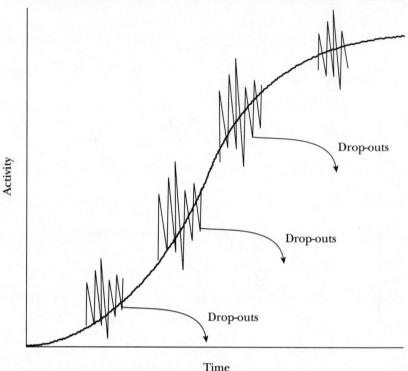

periods of industry equilibrium. At the same time, they're prepared to implement radical, discontinuous change as they approach periods of disequilibrium (Figure 3.3). In short, they have learned that timing is crucial.

My experience suggests some generalizations about the timing of change in relation to the industry change cycles. Initiating change early in the cycle offers no guarantee of success, but it certainly improves your odds. Tushman and his colleagues estimate that companies engaging in change at the leading edge of each cycle stand roughly a fifty-fifty chance of making it through to the other side. Those who fail to act until the end of the cycle are in trouble; their survival odds shrink to somewhere around one in ten. There are several reasons why:

Figure 3.3. Incremental and Discontinuous Change.

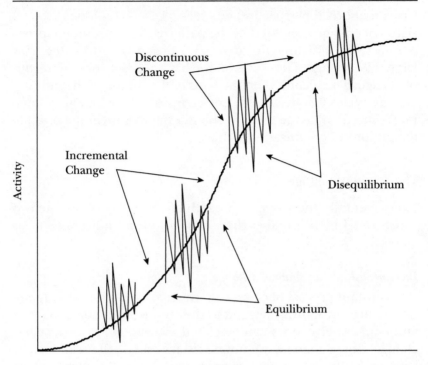

- Early movers—those who initiate change early in their industry's change cycle—can experiment, fail, and still have time to
  experiment some more.
- Early movers have the competitive advantage of influencing
  the direction of market and technology shifts, forcing late-
  moving competitors to adapt to their agenda.
- Early movers have time for their people to learn how to operate in the new environment.
- Late movers, in contrast, often find themselves short of the resources they need—time, money, people, reputation—to make
  profound changes under stressful conditions.

Types of Change

Given that broad perspective, now let's take a closer look at the varieties of change suggested by the patterns described in the previous section. Basically, there are two broad ways to categorize large-scale change. The first is on the basis of scope, or the breadth of change. The second is on the basis of the timing of the industry change cycles just discussed. Let's consider each category separately, and then merge them to create a full picture of the possible dimensions of organizational change.

The Scope of Change

Fundamentally, the scope or breadth of change falls into the two categories I mentioned earlier: continuous and discontinuous change.

Incremental, or Continuous, Change

The constant process of change in which all well-managed organizations are constantly engaged as they try to eliminate problems and improve efficiency can be called *incremental,* or *continuous,* change. These changes are not necessarily small; they can involve large commitments of time, people, and money. But they are part of an orderly flow—hence the term *continuous*—and each step builds upon previous ones. From the perspective of the organizational congruence model, the goal is to maintain fit constantly among all the components of the organization. It's only natural that gaps will appear from time to time: incremental changes help restore congruence.

Incremental change goes on all the time—or at least it ought to. This is the kind of change embodied in the quality management term *kaizen,* or step-by-step continuous improvement. Incremental change can have a major impact on large numbers of people, but that doesn't mean it has fundamentally altered the company's strategy, structures, and operating environment. You can't kaizen your way through a major discontinuity.

Radical, or Discontinuous, Change

Complex, wide-ranging changes brought on by fundamental shifts in the external environment are *radical,* or *discontinuous,* changes.

As in statistics, where the term *discontinuous* as I use it here is rooted, discontinuity suggests the appearance of some factor that disrupts a normal progression. I first began using the term *discontinuous change* years ago, and it has begun showing up in the language of change leaders. For example, Mark Willes, CEO of Times Mirror Company, and Jon Madonna, former CEO of KPMG Peat Marwick, both refer to what's happened at their companies as discontinuous change—I think because the term implies a radical change.

Typically, discontinuous changes require dramatic changes in strategy and abrupt departures from traditional work, structures, job requirements, and cultures, which in turn necessitate a complete overhaul of the organization. This isn't a matter of tinkering with the components in an effort to restore good fit; to the contrary, good fit is almost always the enemy of radical change. A comfortable, smoothly running organization is frequently blind to gradually mounting external threats, and people's satisfaction with the status quo makes it much more difficult to persuade employees that "business as usual" is a prescription for corporate suicide. Radical change means people have to *unlearn* years, even decades of procedures, rituals, beliefs, work habits, and ways of dealing with customers, suppliers, and coworkers—all of which, in their view, have been working just fine.

AT&T's recent history illustrates both kinds of change. The court-ordered breakup of the Bell System in the early 1980s was a classic case of discontinuous change. Spurred by a monumental event in the external environment, the company was forced to make sweeping changes in its strategy, its structure, its workforce, and its operating environment, which was totally unsuited to the demands of a competitive marketplace. The breakup also spawned continuous incremental changes until 1989–90, when Bob Allen fundamentally restructured the company, made major acquisitions, and attempted to remake its basic operating environment. More incremental changes followed until 1995. By that point changes in the competitive marketplace combined with the imminent passage of telecommunications reform by Congress to spur a third period of discontinuous change—the voluntary breakup of AT&T and its spin-off of NCR, its computer business, and its equipment and systems operations that became Lucent Technologies.

AT&T's recent history also illustrates the importance of destabilizing events in provoking discontinuous change. Sometimes the event is as concrete as the court-ordered divestiture of AT&T's regional operating companies or the adoption of the telecommunications bill. In other situations the event is actually a series of developments—in health care, for instance, the explosion in managed care was brought on by the convergence of oversupply, reduced government funding, and corporate demands for controls on spiraling insurance costs. In either case the destabilizing event or trend rocks the industry, creates new alignments, produces new leaders, swamps the laggards, and forces each player to change the way it does business.

The Timing of Change

As I illustrated earlier, timing has to do with where on the S-curve the organization initiates change and whether that change must be incremental or radical. From this standpoint there are again two categories of change: anticipatory and reactive.

Anticipatory

Anticipatory changes are made early in the disequilibrium cycle and often before a period of industry upheaval has even begun. They are made in the absence of any imminent threat from the environment. In a sense AT&T's voluntary breakup was an anticipatory change. Bob Allen and a small group of senior advisors began making serious plans for the breakup in the spring and summer of 1995. The decision wasn't announced to the world until September 1995, as the telecommunications reform legislation was making its way through Congress. By the time the bill landed on the president's desk early in 1996, the breakup was already in progress, CEOs had been named for each of the spin-offs, and the new companies were already beginning to operate independently. Because of the early planning that was involved, Lucent Technologies was in a position to stage the largest initial public offering in U.S. financial history in the spring of 1996—six months before the company technically was spun off from AT&T.

Reactive

These changes generally come either in response to some strategic initiative by a competitor, or in more dire situations, when the organization has its back to the wall. Typically, these changes come toward the tail end of periods of industry upheaval. In the field of health care, Kaiser Permanente—the nation's largest health maintenance organization—basically slumbered through the massive changes that reshaped its industry in the late 1980s and early 1990s. Without the benefit of any single destabilizing event, operating as a not-for-profit organization without dramatic financial indicators like stock price, for example, and inured by decades of serious concern about competition, the organization was slow to comprehend the extent to which private competitors were invading its turf. By the time David Lawrence, who became CEO in 1994, was able to persuade at least some of his people of the need for massive change, the one-time industry leader was left playing catch-up with its competitors.

Four Responses to Change

I've talked about change in terms of scope—incremental and discontinuous change. And I've also described change in terms of timing—anticipatory and reactive change. Now let's combine them to create a matrix that presents the basic responses organizations can make to the four types of change (see Figure 3.4). These responses are tuning, adapting, redirecting, and overhauling. I'll describe each in a moment; first, here's a general introduction to their significance.

Imagine for a moment that you and an opponent are in a sailboat race. You're both sailing along, and neither has a clear advantage. But you realize before your opponent that the wind is shifting; you trim your sails to take full advantage of the wind, and at the same time position yourself to cut off his wind. In our matrix, that's a *tuning* change; you anticipated a change in conditions, and took some fairly routine (incremental) action to exploit it.

Now your opponent has to react; he, too, trims his sails and has to make a course adjustment to find the wind. He's *adapting*, responding to a changed environment but staying within his basic game plan.

Then you detect an impending change in the environment; the sky suddenly darkens, the wind shifts and intensifies, and the marine weather report confirms your suspicion that a major squall

Figure 3.4. Four Change Responses.

	Incremental/Continuous	Discontinuous/Radical
Anticipatory	Tuning	Redirecting
Reactive	Adapting	Overhauling

is approaching. Rather than pursuing your strategy of tacking to make the best use of the wind, you drop your sails, power up your inboard motor, and set a course directly for safe harbor. That's *redirecting*. Responding to what you anticipate will be a radical shift in conditions, you've thrown out your original course, switched to an entirely different source of power, and even redefined what you will consider a successful conclusion to your outing.

The other fellow, misreading the severity of the impending storm, sails on, only to find himself tossed about in dangerous seas and ferocious winds. Pummeled by wind, waves, and driving rain, his strategy becomes one of sheer desperation: he broadcasts an SOS to the Coast Guard. That is a clear case of *overhauling*—a radical change in every aspect of the operation, initiated under crisis conditions in reaction to immediate threats.

In a nutshell, that's what tuning, adapting, redirecting, and overhauling are all about. Now let's apply these change responses to some specific business situations.

Tuning: The Move to ATMs

In the late 1970s, New York's Citibank perceived a strategic opportunity in what was then a new technological development, automated teller machines (which Citibank was then calling customer activated terminals). Bank executives believed the machines could give them a sizable leg up in the competitive world of consumer banking, particularly in New York City. Citibank took the unusual step of buying a company that manufactured the machines, and had them custom designed to offer features unavailable on the standard ATMs operated by Citibank's competitors.

Then Citibank launched Branch '77, a massive campaign—at a cost approaching $1.5 billion—and also took a number of steps unheard of at the time. First, Citibank placed the machines in the vestibules of its branch banks—a major enticement to security-conscious New Yorkers who weren't thrilled about doing their personal banking out on the street, particularly at night. At the same time, Citibank took the enormously expensive step of putting two machines at every location; although there was no way to guarantee 100 percent up time on any given machine, experience showed the odds were slight that both machines would malfunction simultaneously. The dual machines made it possible for the bank to promise its customers twenty-four-hour banking, a new concept at the time.

The whole program was spearheaded with an expensive but effective advertising campaign, which featured the slogan "The Citi Never Sleeps." And then came a historic demonstration of how a little luck never hurts, no matter what kind of change you're involved in. Just as the campaign was beginning, New York was shut down by a massive blizzard; Citibank quickly dispatched camera crews to film snow-bound New Yorkers cross-country skiing to withdraw desperately needed cash from ATMs in the warm, dry, and accessible Citibank vestibules. All in all, a huge success.

What was involved here? From the standpoint of our model, the change encompassed new technological developments and new organizational arrangements. But these were incremental changes. The innovative expansion in the use of ATMs did not involve any fundamental change in strategy, in customer sets, in organizational arrangements, or in people. It was not a small change, by any means; but as I said earlier, incremental changes aren't necessarily small in terms of money spent. This change was incremental because it was a logical extension of the strategy, technology, and procedures already in place; the shock value to the organization was relatively slight. It was a change undertaken not because of necessity but because the organization saw the opportunity to gain competitive advantage. Consequently, it was a classic case of tuning—an incremental, anticipatory change.

Adapting: Chemical Bank Plays Catch-Up

Now imagine you're Chemical Bank, number two to Citibank in consumer banking during the same period. Citibank has just gone into three hundred branches with its highly publicized dual machines. What's your next step? Clearly, if you intend to stay in the consumer banking business in New York, Citibank has just upped the ante—so much so that Bankers Trust, another major player, decided the game had become too expensive, sold off its branches, and basically got out of consumer banking.

But if you're Chemical Bank and you want to keep playing, you too have to go out and put ATMs in all your branches—and fast. You don't have the luxury of designing your own machines—you're stuck with the standard models. You can't remodel your branches that quickly, so many of your machines remain outside—in some cases, to this day. You're in the unenviable position of adapting—carrying out an incremental change in reaction to changes that have already taken place in your environment.

Redirecting: A Revolution in Banking

While all this was going on, Walter Wriston and William Spencer, chairman-CEO and president, respectively, of Citibank, were closely scrutinizing their external environment—looking at the broad issues that might fundamentally reshape their industry. They saw major developments unfolding, including new technology, government deregulation, and a strong upswing in disintermediation—the practice of corporations raising money by going directly to the financial markets rather than borrowing from banks. Wriston and Spencer reached the conclusion that they needed to begin repositioning Citibank, and quickly.

At that point Citibank's most profitable business—generating 100 percent of its profits after also making up losses of other operations that were losing money—was lending to governments and corporations. It was a great business; indeed, Citibank was one of the world's leaders in institutional lending. But the underpinnings of the business were growing shaky. I was present at the strategy sessions with Wriston and Spencer where it became clear that, over time, the role of bankers as middlemen lenders would virtually disappear.

So they reconceptualized Citibank—not as a bank, but as a financial institution. They talked about major expansions into consumer and investment banking, capital markets, and other potential growth areas. Wriston and Spencer saw all this as a very deliberate strategy to change the fundamental nature of the organization over the course of time—as it turned out, it took from 1975 until 1979. It involved a new strategy with major new initiatives, and a completely new organizational structure. It involved enormous changes in people; much of an entire generation of management was moved aside and replaced with younger people more in tune with the new strategy, resulting in people in their late thirties and early forties running major units of the company. And many of the new managers were brought in not only from outside Citibank but from outside the industry, including future chairman and CEO John Reed, an engineer from MIT, and Rick Braddock, who came from General Foods and would eventually become president. They invested heavily in changing the culture, spending enormous amounts of time and money on every form of training imaginable. They modified the entire rewards system.

Eventually, Citibank reworked every component of the organizational model: strategy, work, people, formal structure, informal organization. Some of the things it did worked; some didn't. But the fact is that when the bank found itself in serious trouble in the early 1990s, it was only some of the major changes made in the late 1970s—particularly the strategic move into consumer banking—that kept it afloat. This is an archetype of redirecting—radical anticipatory change. Before Citibank absolutely had to, it acted to meet the changes Wriston and Spencer saw hovering on banking's horizon; many of their competitors, who failed either to read the signs correctly or to make the required course changes, eventually went under.

Overhauling: Chrysler in Chaos

Plenty of corporations, after failing to anticipate and accommodate sweeping change, have been forced to engage in overhauling—the organizational equivalent of amputating several of your owns limbs while undergoing shock treatment. By far, the best example is Chrysler, the corporate basket case of the '80s.

A lot of people at Chrysler were asleep at the switch for an awfully long time. Chrysler had bad strategy, bad organization, and bad output. Throughout most of the 1970s, with Japanese competitors changing the shape of the U.S. auto market, Chrysler remained oblivious to the growing threat; when it finally realized it had to act, it lacked the resources to respond effectively. Ultimately, Chrysler couldn't overcome the dual handicaps of Japanese competition and its own poor management. Staring at bankruptcy, Chrysler had to reach outside to competitor Ford for a new CEO, Lee Iacocca, and then had to endure the unprecedented humiliation of a federal bail-out to stay alive.

Though the exact details of Iacocca's personal role may be in dispute, the fact is that the cumulative effect of his actions brought Chrysler back from the grave. He fundamentally changed the company's strategy from being a full-line international car producer to being a domestic producer of small and medium-sized autos. He replaced nearly all of senior management. He made major changes in the structure, the culture, the operating procedures. He turned the place upside down. He had no choice—it was overhaul or die.

Chrysler's crisis had all the earmarks of a typical overhauling. No incremental change could have brought the beleaguered company back from bankruptcy. There was no time to draft and implement a four- or five-year redirection plan. Chrysler literally had to reinvent itself overnight. Swiftly and simultaneously, literally in a matter of months, Chrysler executives had to remake every aspect of the organization.

Intensity and Complexity

Before moving on, I'd like you to think about change in relation to intensity and complexity—two additional factors that also help us begin to understand the management of change. There are two basic rules governing the relative intensity of change.

1. *Discontinuous change is much more intense than incremental change.* There's more work to be done. There's more stress on individuals. The process drains more energy from the organization. There's more risk for everyone and a higher probability of failure.

2. *Reactive change is more intense than anticipatory change.* As I mentioned earlier, those who initiate change early in each disequilibrium cycle have more resources at their disposal and more opportunities to experiment and fail. Reactive change is a lot like performing a high-wire act without the benefit of either a rehearsal or a safety net.

From that perspective, we can rank the relative intensity of each form of change: tuning as the least intense, followed in order by adapting, redirecting, and overhauling.

The other factor—complexity—has to do with the character of the organization undergoing the change. Lots of the best-known stories about change involve small companies or specific plants—the Harley-Davidson type of success story. It's one thing to create change when you can gather all the employees out in the parking lot and tell them what's going on. It's quite another when your organization is involved in different businesses, different product classes (each of which may be at a different stage in its evolutionary cycle), and different locations around the globe—all factors contributing to organizational complexity.

Charting the factors of intensity and complexity results in the graph shown in Figure 3.5. The vertical axis ranks intensity, with tuning at the bottom and overhauling at the top. The horizontal axis represents increasing organizational complexity. The results are three zones of change, each with different implications for those who manage change.

Figure 3.5. Modes of Change Management.

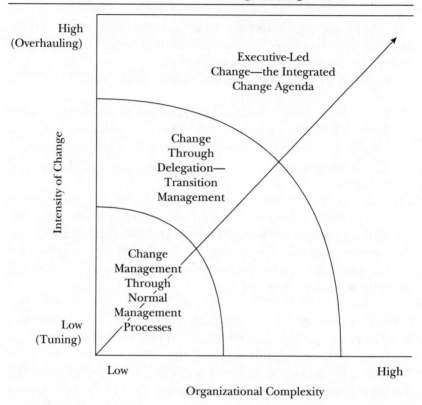

In the first zone—low intensity, low complexity—change comes through the normal management process. Managers set goals, give assignments, oversee the performance of tasks—in short, they run the place pretty much as they normally would. In the next zone— medium intensity and complexity—things get trickier; top management has to start delegating change responsibilities to specific people, because change on this scale just won't happen if everyone is attending to business as usual. This scale of change requires *transition management*—the identification of selected managers who are given the authority, mechanisms, and resources to manage change throughout the organization. In this zone senior management plays a supportive role to the transition team but continues to focus on current operations.

Change in the third zone—marked by the greatest intensity and complexity—is no longer a matter to be delegated. In successful change situations the CEO and the senior team become so personally involved in planning and managing the new strategy and the new operations that they don't have time for the more routine aspects of their jobs. Managing the organization through this period of intense, destabilizing change becomes not only their top priority but frequently their only priority. So in contrast to those managing less intense and complex change situations, the senior executives who have successfully managed complex, radical change have been the ones who delegated responsibility for day-to-day operations to other managers.

The various forms of change described in this chapter can be compared in terms of some important characteristics, as shown in Figure 3.6, summarizing a number of ideas presented so far and clarifying our view of possible change responses.

Clearly, there are concepts that apply to every sort of large-scale organizational change. But the more radical forms—redirecting and overhauling—hold special horrors of their own, problems and pitfalls that demand special attention. So in Chapter Four I turn more specifically to the special challenges that await the leaders of discontinuous change.

Figure 3.6. Comparing Change by Selected Characteristics.

Characteristic	Incremental Change	Discontinuous Organizational Change	
	Tuning/Adapting	Redirecting	Overhauling
Driving force	Internal congruence	Anticipation of future disequilibrium; anticipated crisis	Response to current disequilibrium; performance crisis
Focus of change	Individual components or subsystems of the organization	Most/all of components, including strategy, work, people, structure	Whole organization, including core values
Pacing of change	Targeted to specific requirements	Periphery → core of organization	Rapid; simultaneous systemwide change
Role of senior management	General support; delegate to middle-management	Key drivers, creation of urgency, and persistence are key	Key drivers and making good strategic decisions are critical
Replacements of senior management	No	Some members of senior management are replaced	Large numbers of senior managers usually replaced
Change management requirements	Relatively minor—mostly implementation-planning issues	Major—creating sense of urgency and motivation for change	Major—creating vision and optimism; dealing with resistance

Chapter Four

Reshaping the Entire Enterprise
The Special Challenges of Discontinuous Change

When David Kearns became the CEO of Xerox in 1982, the challenge he faced was, quite simply, survival. Having lost half its market share, Xerox was in danger not only of losing its position as the market leader but of slipping back into the pack of competitors scrambling to find a niche in an overcrowded industry. Thanks to Kearns's deft management of its Leadership through Quality program, Xerox withstood the Japanese onslaught, and the company did indeed survive as the industry leader.

Eight years later, Paul Allaire succeeded Kearns as chairman and CEO—and decided it was time once again for radical change at Xerox. The issue was financial performance and shareholder value. This time, said Allaire, who had served as Kearns's president through several years of the quality change, "It's not enough to survive. We need to succeed."

Kearns, on the one hand, presided over a classic overhauling—radical, discontinuous change in the face of an imminent threat to the company's survival. Allaire, on the other hand, embarked on a full-scale redirecting—a change equal to Kearns's in terms of breadth and intensity, but one undertaken in anticipation of changing competitive requirements, rather than in response to an immediate crisis. In both cases the CEOs envisioned change as a coordinated series of activities that would ultimately touch upon every element of the organization and reshape all of its internal relationships.

Allaire fundamentally changed the company's strategy, transforming Xerox from a manufacturer and supplier of copying machines to The Document Company, providing customers with the advice, technical support, and equipment to improve their use of documents, regardless of physical form. He made significant changes in the company's portfolio, dropping unsuccessful forays into financial services and office computers. He completely revamped the company's structure, changed the very nature of managerial jobs, overhauled the system of rewards and compensation, and made sweeping staffing changes.

"The technology is changing quickly," Allaire explained (Howard, 1992). "The demands of the marketplace are also changing. What's more, they're both moving targets. They're going to continue to change. So we have to change the company itself." And indeed the change was, if anything, even more dramatic and successful than the change from Leadership Through Quality. As I have already noted, over time the effort resulted in a quadrupling of the company's stock price on the New York Stock Exchange. Kearns, in effect, had saved the company; Allaire took it the next step and transformed it once again into an industry power and a thriving enterprise.

Success on that scale required more than a methodical expansion of what was in place when Allaire took over. Merely continuing to do what the company was already doing would not have achieved those remarkable results. It was truly a *discontinuous* change—a fundamental departure from the established course.

Although discontinuous change is disruptive and may require abrupt moves in new directions, it nevertheless has recognizable stages. The final part of this chapter describes the five stages of discontinuous change. In preparation for that discussion I review and reexamine some characteristics of discontinuous changes and some of the forces that cause it. I also describe the corporate Success Syndrome that can blind a company to its need for radical change.

The Elements of Discontinuous Change

In Chapter Three I discussed change in fairly generic terms, applicable both to tuning and adapting, the two forms of incremental change, and to redirecting and overhauling. As you might expect, discontinuous change, because it shatters the framework of the existing organization and scrambles the internal patterns of informal relationships, presents its own very special set of issues for leaders of change.

Let's start by expanding on some central differences between incremental and radical change, ones we particularly need to keep in mind as we set out to deliberately *manage* change in our companies.

Magnitude of change. One defining issue in thinking about discontinuity is the scope of change, which is different from the sheer size of change in terms of dollars spent or numbers of employees affected. Tuning and adapting are the kinds of periodic changes that well-managed organizations make on a regular ongoing basis. In 1996, for example, Microsoft reassigned literally thousands of engineers and programmers to work on new projects involving the Internet. The change involved huge numbers of people—but didn't fundamentally change the company's structures and processes, the nature of its work, or the informal operating environment. Discontinuous change, by contrast, is a jolting departure from the natural order of things. Compare Microsoft's changes with the changes chairman Louis Gerstner has initiated at IBM—changes in strategy, major shifts in product mix, new internal structures and external strategic alignments, and dramatic changes in culture.

Organizational fit. During periods of equilibrium, the goal of management is to maintain fit among all the components of the organization. Indeed, the reason for many tuning and adapting changes is to restore fit between segments of the organization that have gradually drifted out of sync. In radical change, fit becomes the enemy, the force that bolsters the organization's resistance to change. At KPMG Peat Marwick, for instance, Jon Madonna had to nationalize consulting, change the composition of project teams, revamp compensation systems, and alter the makeup of the management team in order to shake up the clublike atmosphere and the long-standing semiautonomous regional fiefdoms.

Strategy and vision. Although incremental change can focus at times exclusively on one or two organizational components within the framework of the existing strategy—improved manufacturing processes, for example, or new systems of compensation and reward—discontinuous change always requires a critical emphasis on developing and implementing a new strategy. Eli Lilly's change in the mid-1990s, for example, began with key portfolio shifts and a complete realignment of the remaining operations around five disease areas—an entirely new focus for the company.

Multiple and concurrent changes. Although incremental change generally involves a single change, or a series of discrete changes, radical change is characterized by a barrage of changes taking place simultaneously throughout the organization. Compare, for instance, Citibank's ATM campaign—a large, expensive, and enormously important competitive move in the area of consumer banking, but one that had little effect on the work, structure, staffing, or culture of the organization as a whole—with Allaire's change at Xerox in the early 1990s, a concerted attempt to transform every aspect of the company. As a result of multiple and concurrent changes, confusion and anxiety increase exponentially, with people often interpreting the changes from a personal perspective as disconnected and conflicting demands.

Incomplete transitions. Incremental change generally has a definable beginning, middle, and end. Discontinuous change isn't that neat; as David Kearns says, "It's a race without a finish line." Because so many changes are happening at the same time, it's not uncommon for some changes to be initiated and then dropped. The organization might launch a major effort to change the culture in a particular business unit only to decide later in a strategy review that the unit ought to be spun off. Indeed, because these changes are, by definition, attempts either to anticipate or respond to periods of disequilibrium, it is inevitable that external forces will necessitate constant alterations in the change effort as it goes along. That's what happened when Scott McNealy restructured Sun Microsystems from a single unit into "the Sun and its planets," a collection of semiautonomous business units. Not all of the changes stuck; some units were eliminated or merged into others, and some new ones were formed in response to the changing marketplace.

Unclear future state. For the same reasons it's often impossible at the outset of a radical change for senior management to present a detailed description of the future state. There are just too many variables. At Lucent Technologies, for instance, CEO Henry Schacht and President Richard McGinn are absolutely explicit in talking to employees about the company's vision, its values, the general assumptions about the basic corporate structure, and a very specific set of financial objectives they refer to as "the five simultaneous equations" that set concrete goals for growth, margins, return on assets, and so forth. But in the early days of the spin-off, they left themselves considerable wiggle room in terms of making long-term predictions about the exact makeup of each business unit because they knew changes in the competitive environment might force them to change the original configuration. They were specific when they could be, and the rest of the time, focused on what Scott McNealy calls "the chalk lines, the ground rules, the big rules."

Time span. An incremental change generally happens within a period of months; the biggest incremental changes unfold over a period of six months to two years. Successful discontinuous change typically takes somewhere from three to five years, and sometimes longer. In the special case of overhauling, the first burst of change generally happens much faster, as the organization moves desperately to save itself. But assuming it survives, the succeeding stages of change continue on for several more years. Both Xerox and AT&T, for example, have experienced successive waves of radical change extending for nearly a decade. During Jack Welch's nearly eleven years at the helm of GE he has led two episodes of radical change and now is heading into a third, centered on providing comprehensive services to support GE's wide array of products.

Leadership. In incremental change it's important for the top executives to fully support the work of the people they've assigned to implement the change while they themselves continue to manage the organization's normal operations. Discontinuous change is different; leadership cannot be delegated. I have yet to see a single situation, either at companies where I've been involved or at those I've observed from a distance, in which discontinuous change succeeded without the active, public, and personal leadership of the CEO and the other people at the very top of the organization.

The Success Syndrome

In Chapter Two I made the observation that discontinuous change is always ignited by changes in the external environment, and I described in Chapters One and Two the major external forces that demand change: industry shifts, technological innovation, macro-economic trends or crises, regulatory or legal changes, new competitive forces, and growth. Any one of these forces can be transformed from a background element in the environment into a factor crying out for radical change when it takes the form of what I referred to earlier as a *destabilizing event* (a term first used by Brian Stern when he was chief strategy officer at Xerox). These single events, or closely related series of events, should act as focal points for companies, drawing attention to some changing situation that can no longer be ignored—telecommunications reform legislation, for example, or President Clinton's attempt to overhaul health insurance in 1993. Even though the attempt failed to produce major legislation, it elevated the health care issue to a prime position on the national agenda, and that prompted a period of dramatic consolidation as health care players jockeyed for position.

Recall that in terms of the S-curve, destabilizing events signal the end of a period of equilibrium and create the *requirement* for discontinuous change. Successful competitors are constantly watching the waves, keeping an eye out for the next change in the cycle so they can be ready before it hits. However, there is a special class of organization that fails to notice the big one until it's crashing around management's ears. Let's look at this instructive phenomenon more closely.

One of the most amazing periods in modern corporate history was a certain eighteen months during 1992 and 1993. In that year and a half, the CEOs of more than a dozen Fortune 500 companies were forced out of their jobs. At the rate of more than one each month, some of the country's best-known and in many cases widely respected business leaders were toppled from the pinnacle of the U.S. corporate pyramid, reflecting immense uncertainty about the future at historically dominant business institutions. Though the pace slowed, the trend continued into 1994; by the time the dust had settled, leaders had been ousted at IBM, General Motors, American Express, Eastman Kodak, Eli Lilly, Allied Signal, Westinghouse, Digital Equipment Company, and Compaq.

What was behind this boardroom revolt sweeping the Fortune 500?

What each of those companies had in common was that they were industry leaders with a sustained record of tremendous success. Indeed, only a few years earlier most of those companies had been regarded as models by the rest of U.S. business. IBM, for instance, had been memorialized on a Fortune magazine cover as "The Most Successful Company in the World" (Hutton, 1986). The other thing they had in common was that each of their replacement CEOs immediately faced the need for radical change upon assuming the job, either a redirection or overhaul. So we can safely assume the need for change had been mounting before they ever took control of their organizations.

My colleagues and I analyzed what was going on at many of those companies, and what we found in each case was more evidence of what we have identified as a special case of discontinuous change we call the *Success Syndrome* (graphically represented in Figure 4.1).

You can see this pattern repeated at different times and in different industries. Companies do certain things that contribute to their success: they make the right strategic moves, for example, or they develop a particularly beneficial organizational structure. But over time, as success becomes ingrained in the company's view of itself, certain troubling characteristics start to emerge in the informal organization:

Codification. Informal ways of doing things, after becoming closely identified with some aspect of success, gradually turn into formal and inflexible policies and procedures. At IBM, for example, the once-useful practice of using overhead slides during meetings turned into a formal procedure, with presenters placing such inordinate emphasis on using slides the right way that meaningful discussion became a secondary concern.

Internal focus. If you believe you're the best in the world at what you do, why bother paying attention to what anyone else is doing? After a while there is a pervasive assumption that all worthwhile knowledge resides within the company. Consequently, the focus becomes inward, marked by an obsession with internal politics and endless concern with who has power, who's up, who's down, who's in, who's out. Conversely, little effort is expended trying to gather information about customers, competitors, suppliers, or market forces such as new technology. At Kaiser Permanente, David Lawrence (1996) says, "neither our managers nor our front-line

Figure 4.1. The Success Syndrome.

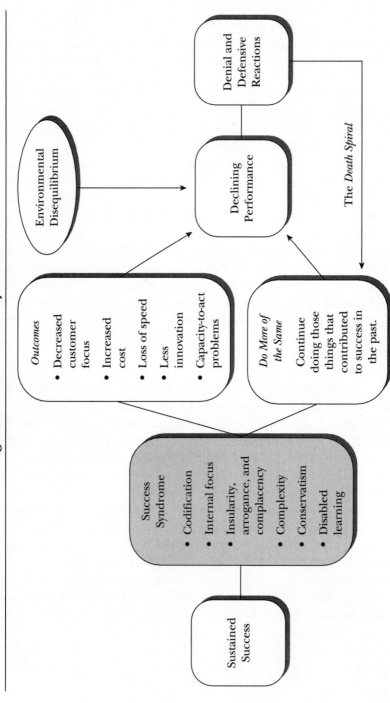

employees really understood the changes that were taking place involving our markets, competitors and customers. . . . They saw nothing to shake their fundamental belief that Kaiser Permanente had an inviolable, God-given right to exist in perpetuity, floating in serene isolation high above the tawdry forces of the marketplace."

Insularity, arrogance, and complacency. A distinctly dysfunctional tone begins to pervade the organization. It progressively cuts off contact with the outside world. Arrogance and insularity lead to complacency and the belief that any competitive problems are merely temporary blips. "We were almost a victim of our own success," says Randy Tobias. "We went through a long period of time where there were some ups and down and bumps in the road, but the financial performance was really quite extraordinary. . . . Until there was a cataclysmic set of events, there was really no catalyst to change." In Eli Lilly's case that catalyst was the loss of $11 billion in market value in just eighteen months.

Complexity. As more and more practices and procedures become codified, and as the focus shifts from customers and markets to internal politics, the organization becomes more bureaucratic and cumbersome. Preserving and expanding power become top priorities; accordingly, the informal structures become more Byzantine and complex.

Conservatism. The longer the company succeeds, the more risk aversive it becomes. Success becomes the norm; failure, even in pursuit of experimentation, becomes unacceptable. The fact is that most people come to conclude that when they are sitting with the winning hand, there's just no percentage in taking risky bets.

Disabled learning. As a result of their complacency, arrogance, isolation, complexity, and conservatism, these successful companies develop the equivalent of institutional learning disabilities. They're unable to try new things, learn from either their failures or successes, or develop new insights.

Sooner or later, this dysfunctional mess in the informal organization results in a pattern of observable and potentially disastrous outcomes:

Decreased customer focus. Not only is less attention paid to customers but when thing go awry there's a prevalent and convoluted belief—a kind of corporate denial—that the problem lies not with the company's offerings but with the customers who are making silly decisions. For years it wasn't hard to find auto executives in Detroit who told each other that the only people who bought small, inexpensive foreign cars were crackpots and weirdos.

Increased costs. Mounting costs come to be regarded as a natural part of doing business. Because there's practically no external focus and little regard for what other companies are doing, benchmarking is unheard of. In the absence of any strong countervailing force, bureaucratic momentum simply builds incrementally upon existing costs year after year.

Loss of speed. Everything slows down—the period from innovation to production, from production to market. The lack of concern about competitors translates into a lack of urgency. The market leader assumes that even if a competitor should bring a new product to market first, the leader's longtime customers will wait patiently for months in order to buy "the real thing." Frequently, that's just not the case.

Less innovation. People present fewer and fewer new ideas for either product or process innovation. Careers, rewards, and power relationships become dependent on maintaining the status quo. There's little incentive to stray from the tried and true; command and control supersede creativity and collaboration as the preferred management skills.

Capacity-to-act problems. Moving down through the organization is a growing inability to act (Shaw and Nadler, 1991). People feel they lack the empowerment, resources, and information to make decisions. They don't feel they'll be rewarded for taking risks. So all the decisions get pushed back up to the top, frustrating and angering the top people who don't understand why their subordinates won't just do their jobs.

In addition to manifesting these outcomes the organization as a whole begins to display a characteristic known in psychology as *dominant response.* People who have just learned some new form of behavior exhibit dominant response when they are faced with a perceived threat and revert to their old behavior. Acting on dominant response is a very powerful and common trait, and successful organizations typically do it too. The underlying ideology of the company becomes "do more of the same. These are the things that made us great in the past, and they will make us great in the future. So if we are threatened, just do more of the same."

A company that enjoys a monopoly or oligopoly can get away with doing more of the same for quite some time. But add disequilibrium and a destabilizing event to the mix and then throw in an environmental factor such as a new competitive force, technological innovation, or government involvement, and all of a sudden the outcomes of decreased customer focus, increased costs, loss of speed, and so on start manifesting themselves in sharply declining performance. That's what happened to the major U.S. automakers, who thought they could somehow protect their markets by conducting business as usual until all three were on the ropes, tens of thousands of workers had lost their jobs, and the government had to rescue Chrysler from bankruptcy. And that's what happened at Xerox, which finally woke up when it realized the Japanese had cut its market share in half.

It is hearing that wake-up call that is the real problem. In the face of declining performance, companies that have enjoyed success for years typically respond first with denial—"It's just not true"—and then with defensive attempts to lay the blame elsewhere. Typically, this takes the form of "the government did this to us" or "the Japanese don't compete fairly." In the most extreme form of defensiveness senior management blames the company's problems on its own employees, as IBM chairman John Akers did when he fired off a memo blaming IBM employees for not working hard enough.

Faced with the very real threat of declining performance, huddled in a foxhole of denial and defensiveness, management continues to revert to the behavior it knows best: "Just do more of the same." Predictably, that leads to continually declining performance, which leads to more denial—a tragic *death spiral*. In the past, many companies caught in a death spiral never pulled out of it. (Try to remember the last time you flew on Eastern Airlines or borrowed money from Continental Bank.) More recently, fewer companies have stumbled all the way into that irreversible decline because corporate boards have grown more aggressive about stepping in and replacing top management while there is still time— the trend we saw during the widespread removal of CEOs in 1993 and 1994. In each case the board then brought in a new chief executive to face the challenge of initiating and leading radical, discontinuous change.

The Five Stages of Discontinuous Change

Given our fluid and competitive environment and the enormous threats external forces pose to every organization, the prospect of discontinuous change presents leaders with three basic challenges:

- *Recognition.* Do you have the capacity to fully recognize changes that are about to happen in the environment—or are already happening—early enough to develop a sufficient response?
- *Strategic choice.* In terms of strategy, can you make the correct choices that will enable your organization to survive or even profit from this period of disequilibrium?
- *Organizational redesign.* Are you capable of reshaping the essential components of the organization in order to implement the new strategic direction?

Just as there are three crucial challenges for you as a leader, there are three all-too-common ways you can fail to cope with discontinuous change:

First, you can *fail to recognize it.* If you're the Big Three U.S. automakers in the 1970s, you completely misread the consumers' growing interest in small, inexpensive, fuel-efficient, high-quality cars. So a watershed period of industry disequilibrium catches you flat-footed, behind the curve, and asleep at the wheel. You're lucky to survive.

Second, you recognize change, you see it coming, you understand the choices it offers—and you *make the wrong choice.* You're Apple Computer, you see competing operating systems squeezing you into a corner, and yet you make an explicit choice to stick with a closed, proprietary operating system, eschewing partners or licensed clones. Again, you're lucky to survive—if, in fact, you do.

In the third scenario you recognize change, you make the right strategic choices—but you *fail to make the organizational changes required to make the new strategy succeed.* Travelers Insurance back in the mid-1980s clearly understood the changes about to sweep over its industry, presenting new threats from banks and other financial institutions but also presenting new opportunities in the field of managed care. The company designed new strategies to address that new competitive environment. Unfortunately, it failed to develop the organizational capabilities—the necessary skills, speed, and flexibility—to make the new strategy work, and ultimately was acquired by Primerica during a period of industry consolidation.

The point should be obvious. In turbulent times leaders must avoid the three common errors but also actively confront all three challenges; failure to meet any of the three could prove fatal. Over time those three challenges are played out in a cycle of discontinuous change that roughly breaks down into five phases (see Figure 4.2).

- Recognizing the change imperative
- Developing a shared direction
- Implementing change
- Consolidating change
- Sustaining change

When you're in the middle of massive change, it never looks this neat or well defined. In practice, the phases tend to merge and overlap. Nevertheless, the change cycle follows a logical flow and provides a general road map for planning and managing even the most complex discontinuous change. In the following chapters I'll take up each of the five phases in turn and describe them in considerable detail. For now, let's begin with a general overview.

Recognizing the Change Imperative

The easy description of this stage is simply that it answers the question, What's going wrong here? Of course it's not that easy. The essential first step is to use the congruence model to analyze each of the organization's components and how they fit—or don't. That requires examining the strategy, the work, the people, the formal structures and processes, and the informal environment, and then asking the question, What's working and what isn't? It means going

Figure 4.2. Cycle of Change.

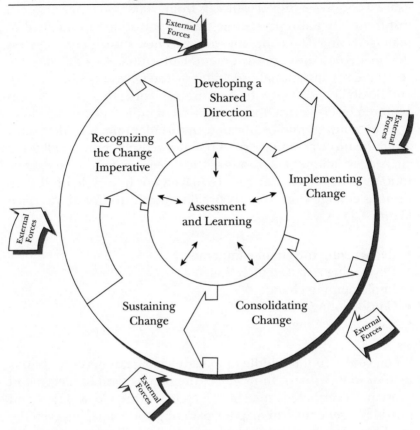

back, as I suggested earlier, and comparing the strategic objectives with actual performance and determining where things are falling apart.

As important as this diagnosis is to every organization, the reality is that it rarely occurs as a normal part of doing business. Executives who contact Delta Consulting because they know we specialize in managing change generally fall into one of two categories. One group includes senior executives who have just found out they're going to become the CEO of their company—sometimes as much as a year in advance of actually assuming the job—and want help in figuring out precisely what they want to achieve, what goals to set, and how to move the company toward those goals. The second group consists of CEOs who are still fairly new in their jobs but, after failing at their first attempt to initiate widespread change, have come to grips with the full horror of the task at hand. In many cases they liken themselves to a captain standing on a bridge who knows where he wants the ship to go, but as he barks orders, pulls levers, and pushes buttons, nothing happens. The crew doesn't pay attention, and the controls don't seem to be connected to anything down below. These CEOs are finding, as Henry Schacht says, that "exhortation will get you only so far."

I remember the frustrated new CEO of a Fortune 500 company who had launched a fervent campaign to improve quality, cut costs, and sharpen customer focus. Four nights a week he was out giving speeches, trying to rally his troops to the cause. "Everybody is agreeing with me," he said. "Everybody is smiling, everybody is nodding, everybody is saying, 'That's right.' And nothing is happening. Nothing."

That's much like the situation I encountered when I first started working with Xerox. Toward the end of his first year as CEO, David Kearns described to me how his intense effort to transform the troubled company through an emphasis on quality was having no impact whatsoever. Kearns had already done much of the necessary preliminary diagnostic work during his first year. The problem he found, in a nutshell, was that Xerox was rapidly losing market share because its Japanese competitors had decided to make quality a competitive weapon, which gave them advantages both in cost and customer satisfaction. Kearns came to the conclusion that they were right and that if Xerox were to survive, it too would have to make quality its top priority.

In other cases the underlying causes for an organization's poor performance may not be quite so apparent. When Bob Allen took over at AT&T in 1988, he knew he faced huge problems, but it took him six months of visiting field locations, talking to employees, burrowing into details, and employing the help of our firm and others before he felt he had a clear picture of what was going wrong.

Developing a Shared Direction

Having recognized the need for change and diagnosed the problem, CEOs face a two-step second stage: providing clear direction for change and building a coalition that will provide the support essential to the success of any radical change effort.

The first step involves the communication of a fundamental direction for change. Details come later, as the plan develops and adapts to changing market conditions. But the expression of some basic direction is essential. It might be Scott McNealy's "Sun and its planets" reorganization or Chairman and CEO Alex Trotman's Ford 2000 blueprint for speeding product design and development and focusing on global markets at Ford Motor Company or Corning CEO Roger Ackerman's "Growing Corning" initiative, aimed at improving performance and reshaping the operating environment.

Beyond that is the crucial need to build a coalition at the top of the organization to support the need for change and the direction to which the CEO is committed. The participation of the top circle of executives in this effort is absolutely essential. I worked with the CEO of a health care company who found that out the hard way in late 1994. He had spent two years working with another consulting firm on a very sophisticated, comprehensive plan for changing the company. But when he unveiled the finished product to his top executives, he ran into a brick wall. "No way," they told him. "It won't work." The issue of whether or not it was a good plan was irrelevant; having been left in the dark for two years, the executives felt no sense of ownership for a plan they felt was being forcibly imposed upon them. In fact much of the plan made perfect sense, but the senior executives, having been excluded from the development of the plan, didn't understand the line of reasoning underlying specific recommendations. It's also worth noting that other portions of the plan clearly reflected the absence of input from people with hands-on field experience.

In my experience this is the stage at which most CEOs make their first major mistake—failing to involve enough people and build enough initial support. The reason is simple: involving others takes time, and CEOs, by their very nature, tend to be impatient people. What those who make this mistake fail to realize is that the amount of time involved in developing the plan the right way the first time around pales in comparison with the time and effort required to correct and resurrect a stalled plan devised in secret.

Implementing Change

In some ways the step of implementing change overlaps some of the others in that the processes employed in the early stages of diagnosis and strategy development are also keys to implementation. The steps in the implementation stage can be broken down this way:

- Redefining strategy and rethinking the nature of the work required to employ that strategy
- Redesigning the organization's formal structures, systems, and processes
- Rebuilding the operating environment of the organization and creating informal arrangements that support the new strategy and work requirements
- Restaffing: making sure the right people are in the right jobs in keeping with the new strategy, structure, work, and culture

These steps are crucial, and I'll devote an entire chapter to each of the four. For now, I merely want to emphasize that all four are important elements in any change. If you're involved in leading change, the truth is there really are a limited number of buttons you can push. You can change strategy and structure, but you can't do that every day or you'll create chaos. You can change the culture, but as I'll describe in Chapter Ten, that's exceptionally difficult and can only be accomplished over a protracted period of time.

In many ways the easiest—and the most potent—device for sending signals about change is staffing. Reassignments, promotions, demotions, and dismissals all send powerful messages that are closely read by everyone in the organization. Yet in countless change situations such opportunities are lost. Too often the senior executives end up saying, "OK, we're done. We've changed the strategy and the structure. Now let's just figure out who we should put in all these jobs." That's a huge mistake. Staffing issues should be handled as an integral part of the change process, not as an afterthought.

Consolidating Change

This stage essentially involves three major activities. The first is communication and diagnosis. It's essential for the senior team to actively find out what's working and what isn't. Team members can do this through a variety of techniques, both formal and informal. They should use structured tools such as interviews, surveys, focus groups, and formal assessments. But just as important is face-to-face communication between top leaders and employees throughout the organization.

Refinement, the second activity, or step, simply means processing the information gathered with all those tools, figuring out which aspects of the change are working and which aren't, and then going back and fine-tuning the plan accordingly. This is where Henry Schacht's concept of "roughly right" comes in. He, like most CEOs, assumes it's unlikely that you're going to come up with the right answer to everything during a large-scale change effort. What you ought to aim for, Schacht says, is to get it "roughly right," and then to come back and refine it once the change is up and running. Interestingly, Schacht believes the aspect of change that almost always needs later refinement is governance; the relationship between corporate headquarters and the operating units will almost certainly be too tight or too loose, but the only way to find out is to get started and adjust things as you go along.

The consolidation phase is when what was once new and radical starts getting baked in to the fabric of the organization, and this is the third activity. As I'll describe in Chapter Twelve, it requires a wide range of techniques, ranging from political activity aimed at broadening and deepening support to using all the assessment, compensation, staffing, and training processes to support the strategy, work requirements, and desired operating environment. This is when it's so important for leaders to walk the talk, to reward those who support the change and help—or, if necessary, remove those who are still resisting.

Sustaining Change

In this final stage it is vital for top leaders to maintain their vigilance while the organization around them begins to gear down and life gets back to normal. It remains crucial for the lines of communication to stay open if leaders are to figure out which aspects of the change are working and which will "stick." One of the major dangers at this stage is renewed rigidity: leaders at the top may come to view change as a way of life, but most other people will be searching for stability. Many are eager to grab hold of the new strategy, structure, and work and say, "Oh, we get it, this is the way things are going to be from now on." Consequently, the experimental or transitional practices of the change period become as formalized and codified as the practices they replaced, much as we saw earlier in the discussion of the Success Syndrome.

At the same time, managers have to anticipate and be prepared to deal with the inevitable emotional letdown that follows a period of dramatic change. Though a steady diet of upheaval, reassignments, new responsibilities, and staffing changes can be stressful, it can also be exciting. When people have grown used to coming to work each day and finding out they have a new supervisor or there have been dramatic departures from the executive committee or the company has sold a division or bought a competitor, business as usual can be downright boring. It's not unusual for people to start suffering from mild depression and emotional fatigue in the aftermath of sustained turmoil, and management has to find ways to revive and sustain the sense of challenge, both on an individual and an organizational level.

This final sustaining stage also continues the consolidating stage, in that management needs to constantly reassess the effectiveness of each element of the change program and stay sufficiently flexible to modify the plan when necessary. This is the time to iron out the fit—to reconnect the web of relationships among organizational components that had to be ripped apart to clear the way for radical change. In the symmetry of organizational change, this is the time when the enterprise sustains and smooths the edges of radical change through a series of incremental changes and makes the midcourse corrections that maintain growth and success and position the organization for the inevitable next period of disequilibrium and radical change.

Once again, it's important to think about discontinuous change as a cycle rather than as a linear process with a beginning, middle, and end. The final stage of a change cycle always contains the seeds of the next cycle. One of the most vital responsibilities leaders have, even as they're enjoying the fruits of a successful change that's settling into place, is to renew their vigilance for changes in the external environment. It's incredibly easy in the wake of a well-executed change to become a prime victim of the Success Syndrome. Instead this is precisely when leaders should be raising their antennae and searching the competitive landscape for the "next big thing."

Organizational change would be a good deal easier if it were a neat, orderly process, a logical progression from step one to step two and on to step three. Unfortunately, it isn't. Even though I've framed my description of change in terms of a five-stage process, organizational change in the real world is neither linear nor serial. Each phase overlaps both those that preceded it and those that follow. It's a cycle; and as you'll soon see, it inevitably leads you back to the point where change begins all over again.

Now, as we press on with our exploration of leadership and change, it's time to leave behind the realm of theory—"where the rubber meets the sky," as a colleague once said—and get down to the real-world business of leading change. We're at a point in the book that's a little reminiscent of the old roadside circuses that once roamed rural America. To get customers inside the tent, the circus had signs and barkers advertising its big attraction: the dancing bear. Inside, after each act, the ringmaster would continue to promise that before long the lucky audience would be astounded and amused by the remarkable dancing bear. After a while the audience would grow impatient, and finally some heckler would stand up in the bleachers and shout, "Bring on the bear!"

Here comes the bear.

Chapter Five

Winning Hearts and Minds

Overcoming the Obstacles to Change

The first thing leaders of change have to realize, as they prepare to turn everybody's life upside down, is this one simple truth: for the foreseeable future nobody is going to love them for what they're about to do. Just ask Jamie Houghton.

In October 1983, six months after becoming CEO of Corning Inc. (then called Corning Glass Works), Houghton called his first meeting of the company's top 150 executives from around the world. Convinced that the company was in deep trouble, Houghton was determined to set a tone decidedly different from the convivial gatherings of the past.

"So my opening speech was not polite," he says. "I pointed out that our financial results were appalling, the organizational morale worse, and that as organizational leaders we were disgraceful. I said that our first task was to admit we were at the bottom and had nowhere to go but up." After comparing the company to an alcoholic who must first admit to the seriousness of his problem before having any chance of recovery, Houghton walked off the stage—to dead silence.

After dinner that same night, Houghton met again with the somber group and announced the first step to recovery would be "a major investment in total quality management. I said we were going to spend several million dollars in setting up a quality institute, in training all our people around the world, in establishing a corporate director of quality, and on and on."

Corning's top executives still weren't in any mood to stand and cheer. In truth, Houghton recalls, "I was a very lonely fellow. The organization was demoralized and very cynical. How could we spend that much money when we were just breaking even? Was this 'quality' idea just the new chairman's way of trying something out? I believe they looked upon the suggested quality initiative as being just another 'new flavor of the month'" (Nadler, Shaw, Walton, and Associates, 1994, pp. 251–252).

Houghton's recollections illustrate what may be the single most important concept involving change. In the words of Chase Manhattan CEO Walter Shipley, who has engineered some of the biggest mergers in U.S. banking history, "People fundamentally don't like change. None of us likes change."

For most people the notion of dramatic change is downright scary. Just ask any CEO who has tried to persuade employees to join him or her in a collective leap into the corporate abyss. The natural response is resistance; it might not always be obvious or overt, but rest assured it's there.

The depth of this resistance bears a direct correlation to the scope and intensity of the change at hand. Resistance to tuning and adapting tends to be relatively mild and largely localized within those portions of the organization directly affected by the change. As an organization moves up the scale to redirecting and overhauling, resistance grows broader and deeper.

Because resistance is so common, learning to overcome it is crucial to managing change at every level. In this chapter I focus on some specific techniques for doing that. To set the stage I describe the important notion of the transition state—the turbulent period that lies between where you are today and where you hope change will take you tomorrow. I talk about the initial responses evoked by change—instability, stress, and uncertainty—and about the huge problems they pose to management in terms of power, anxiety, and control. Then I turn from problems to solutions, and suggest twelve action steps successful leaders have used to manage their way through this perilous period.

The issues inherent in transitions present problems and challenges that no CEO can handle without the active support of senior executives and middle managers up and down the line. What's more, these issues apply, though with varying intensity, to all four change responses: tuning, adapting, redirecting, and overhauling. Consequently, they concern practically every organization in today's competitive environment.

Here's what I mean. Consider this list of the most common kinds of corporate change:

Strategic change

Structural change

Cultural change

New technology change

Merger and acquisition change

Breakup and spin-off change

Downsizing change

Expansion change

These are the changes that make news on the business pages every day; these are the squiggly lines on the S-curve. How many of these changes is your organization experiencing right now? One? Two? Perhaps three? When I ask managers that question, nearly three-quarters of them tell me that *four or more* apply simultaneously to their organizations. Clearly, at any given time a majority of organizations or major organizational subunits are in some stage of transition.

The Transition State

In 1993, as Randy Tobias met with Eli Lilly employees to explain the corporate change he had begun, he would start by talking about "the old Lilly." He would draw an organizational congruence model illustrating the company in terms of its strategy, work, people, structure, and culture. In change management terminology, he was describing the *current state*. Then he would talk about the remarkable changes washing over the health care industry, and he would describe "the new Lilly" he believed would be required to meet the new threats and opportunities. And he would explain every component of the new Lilly—the new strategy, the new culture and values, the new skills and attitudes that would be required of its people. To Tobias, that picture was crystal clear, and he could easily describe it to others. It was his vision of Lilly's *future state*.

The problem for every company undergoing major change comes when it reaches the point where Lilly was about that time—

when it is no longer in the current state but hasn't yet fully entered the future state. It is now in the condition first described in the late 1970s by Richard Beckhard of MIT (Beckhard and Harris, 1977) as the *transition state.* It is that transformational gray area David Kearns was describing during the change years at Xerox when he told his colleagues, "We are no longer the company we were, but we are not yet the company we need to be."

In most cases, you can get people to continue managing the current state—that just means doing things the same way. You can generally count on finding people to plan for the future state—in fact, many find that exciting and challenging. It's the transition state where so many organizations stumble and fall, simply because they didn't think it through in advance. Over and over I've seen managers labor under the mistaken notion that once they've come up with a design and strategy for change, the heavy lifting is done. Nothing could be further from the truth: implementation is always the key. As Sun's Scott McNealy says: "A bad strategy, well executed, will win every time. And a good strategy, poorly executed, will fail every time."

Given enough time, CEOs can fix bad strategies. But the most brilliant strategy won't work if the transition state is a disaster. As Randy Tobias once told me, "As I look around at the industry and at our competitors, I see many of the failures not as failures of strategy—it wasn't that the ideas were bad—but failures of implementation."

Based on years of close observation, I can assure you that transition states always feature three characteristics that if ignored, carry the potential to kill any change initiative. Their intensity will vary, depending upon the nature of the change and the culture of the organization—but I guarantee you they will be there.

Instability. You can always count on instability. The transition state begins the moment the first rumor of change starts making the rounds. At that point all of the formal and informal organizational controls start to disintegrate. If you think there's a good chance you'll be in a different job next year, or the unit you lead might be merged or wiped out, then how are your bosses going to measure your performance? The result is *transition paralysis,* the behavior people exhibit when they are so staggered by instability that they burrow into their foxholes and keep their heads down. It's a common phenomenon; people start to think there's no guarantee of reward for doing "the right thing," and too many risks associated with doing "the wrong thing." So they play it safe and do nothing.

Uncertainty. Transition states always spawn uncertainty. In the absence of concrete information about the future, uncertainty runs rampant. All of a sudden people haven't a clue as to which of their assumptions about their future—or that of the company—have any validity.

Stress. The result of all this uncertainty and instability is stress, both for the leaders of change and those they're trying to lead. Looking back at KPMG's transition period in the mid-1990s, Jon Madonna believes much of the opposition he encountered resulted not so much from his new strategy as from the instability and uncertainty involved in getting there: "People were thinking, 'There's got to be an easier way. Isn't there a pill I can take to get through this?'"

However, there is a flip side to all of this. Just as a poorly planned and badly managed transition state can be disastrous, one that's handled well can generate enormous excitement. People not only see new opportunities for the organization but also feel personally challenged; they see new prospects for growth and advancement, and they feel good about being part of a reinvigorated organization. That kind of enthusiasm is contagious, and leaders should constantly be on the lookout for ways to leverage it.

Nevertheless, the three characteristics of instability, uncertainty, and stress inevitably lead to three problems that require painstaking management during any transition period. Let's consider each of them.

Power

Every organization is a political system. Every organization has identifiable groups, cliques, and coalitions, each of which holds fast to its own values and beliefs. Each faction works to accumulate and exercise power in pursuit of its own vision—and not incidentally, in pursuit of power for the leaders of those groups. At any given time there is a relative distribution of power—some groups have more, some have less.

During periods of change, there's a tectonic shift in the distribution of power. The result is an upsurge in political activity. Those who have power worry about losing it and work to tighten their control; those with less power see new openings and begin maneuvering for a bigger share of the pie.

Consequently, the early stages of major change are always characterized by intense, nonproductive political activity stimulated by changes in the informal organizational structure. It consumes enormous amounts of energy, most of which—theoretically—would otherwise be channeled into work. You can easily tell when you're at an organization going through this phase. You can see it in the hallways and hear it in the cafeteria. People are griping. They're furtively huddling when they think no one is noticing. They're whispering into their phones, making lunch dates with former colleagues. Few are thinking about their work or their customers.

Political activity is most intense when the impending changes strike at core values. As Kaiser Permanente tried to overhaul itself in the early and mid-1990s, there was tremendous resistance to the idea of shifting power from regional operations to national headquarters. There was a perception that the organization was stepping back from the lofty ideals of its social mission as a not-for-profit health care system to compete in the grubby competitive marketplace. Some people felt the organization's traditions and values were at stake, and political resistance was immense.

Similarly, political resistance is common when reorganizations significantly alter established patterns of control. Jon Madonna ran into that when he shifted power from KPMG's one hundred local offices to corporate executives in New York; so did Scott McNealy when he decentralized corporate power through the creation of Sun's independent business units. "I got every reaction in the book," McNealy says. "I even had a lot of people subvert it for many years, and fight it—in fact, some of them still are fighting it."

Anxiety

Let me share two incidents that illustrate how anxiety comes into play during transitions.

A few years ago, I was consulting on a change project at a well-known oil company. After months of planning and preparation the president met with his thirty top executives and unveiled his comprehensive blueprint for changing the company's strategy, structure, and portfolio. At the end of his presentation he asked for questions, and one of the most senior executives rose to his feet.

"Sir," he said. "I want you to know there are nine questions on everybody's mind."

"Nine questions?" asked the president, somewhat taken aback.

"Yes, sir, nine questions," the executive repeated. "The first question is this is all very interesting, but what's going to happen to me? The second question is what's going to happen to me? The third question is what's going to happen to me?" (The other six questions, in case you're curious, were why? why? why? and when? when? when?)

Some years prior to that incident, in the early 1980s before the Bell System breakup, I was doing some work with Mountain Bell. At the time each of the state phone companies within Mountain Bell operated as an independent unit. Now they were being combined and restructured into three operating units based on market segments—business, residential, and network—rather than on geography. The state companies would be reduced to the status of regulatory overseers, while the real work would be done by the new business units. Under the new plan, for example, the top executive in Colorado would go from leading an operation of twenty-five thousand people to supervising a staff of forty. Needless to say, the restructuring was playing havoc with power relationships throughout the organization.

One of my jobs was to help Bob Timothy, Mountain Bell's president, craft a clear, thorough statement that would explain what was happening, why, and when. I listened as he gave his presentation to the company's top executives, and I thought he did a marvelous job.

The next morning, waiting on line for coffee in the executive dining area, I overheard two people talking.

"Did you hear Timothy's speech yesterday?" one fellow asked the other. "What did you think of it?"

"I don't understand," the second man replied. "Why are we doing all this?"

"I don't understand it either," admitted the first. "I mean, exactly what is it that's going to happen?"

Having written what I thought was a classic piece of descriptive oratory, I was stunned and disappointed. Quickly I used some surveys and interviews to get a better handle on reaction to the speech. The results were consistent and the lesson was clear: most people could not hear and integrate a major message involving dramatic change until they had heard it on three separate occasions. As a result, my colleagues and I designed a process requiring that every major message had to be delivered at least six times—a practice our firm has continued wherever we've been involved with major integrated change.

What do these two episodes have in common? Anxiety and stress. The moment someone stands up, starts talking about change, and can't answer the question, What does this mean to me? (and odds are the person can't answer because he or she doesn't know) we all experience stress and anxiety. And we stop hearing.

Some managers are convinced that anxiety and stress improve performance. That's true, but only up to a point. Too much anxiety and stress can dramatically diminish performance, starting with the ability to process information. Employees caught in the throes of change-induced anxiety just can't hear you. They can't figure out what's going to happen. They have no idea how to act or what to do.

Control

Because the organization usually starts to dismantle the current state before the future state is up and running, the current state collapses in the minds of employees long before its formal structures have disappeared. The moment people suspect that a major change is in the offing, they start to believe all bets are off. At that point, management begins to lose control.

That's particularly disastrous where people deal directly with customers. The classic control problem—at AT&T, IBM, Xerox, and just about every enterprise that's undergone major change—is that almost any time the salesforce is reorganized, the company loses customers. There are just too many questions: What's happening to the compensation plan? Will I keep my coverage area? Am I going to have to start selling products I've never heard of? Managers soon find that pushing the usual buttons doesn't accomplish anything; rampant uncertainty has dulled both the fear of punishment and the hope of reward.

Keep in mind the connection between the problems of power, anxiety, and control and the congruence model(see Figure 5.1). Given major changes in either the strategy or the work processes, or both, the redistribution of power shakes the informal organization. Anxiety warps individual behavior. And the formal organization suffers from a breakdown in the normal structures, processes, and systems.

**Figure 5.1. Power, Anxiety, and Control
and the Congruence Model.**

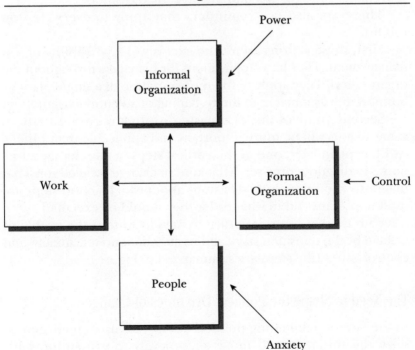

More specifically, if unaddressed, the problems of power, anxiety, and control can cripple the organization. They bog people down in dysfunctional office politics, divert focus from competitive demands, and seriously damage relationships with customers and suppliers. The good news is that it's possible to design a coordinated plan of attack that addresses all these issues and paves the way to successful change.

Managing the Transition: Twelve Action Steps

Having watched dozens of organizations wrestle with these three problems, my colleagues and I have had the opportunity to judge firsthand what works and what doesn't. We've distilled those various approaches into a dozen action steps for overcoming resistance to change.

We also found that the twelve steps can be subdivided according to the organizational and leadership needs they imply: the need to shape the political dynamics of change, the need to motivate change, and the need to manage the transition.

There are also two reminders that apply to every step on this list.

First, these actions aren't the exclusive responsibility of top management. They have applications for managers throughout the organization. They apply to the reorganization of a single plant or business unit as much as to the reshaping of an entire corporation.

Second, think of this as a master list. In any given situation, some actions will be more important and applicable than others. As I'll explain later, one of the earliest steps in any change situation is to diagnose precisely what kind of change is called for. That diagnosis should include decisions about which action steps are most important and in what order they should be executed.

With those caveats, let's turn to ways to address the problems created by the transition stage and its attendant power, anxiety, and control issues (the steps are summarized in Figure 5.2).

The Need to Shape the Political Dynamics of Change

In the face of debilitating political activity, it's up to managers to seize the initiative and move aggressively to win support for change. Kaiser Permanente's David Lawrence employs a useful

Figure 5.2. Responses to Power, Anxiety, and Control.

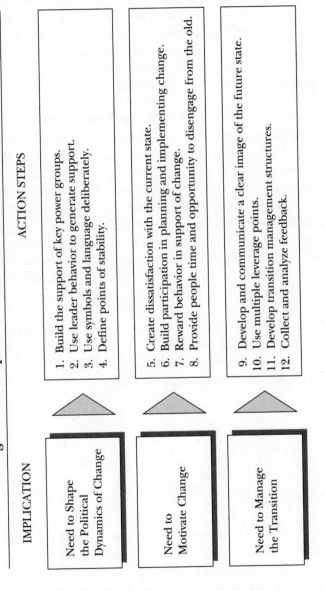

IMPLICATION

ACTION STEPS

Need to Shape the Political Dynamics of Change

1. Build the support of key power groups.
2. Use leader behavior to generate support.
3. Use symbols and language deliberately.
4. Define points of stability.

Need to Motivate Change

5. Create dissatisfaction with the current state.
6. Build participation in planning and implementing change.
7. Reward behavior in support of change.
8. Provide people time and opportunity to disengage from the old.

Need to Manage the Transition

9. Develop and communicate a clear image of the future state.
10. Use multiple leverage points.
11. Develop transition management structures.
12. Collect and analyze feedback.

metaphor: he likens this aspect of change to a political campaign, an all-out effort to win people's hearts and minds. And he reports, "We made numerous errors because we failed to invest heavily enough in planning the campaign aspects of our change. We started out with the assumption that once we had the mission, values, strategies, and some tactics, that our work was done. All we would have to do is implement. We were wrong."

Let's look at four ways to plan a campaign that addresses the issues of power.

Action Step 1: Build the Support of Key Power Groups

Assuring support for change among key power groups should begin well before the change is announced. In early 1983, when Xerox executives finally agreed to initiate a massive quality-based change effort, one vice chairman urged that the decision be announced immediately. Others, myself included, urged a delay. In the end the announcement was held off for nine months—a postponement that proved enormously beneficial. During that time key executives enlisted the aid of unions. They lobbied the heads of major business units. They identified key opinion leaders and signed them up as supporters long before the change was publicly announced.

Of course, it's impossible to win everyone over, no matter how hard you try. And the ones you do win over will join you with varying degrees of enthusiasm. Beckhard (1969) uses these four categories to describe the range of response people have toward change:

Those who make it happen

Those who help it happen

Those who let it happen

Those who get in the way

In any situation, there are only a few people whose active participation is absolutely essential. There are others who could be extremely helpful but aren't necessarily crucial. Successful managers target the really essential people at the outset, and then employ a range of techniques to attract involvement by other key players. In descending order of importance, these techniques are

- Participation
- Persuasion
- Incentives
- Isolation
- "Ventilation"

Let me explain each.

Participation is far and away the most important technique. I can't overstate how important it is to bring crucial people into the process and win their enthusiastic support. "It's better to take more time at the beginning to make sure everybody's on board than to rush it," says Henry Schacht. "I'm a great believer that if you don't have everybody on board, you're not going to get there. You're pushing a boat through the water sideways. You're far better off to get the boat turned around, get everybody pulling the oars, and then go like hell."

I'll repeat this notion throughout this book, but think about participation in terms of concentric rings. The way to build participation—and this is true at every level of the organization—is to start with a small, trusted, cohesive group, get the people in that group totally committed to the vision and objectives of the change strategy, and then let them gradually engage successive groups of people, constantly pushing the participation out into the organization.

The technique of *persuasion* can sometimes be used to win the support of people whom you might not want to involve directly in the initial, sensitive stages of designing the change. These people might be won over through persuasive appeals to a shared sense of the organization's core values.

Both *formal and informal incentives*—an opportunity for a new assignment, opening of a new career path, perception of increased status—are often used to win support. Keep in mind, however, that the support you engender with rewards tends to be less intense than the support you get from people who feel personally involved and ideologically committed to the change.

Isolation is a technique sometimes used with people who are important to the organization but unlikely to support the change, no matter what. The idea is to keep them on board but reassign them somewhere far from the initial change activity during its fragile stage.

"Ventilation" is a euphemism I heard used by the human resources chief at a major company. His actual statement was, "We're opening a retirement window and we think we're going to ventilate about two thousand people." (It's hard to find a euphemism for getting rid of people that isn't distasteful. I recently heard an executive say that a colleague had been "changed out," which is the sort of thing that gives change management a bad name.) In this context, I'm talking not about massive layoffs but about the replacement of small numbers of very senior people. I can virtually guarantee that if major change is to succeed, some alteration in the cast of senior characters is unavoidable.

As David Lawrence says, "It is inevitable in most change situations that some people just are not going to make it. Perhaps it is just not in their nature to handle change well. Or, because of their background, attitudes, ideology, or style, they are not going to be a good match with the new structures, processes, or culture. There are lots of reasons why very smart, able, and well-meaning people cannot succeed in their old job in a new era."

Action Step 2: Use Leader Behavior to Generate Support

The second technique for designing the campaign for change is to employ leader behavior to create support. The visible actions of respected leaders are crucial to creating widespread support. I'm talking about how leaders use rewards and punishment, how they employ language and symbols, how they act in public. During the early stages of change, leader-watching becomes one of the organization's most popular spectator sports.

"Everything counts," says Henry Schacht. "Every signal counts—little signals, big signals, intentional signals, unintentional signals." Managers have to be keenly sensitive to the possible ramifications of everything they do and say because people will try to read signals even when no signals are being sent. I have seen inadvertent grunts, grimaces, and symptoms of indigestion by senior executives misread and widely misreported as opposition to change.

Conversely, during this period of intense leader-watching, simple acts can send similarly powerful messages in support of change. I once worked with a CEO who was hired to overhaul a traditional manufacturing firm. In the past, key company decisions had always been made in secret, quite literally behind the closed doors of executive offices that extended down a series of long, empty corridors. Two weeks after taking over, the new CEO brought in a construction crew one weekend and had them rip out all the office doors. Nothing he might have said could have sent as clear a signal and engendered as much support among the rank and file.

Still, it's not enough for the CEO to send big messages; during the transition more than at any other time, every leader has to walk the talk. People are searching for signs that perhaps not everyone in management is on board and perhaps the change isn't a foregone conclusion. It's a time when people seize upon every fragment of rumor and gossip, every anecdote from supposed "insiders" who claim to have well-placed sources. In this environment it's essential for managers to make sure that every action and utterance is consistent with the change agenda.

Action Step 3: Use Symbols and Language Deliberately

The third technique for building support lies in the deliberate use of symbols and language. Think of mass political movements; throughout history, the most successful ones have skillfully employed symbols and language systems to build support. Consider the emotional responses evoked by national flags and patriotic songs. Think about the political slogans that become conceptual shorthand for complex concerns—slogans like "family values" and "character counts."

Similarly, organizations involved in change can create new symbols and language systems that encapsulate primary themes and then find creative ways to insinuate those new words and symbols into the workplace. Some successful organizations make it impossible to function in the workplace without using the new vocabulary. Over time the continued use of the new terms conveys implicit support of the change. And the more people hear the supportive language all around them, the more they believe in the reality and the legitimacy of the change. One of the enduring strengths of the total quality movement, in fact, has been its capacity to induce large numbers of people to start using its distinctive vocabulary—terms like *continuous improvement* and *process discipline*. Before long, the concepts embodied in those terms take on a life of their own.

Symbols likewise can effectively convey a sense of widespread acceptance of a change. When Corning launched its quality effort in the 1980s, executives searched for a symbol that would clearly say "quality" but also incorporate some characteristic unique to their company. They came up with the Quapple, a stylized letter Q that not only stood for quality but also resembled an apple, in recognition of Corning's roots in rural Steuben County, New York. Before long, Quapples were showing up as lapel pins, factory banners, and quality control stamps on assembly lines.

Over time, the Quapple worked because it meant something. At GTE, which launched its own quality program at about the same time, the results were considerably different. The program was called The Best, signifying that the company wanted to be the best at offering quality to its customers, and all the employees were given "Best" buttons. When the quality effort sputtered, the "Best" buttons became merely embarrassing reminders of a failed program. (A second effort a few years later proved to be much more successful.)

Action Step 4: Define Points of Stability

The fourth technique for shaping the political dynamics and building support is to define points of stability. People need to know that those in charge—some of whom might be newcomers—aren't discounting the value of everything—and everyone—connected with the past. By maintaining some sense of continuity, leaders can reduce concern about wholesale changes in power relationships and core values.

Consequently, in the course of explaining change, leaders should be just as clear and emphatic about what isn't changing. In 1996, as Corning Clinical Laboratories was being spun off from Corning Inc. as the independent company Quest Diagnostics, the senior team hammered out a new list of corporate values for the new venture. In the end, four of Quest's six values were the same as the parent company's Corning Values—a point Quest CEO Ken Freeman was careful to highlight as he introduced them in a companywide video. "We believe the Corning Values represent a proud part of our company's heritage, an element of our past that should help shape our future," he told employees.

Maintaining important links to the past is particularly important in merger and acquisition situations. "It's like your grandpar-
ents died at the time of the merger," says Chase Manhattan's Walter
Shipley, who's had the experience of being both a junior manager
at a small bank swallowed by a larger one and then a top executive
managing mergers with other banks. "What I talk about a lot with
our people is the wonderful heritage of the old Chase and the old
Chemical and the old Manufacturers Hanover, and that it's very
important to honor and respect and revere those histories, but not
to dwell on them, not to hang onto them."

The Need to Motivate Change

In the face of the widespread anxiety that accompanies major
change, managers must constantly emphasize that change is necessary and that constructive behavior in support of change will
ultimately result in a better organization. Here are four ways to
do that.

Action Step 5: Create Dissatisfaction with the Current State

To get to a desired future state, first create dissatisfaction with the
current state. Change runs directly counter to our normal desire
for stability. As David Lawrence (1996) puts it, "People are not
going to buy into change until they have become thoroughly convinced that standing pat is not an acceptable option. They might
smell smoke, but they are not going to leap from the burning
house until the flames are licking at their heels." Stuart Blinder,
when chief financial officer at Lever Brothers, used a similar
metaphor—"the burning platform"—to impress upon people the
dire need for change. In a classic bit of understatement, Blinder
suggests that "imminent death will catalyze the organization."

Yet in the absence of imminent disaster, few people are willing
to abandon what they have, no matter how bad it is. So an essential job of change leaders is to make people understand the necessity of letting go of the current state. This understanding must
be addressed both intellectually and emotionally.

On the intellectual level, one strategy is *disconfirmation*, giving
people information that makes it clear the current situation either

isn't what it should be or isn't what they thought it was. Benchmarking is essential. Most people tend to assume their performance is pretty good until they're hit with comparable numbers from elsewhere—the cycle time for a new product, customer satisfaction percentages, total sales per employee—and realize they've been kidding themselves.

At Kaiser Permanente, David Lawrence had an unusual problem. As a not-for-profit driven by social objectives, Kaiser lacked the stark empirical indicators such as stock price that normally trigger institutional alarms. "In our case," he says, "conveying that dire need for change was unusually difficult." What finally worked was getting outside consultants to work with Kaiser's people—region by region, market by market—to do extensive comparisons with their competitors and to survey present and past customers. Only after they'd gone through that process did local managers realize how perilous their situation had become.

"The lesson we learned was that real change cannot possibly begin until the organization as a whole has developed a readiness to move forward and a common understanding of what kinds of change are required," Lawrence says. "That readiness comes through a process of education; people have to be guided to their own conclusion that change is essential. You cannot dictate readiness from the executive offices" (Lawrence, 1996).

Frequently, facts and figures won't get the job done; it's often necessary to drive home the need for change on an emotional level too. One common technique is the *disaster scenario*—presenting people with the likely result of business as usual. I remember a division manager at one company who called his people together and told them that if the unit failed to turn things around within eighteen months, "they'll pull buses up to the door, close the plant, and cart away the workers and the machinery." That got people's attention. On a somewhat more subtle level, Xerox gathered its people and showed them charts depicting the fate of the U.S. television industry, the U.S. motorcycle industry, and other sectors decimated by Japanese competition. Then they displayed a chart showing similar trends for the U.S. copier industry—a depressing scenario but an effective wake-up call.

A word of caution: don't oversell the disaster scenario. If you're too effective, people can panic. Your best people, being the most marketable, will lead the stampede to the exit if they get the idea that the place is on the verge of free fall. At Eli Lilly, Randy Tobias says he felt he had to keep giving out "a simultaneous dose of optimism and a real sense of urgency about what had to be done." Similarly, at KPMG, Jon Madonna says he was "constantly balancing scaring with hope. You've got to be careful not to push the scare button too far, because these guys can run pretty quickly."

Frequently—and the more senior the people, the truer this is—it takes more than a disaster scenario to sell the need for change. Frontline employees have a front-row seat on disaster. Senior executives rarely smell the smoke from the trenches. That was certainly true at Xerox in the 1980s. Despite all the terrible numbers, life went on as usual at corporate headquarters. There was no sense of impending danger; there were no signs of pillaging barbarians on the outskirts of Stamford. Our challenge was to smash through the defenses of the executive bunker and let in the full horror of what most employees were experiencing every day. To do that, we turned to the customer service desk.

We arranged to have all the calls to the customer service desk—in reality a phone room located far from the executive offices—channeled directly into corporate headquarters in Stamford. For one day each month, each executive was responsible for the "complaint desk." Any call on that line was directed to his line, and he had to drop whatever else he might be doing and handle the call. And that didn't mean just listening to the complaint; it meant solving the problem.

That grabbed everyone's attention. There's nothing like a little personal interaction with an angry customer to cut through the corporate fog. At meetings to review their experiences I heard executives say things like, "I don't understand why these people do business with us. Some of them are just determined to deal with us despite all the things we do to them."

Action Step 6: Build Participation in
Planning and Implementing Change

Because there is absolutely no doubt that the more you can engage people in a process, the more successful it will be, build participation in planning and implementing change. There are three reasons why participation breeds success.

First, as people participate they develop a sense of ownership. Rather than perceiving change as something that someone is doing to them, they see it as something they have a hand in creating. If someone is imposing the change upon them, they derive a sense of power from messing it up; if they feel ownership, they get a sense of accomplishment from making it work.

Second, participation builds understanding. People working through the process are much more likely to truly hear important messages. And few activities boost understanding more than working on a script that will be used to explain the change to others who weren't involved.

Third, participants may have some good ideas. Unlikely as it might seem to the original crafters of the change initiative, others in the organization do, from time to time, have different perspectives and insightful ideas that can actually improve upon the original plan. Amazing, but true.

Of course, someone has to make decisions about who should participate and when. It's literally impossible for everyone to participate, and it's important to figure out which people have the information and capability to make a significant contribution. Moreover, certain matters can't just be turned over to large groups. I'm certainly not suggesting that you get three thousand people in a room and ask, "Who wants to sell the Shreveport plant?"

The issue this point raises is the difference between participation and consensus. Virtually every CEO I know recognizes—or certainly purports to recognize—the vital importance of widespread participation in planning and implementing change. At the same time, each is absolutely adamant about drawing a line between participation and making decisions by consensus.

"There's a distinction between consensus building and consensus decision-making," says Randy Tobias. "Consensus building is very important. Consensus decision-making is awful."

At Sun Microsystems—a company often depicted in the press as a wacky outfit where no one cares if men wear skirts to work and the whole staff engages in water-pistol battles out behind the headquarters building—CEO Scott McNealy deliberately describes himself this way: "I'm an incredibly participative but not at all consensus-oriented manager. I don't set any expectations that this is a democracy, that this is a consensus-oriented place, that this is a feel-good place. I explain on a regular basis that they don't call it work for nuthin.'"

When he redesigned the company's entire structure a few years ago, McNealy says, he had lots of group brainstorming sessions and one-on-one meetings with each of his top managers. He then went off by himself over Christmas, returning in early January to announce to his staff: "This is the new organizational structure starting July 1. Let's figure out how we're going to get from here to there." The fact that his managers, by McNealy's own admission, were all surprised by what he came up with would argue that the participation could have been more intense. Still, there was never any expectation that the final decision would be put to a vote.

Action Step 7: Reward Behavior in Support of Change

The third technique for overcoming anxiety is to reward behavior in support of change. Research and common sense both will tell you that people are motivated to do those things they believe will lead to desired outcomes. These can be internal outcomes, such as comfort and security. They can also be external outcomes (things other people give you), in the form of pay, promotion, and recognition.

However, motivation can get tricky. Researchers have shown that a fairly easy way to cause mice—and people, for that matter—to go crazy is to set up a system that directs them to do one thing and then rewards them for doing something else. Similarly, people often develop anxiety or feel uncertain about their actions during periods of change because they are told to start doing their jobs differently, yet the reward system lags behind and remains pegged to old standards and objectives.

Years ago, I was at a Corning plant during the transition period when Jamie Houghton was trying to instill quality as a guiding principle in all operations. Everybody was talking quality, everybody was learning quality—in hindsight, there were probably Quapples all over the place. Everybody agreed that quality guided everything that happened there—except during the last few days of the month.

Why? Because at the end of the month everybody was focused on meeting targets. And even though the talk was quality, the targets were volume—sheer volume of Corning Ware leaving the plant. So the rule of thumb at the end of the month was "ship the Ware." I would ask people, "Wait a minute, what about quality, and defects, and just shipping the good stuff?" And the answer would come back, "Yeah, that's fine, but the last couple of days of the month, we ship the Ware." It was a clear example of a transition state in which the new objectives were being undermined by the old reward systems.

Action Step 8: Provide People Time and Opportunity to Disengage from the Old

Finally, in motivating change it's essential to provide the time and opportunity for people to disengage from the current state. As I said earlier, it's imperative early in the process to pry people loose from their familiar organizational surroundings. But it's equally important to give people the opportunity to mourn and let go—a situation not unlike the loss of a loved one.

Think back to the situation at Mountain Bell, where the well-entrenched state phone companies were giving way to new customer-focused business units. At one point during the transition in the early 1980s, I was invited to a luncheon with Mountain Bell president Bob Timothy at the corporate headquarters in downtown Denver. Seated in the dining room were Mountain Bell's board of directors, the company's senior executives, and the directors of the state companies. Timothy welcomed everyone, and then we ate lunch, looking out over a panoramic view of the snow-capped Rockies. Then a few people were asked to make some brief remarks.

One by one, executives began recounting stories. One recalled the hazards of running a toll line over the Continental Divide during a blizzard back in the 1950s. Similar stories followed. And then Timothy began handing out mementos—framed collages made up of fragments of stock certificates from the old companies like the Rocky Mountain Telephone and Telegraph Company that had eventually become Mountain Bell. Suddenly I realized what was going on: Timothy was holding a funeral for the old Mountain Bell.

It was like a wake. It felt good. People were saying a fond good-bye to a company they'd been part of for years. They had the chance to say good-bye without guilt, without remorse, without unsurfaced grief. From that point forward, I never heard any talk of the good old days.

The Need to Manage the Transition

As formal and informal structures buckle under the pressure of anxiety and uncertainty, the organization has to focus on maintaining effective management throughout the transition state. Again there are four basic things for leaders to keep in mind during this turbulent period.

Action Step 9: Develop and Communicate a Clear Image of the Future State

It's up to the leaders to develop and communicate a clear image of the future state. It's almost impossible to manage the transition if people have no sense of where changes are headed. Yet painting a clear picture for them can be terribly difficult; the truth is that many organizations head into the transition state with nothing more than some basic goals and cherished values to guide them on their journey. That gives leaders the flexibility they need to be truly creative and open-minded in selecting a future path; but for the followers it can be frightening. So it's important to describe the future state as fully as you can.

During this stage, communications continue to be absolutely critical. Successful CEOs and their top managers spend incredible amounts of time meeting with people one-on-one, in small sessions, and in massive group meetings with literally thousands of people. They regularly produce videotaped messages that are played at staff meetings at locations across the country and around the world.

Increasing numbers of leaders—for example, Scott McNealy at Sun Microsystems and Lou Gerstner at IBM—encourage employees to communicate directly with them; McNealy says he gets more than two hundred internal electronic messages a day. He posts information on company Web sites, and employees can listen on the company Intranet at their convenience to "The McNealy Reports," his twice-monthly in-house radio show in which he personally interviews researchers, customers, and his own managers about new programs or developments of interest. Obviously, these and other communications techniques aren't limited to change situations—but every one of them should be used in a coordinated effort to describe where the organization is headed.

Action Step 10: Use Multiple Leverage Points

Use multiple leverage points to achieve change. In other words, don't forget the systems model of the organization and the overall concept of integrated change. In terms of the congruence model, every component of the organization should be involved, and should be seen as an opportunity, leverage point, for influencing and advancing change (even if you're dealing with tuning or adapting as opposed to redirecting or overhauling). Too often managers address only a single component—strategy or structure, for instance, or address only one of a pair of concerns. They deal either with the *hardware*—the work and formal structures—or with the *software*—the people and informal arrangements.

Focusing on hardware to the exclusion of software typically produces change—but change plagued by enormous resistance and poor performance because people lack the skills for handling new jobs and the cultural framework for operating in new ways. At organizations that focus exclusively on software, I watch people go off for a week in the woods to iron out their social problems and come back with a warm fuzzy glow. But the work, the structure, and the rewards systems haven't changed. So a week or two later, everything is back to normal.

Action Step 11: Develop Transition Management Structures

Be prepared to employ transition management structures. What frequently happens is that top management is fully engaged in managing the current state and planning the future state. So who is figuring out how to get from here to there? Answer: nobody. Successful organizations create transition management programs that include most or all of these four elements:

- *A transition plan.* Surprising numbers of organizations begin stumbling toward the future state without a step-by-step transition plan. Before anxiety and uncertainty begin paralyzing the organization, you have to be ready with concrete plans explaining who's in charge, who's involved, who's doing what, and by when.

- *A transition manager.* Unless one person is handed the responsibility for managing the transition, it just won't succeed. The transition manager has to be a senior manager, preferably one with close ties to the CEO, and someone who has demonstrated the ability to manage stress and ambiguity.
- *Transition resources.* Effective transitions are expensive. They require time, training, often the use of outside consultants, the diversion of key people from important day-to-day responsibilities, off-site meetings—the list goes on and on. This is one of those "pay me now or pay me later" situations. Once again, the costs of mishandling the transition dwarf the price tag for doing it right the first time.
- *Transition structures.* No transition manager can do the job without help. And it's unrealistic to expect an entrenched bureaucracy, which has spent years protecting the status quo, to go out of its way to help someone turn its world upside-down. So the transition manager needs the support of a designated transition team. It's also essential to create mechanisms outside the formal structure—special task forces, design teams, and experimental units, for example—to focus on specific objectives during the transition period.

Action Step 12: Collect and Analyze Feedback

One of the normal processes that frequently runs aground amid the confusion of the transition state is the routine collection of data and feedback. Managers should develop an array of sensing devices that constantly take the temperature of the organization and help them figure out what's working and what isn't—both in the day-to-day operations and the change activities.

Some of these feedback techniques can be formal and fairly structured: surveys, focus groups, formal interviews. Others can be less formal, more personal. When Citibank launched its ATM offensive in New York, rival Chemical Bank retaliated with a major overhaul of its own. Robert Lipp, then the head of Chemical Bank's Consumer Banking, made it a point each morning to stop on his way to work at one of Chemical Bank's branches and do a piece of personal business. It was his way of getting his own read on what was actually happening out in the field.

One final reminder: the twelve action steps are not a recipe for transition management. They're a template to be overlaid on each organization and adjusted to its unique set of circumstances. If implemented in conjunction with a thorough diagnosis of the organization, its current circumstances, and the nature of the change to be achieved, they can provide powerful tools for managing the turbulent transition period.

In the first four chapters I talked about change in fairly general terms, looking at its causes, dimensions, and varieties. In this chapter the focus shifted to the human dynamics of change, and ways to address people's inevitable resistance. Starting with Chapter Six we'll proceed through the five phases of the change process, beginning with how successful change leaders recognize the need for large-scale change and how they go about diagnosing their organizational ailments.

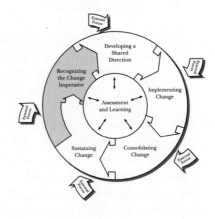

Chapter Six

Setting the Stage
Recognizing the Change Imperative

If the most fundamental principle of change is that nobody likes it, the second principle is that it's better to be a driver of change than its victim. Organizations are infinitely better off initiating change on their own terms, according to their own timetables, in a thoughtful and orderly way. Anticipation and preparation are everything; in their absence change becomes a frenzied last-minute tap dance along the edge of the precipice.

Most of the executives with whom I work understand that. They're people who are fairly sure that even if things seem fine at the moment, important change is almost certainly lurking somewhere just over the horizon. Scott McNealy used to say that the thing that kept him awake at night was wondering whether, in his frantic scramble to build the company, he ran the risk of failing to recognize "the next big thing." Even now, with Sun Microsystems well established and enormously successful, "it's still a legitimate concern," he says. "You don't do something about it if you're not worried about it. I never feel good. I don't get paid to feel good."

Executives are rarely certain about what form the next wave of change will take, how soon it will arrive, or even whether it might help or hurt their organization. All they know for sure is that it's out there, somewhere. And given the volatility of today's environment, they're almost certainly right.

What they want to know from a company like Delta Consulting is, How can we figure out earlier what problems are out there? How can we anticipate change earlier? In terms of industry cycles and the S-curve, what they want to figure out is how to position their organizations at the leading edge of disequilibrium, rather than being forced into a reactive change at the end of a cycle. It's one of the most crucial issues faced by the leaders of any organization.

The answer lies in the first phase of the change cycle: *recognizing the change imperative*. This work of this phase begins with an intensive scan of the external environment for any clues suggesting that fundamental change is on the way and an analysis of what that change might be. If a major shift is indeed in the offing, then the question becomes one of how it will affect the organization and its core competencies.

Will the organization benefit from happening to be in the right place at the right time to cash in on shifting consumer demand? In the 1980s, for instance, would it have been positioned to churn out, say, minivans and sport utility vehicles to meet the new demands of baby boomers and their growing families? Or will it experience the opposite scenario? In the 1990s, is it, say, locked into a strategy of personal computers, based on a single operating system at a time when more and more businesses are moving to the open architecture of the Internet and intranets?

Will the change require you to substantially alter the goods or services you offer? Will it require you to modify your relationship with customers? Can the organization as presently constituted—its structure, its processes, its people, and its operating environment—cope with new demands, new competitors, and new opportunities?

Needless to say, effective managers are always trying to look past tomorrow and anticipate change, just as they are constantly scrutinizing their organizations and looking for ways to improve them. That's what enables organizations to make the successful incremental changes we discussed earlier. But tuning and adapting, by definition, are insufficient to meet the demands imposed by seismic spikes in the environment that fundamentally alter the rules of the game.

Recognition: Scanning the External Environment

The key to recognition lies in two words: *external focus*. Think back to the Success Syndrome. A major reason why traditionally dominant market leaders are often overwhelmed by change is that they're so seduced by their own success that they fail to keep an eye on interesting developments in the outside world. The organizations that successfully anticipate change are those that look, think, and communicate with an external focus. That focus not only helps them identify and understand important changes in the outside environment but also gives them a clearer picture of how well positioned they are in the overall marketplace to meet those new challenges.

At forward-looking organizations, that focus on the external environment borders on obsession. It is part of the fabric of the enterprise. I keep coming back to Sun Microsystems because such a major factor in its success has been its intensely competitive strategy and culture—the two have become inseparable. Keeping a close watch on the competition is a way of life. "We spend a lot of time watching the train wrecks of our competitors," McNealy explains.

> There's been a lot of spontaneous combustion in our industry. A lot of different companies have hit the wall—big time. And we've very, very carefully watched, and methodically done a post mortem on them in our staff meetings. We spend a lot of time really trying to understand. We don't even do it formally any more. When somebody splats against the wall, the "hallway conversation" of my staff meetings is, "Can you believe they did this?" It's just what we do now. And now we're at the point where we actually predict a lot of it. We look at it and say, that strategy's not going to work. That's all part of our strategy discussion, it's very competitive. We look at the whole world as a chess board.

The fact of the matter is that too few companies have such competitive instincts embedded in their normal operating environments. In most cases, top leaders have to initiate the recognition process.

What to Look For

Typically, leaders get the process under way, as I have been describing, with a detailed scanning of the environment in search of the leading indicators of fundamental change. In a sense this is a massive job of data collection that entails throwing out a huge net to gather as much information as possible. If the scan is both wide and deep, some important blips should show up on the screen.

Major shifts in market structure. Changing preferences, competition, and distribution patterns suggest enormous dislocations throughout a market. Consider the waves that have swept across the movie business since the days when audiences could see feature films only by going to theaters. First network television, then cable, home videos, and satellite and pay-per-view TV have completely restructured the economics of the industry. Before long, the ability to obtain movies on demand over phone company lines could transform the business—along with cable TV and video stores—once again.

New competitors who have a whole new basis for competition, such as significantly lower production costs, higher quality, more efficient distribution. Daily newspaper advertising is taking a beating, for instance, from target marketers who can deliver printed advertisements, at much lower cost, directly to the homes of specific groups of customers targeted by demographics and geography. What's more, on-line services threaten to devastate large segments of the lucrative business in classified advertising. Those developments have newspapers scrambling for new technology that will allow them to design and deliver a customized daily product to the home of each reader. Newspapers that are first to acquire this capability will leave competing papers at a tremendous disadvantage.

Innovations in products and processes. For example, the onset of digitized information forced Xerox to rethink its reliance on printers and copiers based on light-lens technology. Through the late 1980s, many in the company were insisting that the digital office was a pipe dream; by 1997, more than 30 percent of Xerox's sales revenues came from digital equipment. Now the company faces a new wave of innovation-fostered change as the electronic distribution of digitized documents diminishes the need for large, high-volume office copiers.

External developments that change the rules of the game. These could involve government action, economic trends, or currency fluctuations, for example. Probably the clearest example continues to be the area of telecommunications, where deregulation and legislative action continue to reshape the competitive landscape for local phone companies, long-distance providers, and cable operators. U.S. automakers are constantly on the lookout for changes in the relative strength of the dollar and the yen and their direct impact on pricing strategies.

Changes in customer demands and characteristics. Department stores and shopping malls around the country are feeling intense pressure from catalogue merchants, who have capitalized on consumers' preference to shop from the comfort of home. The failure to closely monitor and accurately predict consumer trends can be costly—just ask the Quaker Oats executives who paid a premium price to acquire Snapple nearly a year after others in the industry were (correctly) predicting the flavored fruit drink fad had reached its peak.

Who Should Be Assigned to Look

The textbook procedure for environmental scans in such areas is for senior executives to assign the job to the strategic planning staff. But that's not enough; the experience is far too valuable to be handled as a routine staff assignment. Successful organizations may well put their strategic planners to work, but at the same time they'll do some other important things—specifically, getting the CEO and the executive team to go outside the company and talk to people they don't normally see and who are willing to tell them the kinds of things they don't necessarily want to hear.

The fact is that many CEOs, and to a lesser degree their top executives, live in a hermetically sealed environment that bears little resemblance to the rest of the organization. They are carefully insulated from bad news—partially because of corporate politics, partially because of their subordinates' self-preservation instincts, and largely because nobody particularly likes to be the bearer of bad news. By the same token, though most CEOs say they want to hear all the important news, both good and bad, the truth is that none of them wants to be relentlessly battered by worrisome developments. So though they may say they want to hear the worst, they're frequently sending signals to the contrary, some subtle and some not. Consequently, up and down the organization there's a kind of tacit collusion to bury bad news or at least muffle it.

Moreover, CEOs of companies offering consumer products or services rarely use their own products. In many cases that's not particularly surprising; no one should have been shocked to read in a *Fortune* interview that Arthur Martinez, CEO of Sears and formerly head of its retail operations, buys his suits at Paul Stuart and Neiman Marcus. That's what you'd expect of the CEO of one of

America's largest retailers. But it also distances Martinez, unavoidably, from customers who buy their suits at his stores.

When CEOs do use their own products, it's often in an abnormal setting. For years top executives of Detroit's auto companies were routinely provided with the newest models of their company's cars, at no charge, for their personal use. They never had to go into a showroom and haggle with a salesperson. They never had to deal with the cost, inconvenience, or frustration of getting a car serviced; they'd park their cars each morning in their reserved spaces in the company lot, and by the time they were ready to leave in the evening, the cars had been washed, fueled, and serviced. In short, the people responsible for charting the course of the U.S. auto industry were completely insulated from the reality of buying, owning, maintaining, and selling a car.

Similarly, it's not unheard of for some newspapers' production departments to produce a special batch of papers each night, sometimes referred to as *executive copies*. Under the supervision of a top production manager, several dozen papers are produced under the toughest quality control standards and then delivered to the homes and offices of the company's top executives. When readers complain of poor color quality or fuzzy printing, those executives assume the readers either have no valid cause for complaint or else had the bad luck to receive one of just a few poor-quality papers to come off the press.

If CEOs of consumer product companies are buffered from the realities of handling their products, leaders of companies that deal directly with other companies or institutions are even more isolated from reality. Their customer calls generally take the form of ritual state visits between corporate potentates, with one CEO meeting directly with another. Their conversations invariably are characterized by polite generalities—although if the CEO of an office equipment manufacturer were to wander off to the copy room and ask a secretary what she thought of the machines, that CEO might well get an answer he or she wouldn't like. But CEOs rarely hear the direct unfiltered comments of people who actually use their products every day. CEOs talk to other CEOs, and they're all members of the same exclusive club, in a figurative sense—and sometimes literally too. At a certain level they may both be members of the Business Roundtable and the Conference Board; they may play golf together. And so they become partners in an unconscious conspiracy of politeness; causing another member of the club to lose face just isn't done.

Luckily the converse is true too: numerous top executives seem to have an absolute passion for talking with their customers and satisfying their own curiosity about their products. While CEO of Xerox, for example, David Kearns arranged a roundabout system for having each new piece of Xerox office equipment delivered to his house without the knowledge of his employees. With the help of his sons, he would assemble the machines in his basement and try them out.

But in the many situations in which this is not true, it's essential to get the CEO and his or her senior team in firsthand situations where they can gather raw information, about both their own company and the larger environment, where they can ask their own questions and make their own assessments of the information's reliability.

Sources of Raw Information

I've found that the following sources of information can be particularly helpful in guiding senior teams toward their own external perspectives:

Customer Data

Senior executives should do their own analysis of customer data. This ranges from data in the form of sales numbers and market research to information from specially arranged surveys, interviews, and focus groups. Moreover, I constantly look for ways to create personal interaction between senior executives and their customers—the actual users of their products or services, rather than other CEOs. Consumers are rarely awed by CEOs and can generally be counted on to give their honest assessment of a product or service if asked under nonthreatening conditions. Interactions like the one described in Chapter Five, where Xerox top executives staffed the customer service phone lines, can be tremendously effective.

Financial Analysts

If you're looking for a guaranteed source of candid assessments, unvarnished by excessive politeness—or in some cases by even minimal social skills—the first people to turn to are industry analysts.

Obviously, some are more knowledgeable than others, and they all view each company and its industry sector from a particular perspective—but it's an important perspective nonetheless. Years ago, as Chemical Bank was working on its competitive strategy, a group of analysts was gathered and asked to talk about the banking environment and in particular Chemical Bank. A videotape of the session was later shown to the bank's senior team, which found it highly instructive.

Recent Hires

Employees who have only recently joined the organization are a rich source of unusual and perceptive views, combining both internal and external perspectives. Some companies put together regular seminars with new employees, that is, people with the company for less than six months; after that, for all intents and purposes, recent hires are no longer new. When my colleagues and I do this, we sit the new people in a room and bring in either the CEO or the unit president, who tells them: "You people are valuable. You see things we don't see. We believe that when you ask, 'Why do you do things that way around here?' that's one of the most valuable questions that can be asked. And we want to benefit from that."

Then we put the following series of questions to each of the new hires and encourage them to compare and discuss their respective responses:

What were your impressions of this company before you were ever contacted by us? What did you think it did well and not so well?

When we first called you, what were your immediate responses?

What impressions of the company did you form during the interview process?

What made you decide to come to work here, and as you prepared to start, what were the things that most concerned you?

Talk about your first couple of days here: What struck you most? What were your biggest surprises?

Subsequent questions progressively focus on more substantive issues of the company's strengths and weaknesses, its formal struc-

tures, and its informal culture. And the answers prove fascinating—
and radically different from those the company might elicit from
longtime employees.

Outside Experts

Some companies regularly bring in outside speakers to give the top
people unusual perspectives on a wide range of issues. Corning
does this regularly for its top three dozen or so executives. Past
speakers have ranged from former White House national security
adviser Zbigniew Brzezinski talking about developments in Eastern
Europe and their implications for international business to Super
Bowl–winning coach Bill Parcells describing his team-building techniques. Corning, with its headquarters tucked away in upstate New
York, feels a particular need to give its top executives personal contact with a variety of thought-provoking people from the outside
world; as a result, its executives probably see more of such outside experts than the executives of most firms located in midtown
Manhattan do.

Home and Away Visits

I've found it useful to set up a series of sessions involving the senior team of one company and its counterpart from another, at al-
ternating locations. For instance, the top Xerox people came to
Corning, New York; after which the Corning executives traveled to
Stamford. More recently, the top executives of Lucent Technologies as it was in the process of being spun off by AT&T and of
Quest Diagnostics as it was being spun off by Corning met and
compared notes at a time when both companies were dealing with
similar challenges. Executives almost always find these opportunities to share experiences and insights to be more than worth the
time and inconvenience involved in the trips.

Scenario Planning

Some organizations have found it particularly useful to involve
their top executives in regular "what if" exercises—examining possible sources of instability in the environment, "thinking through
the unthinkable," and developing a range of possible responses.
Shell Oil has been particularly adept at this. One of that company's
early exercises focused on what would happen if the Middle East

oil supply were suddenly shut off. When that "unthinkable" situation actually arose, Shell was in a much better position to deal with it than the company's unprepared competitors were.

Scanning Strategically

Exploiting all these potential sources of information lies at the heart of a process I call *strategic recognition*. In an era of constant change, leaders have to work at remaining constantly tuned in to environmental shifts in order to dodge threats and capitalize on opportunities. At successful organizations, this work doesn't occur as sporadic, isolated exercises; instead, it becomes an integral part of the way the enterprise does business. As John Kotter of the Harvard Business School has pointed out, the most successful organizations are those with *cultures* that are externally oriented and most open to information and ideas from the outside (Kotter, 1990). Now more and more companies have begun seeing the benefits of making scanning an explicit process.

In 1978, for example, Citibank chairman and CEO Walter Wriston asked George Vojta, his planning director, to do a major environmental scan. It was that exercise that alerted the company to the fact that its biggest and most profitable business, disintermediation, had no future and that Citibank had to redefine its strategy before that fast-approaching future arrived. Xerox, as I'll describe shortly, has engaged in three extensive projects since the mid-1980s, each aimed at envisioning the competitive landscape ten years into the future. More recently, a yearlong scan at AT&T in 1994–95 led to the conclusion that an inevitable destabilizing event was approaching—the entry of the regional Bell operating companies (RBOCs) into the long-distance market—and that it would drastically reduce the margins in AT&T's core operation. The implication was that AT&T would have to become a major provider of other goods and services if it was to remain a major player in the information services business. Moreover, people at AT&T took the results of that scan very seriously. Alex Mandl, who directed the strategic scanning project before briefly serving as AT&T's president from 1995 to 1996, predicted the RBOCs would enter the long-distance business sometime around January 1, 1997. On the wall of his office, right next to his conference table, was a huge calendar-like chart showing every week leading up to that date, and each week he crossed off another week. The message at the top of the calendar was brief and to the point. It said, "Time Is Short."

Diagnosis: Sizing Up the Organization

Assume, then, that you find yourself in a situation in which the need for radical change is obvious. You might have a mandate from the board of directors or from your corporate chiefs. Your external scan might have detected a gathering wave of change, and you're intent on acting before it arrives. Or perhaps you've been hired with the specific mandate to initiate major change.

Recognition began with an external scan, but you now quickly shift to an internal scan, or *diagnosis*—figuring out precisely what it is in the organization that has to change and weighing the most appropriate approaches to leading change. In reality, that's much harder than it seems, because the pressure from everyone else—and possibly your own inclination—will be to dive in and start changing things as fast as you can. Henry Schacht, one of the most successful leaders of organizational change, recommends the opposite.

> My advice to anybody who wants to be a change agent is to do the reverse of what everybody says. Everybody says, "Get in there and get busy." I say, "Stop right where you are, before you do anything. Stop!" Do not take a step further. Think first: What is it you're trying to do, what is the current topography, what's going on, where are you, what do you need to do first, and why? Of all the experiences you've had, of all the methodologies you've tried over the years, what is most likely to work here and why? And what are your priorities? There are only so many hours. A lot of things are going to go untouched for long periods of time, so where do you want to spend your time?

The range of possible approaches to any change situation is incredible. The only way to know how to start is by carefully diagnosing the situation. That means determining what kind of change is needed, how drastic it must be, how soon it must happen, and which components of the organizational model can best be leveraged to accomplish the necessary change.

Sources of Diagnostic Information

The success of any diagnostic process lies in first collecting the right information. There are several vital sources:

Internal Data

The obvious place to start is with the basic financial data already available internally, and then to peel back the onionskin layers to figure out what's really going on. One seemingly obvious issue is to determine which operations actually make money and which don't. That might seem ludicrous, but it's amazing how many companies don't really know where their money comes from. Because their internal reporting procedures are so imprecise—or in some cases intentionally convoluted—they simply don't know where the true profits are being generated.

Similarly, it's essential to look at costs and try to wade through the web of transfers and reallocations that often obscure the true size and source of expenses within the organization. I recently worked with a company where for years managers had analyzed field units on the volume of orders processed and capacity utilization; it wasn't until a new set of eyes analyzed the statistics from a different perspective that it became obvious the company was actually losing money on many of those orders because of high discounts offered to keep the business coming in the door.

Benchmarking

Once you've collected those internal data, it's essential to use them as benchmarks, pinpointing the organization's shortcomings in comparison with competitors and other comparable organizations. Benchmarking has become increasingly prevalent in recent years, and because information about it is readily available, I will not go into it here in any depth. However, I do want to underscore its importance as a key diagnostic tool.

Frontline Employees

When it comes to analyzing how the organization's strategy is actually playing out in the real world, there's no substitute for soliciting the insights of people such as the sales and service employees who are out in the marketplace each and every day. Though they see a small slice of the operation through the prism of their own interests, bias, and experience, they see it in practice, not on spreadsheets or overhead slides.

A case in point: at many daily newspapers it has become axiomatic that most delivery truck drivers, the people who actually drop papers at stores and coin racks each day and retrieve the unsold copies the next day, have a better sense of what readers want than editors or market researchers sitting in a downtown office. And as long as their information is viewed in the context that what they know are the buying habits of a particular kind of reader in a particular geographic area, this axiom holds true. Given these limitations, they can predict more precisely than any news executive how well a particular edition of the paper will sell. They can also tell you in incredible—if anecdotal—detail about the changing demographic, economic, crime, and traffic patterns of the neighborhoods they work. Sensibly and knowledgeably used, they are valuable sources of information about both the organization and the environment.

The Workforce at Large

As I said earlier, for CEOs seeking to understand the fundamental organizational issues, there's just no substitute for obtaining first-hand information. Sometimes it's best obtained through structured devices such as surveys, attitude assessments, and focus groups. However, those data should always be supplemented through face-to-face interactions, both formal and informal, with employees at every level throughout the organization. That can be time-consuming, physically demanding, and sometimes highly unpleasant. But if we're going to apply David Lawrence's metaphor of change as a political campaign, then it's essential that the leaders get out of their offices and find out what employees really have to say, without the filters of politically sensitive supervisors and bureaucrats.

Three Methods of Collecting Data

How this information is collected becomes an important issue. There are essentially three ways to do it. First, the CEO can elect to do it himself or herself—read the reports, view the focus-group videotapes, interview the employees. Second, the CEO can assign staff people and special teams to do it, which in some ways is more efficient but is less effective in the long run. It also has the inherent problem that each of these collectors will see and interpret data through their own particular lenses, and often they will use the lenses of the past to try to figure out the problems of the future. Third, the CEO can bring in outside help (consultants) to obtain and interpret internal information from an external perspective.

I strongly advise using a combination of all three. In my experience, consultants can be particularly helpful in three areas: first, in producing research-based analysis of industry sectors and particular markets; second, in facilitating and guiding recognition and diagnosis, with the actual work being carried out by senior executives; and finally, by training people within the organization to find and collect the wealth of data that is available internally.

Interpreting the Data

The outcome of all this information gathering should be some clear indications about what's going on in the environment, what's going wrong within the organization, and what needs to be changed. For that to happen, you need a way to interpret all the raw information—and that's where the congruence model (see Figure 2.4) comes into play. Indeed, there's a certain logic to moving methodically from left to right across the model: first you fix the strategy, then you work on reshaping the other organizational components to fit the strategy and each other.

Frequently, that's just what happens. Very often the diagnostic work makes it perfectly clear that what's called for is a radically different strategy. That new strategy, if it's sufficiently far removed from the old one, inevitably calls for new work requirements, formal structures and processes, staffing needs, and operating environment. But a new strategy is not always required. I've also encountered situations in which the existing strategy, given what's happening in the external environment, is right on target, but the existing organization is absolutely incapable of executing it. Or—a third scenario—the strategy may be an absolute disaster, but it would be a waste of time even to try hammering out a new one until the existing organizational structure has been burned to the ground and a new cast of characters is in place to make the strategic choices. In those cases it's premature to start rethinking strategy before you have the right people sitting around the right table thinking about the right kinds of strategic issues.

That was the case at AT&T in 1988. The chaos created by attempts to transform a heavily regulated monopoly into a streamlined competitive business meant that the first step had to be figuring out precisely which businesses the company was in. Then each business unit had to figure out what its strategy was. At that point, and only then, could the corporation look at its portfolio and figure out which operations to abandon and which to pursue. Up to that point, no one had a clue; executives literally had no idea where they were making money and where they were losing it. Because of their unique regulatory environment, reporting procedures intentionally obscured the way operations were cross-subsidized. The highly profitable long-distance operation, for example, was paying for local service, which was a money loser. The Network Systems operation—providers of the PBX (switchboard) systems used by businesses had also been losing astronomical sums for years. Now all that had to change; AT&T had to run itself as a real business.

In cases like that, the organizational model can be a useful tool in determining which problems to attack and in what order—for AT&T it all came back to strategy. The model is also useful in discriminating between problems and symptoms. A common example: organizations typically take a superficial look at their operations and decide their problem is excessive costs. But that diagnosis is generally wrong.

Based on experience, I can tell you that attacking costs as a root problem solves nothing. What appear at first blush to be unreasonable costs are almost always a symptom of more profound problems. Often costs are high because of flawed organizational structures, inefficient processes, inattention to quality, inadequate training, or a dysfunctional work environment. Budget slashing and payroll cuts rarely, if ever, address any of these underlying issues. Moreover, I've seen countless situations where purportedly high costs were in fact quite reasonable; the real problem was insufficient revenue, which requires much more creative solutions than tossing some people out on the street and exhorting the survivors to work harder.

Indeed, the American Management Association reported in 1996 that only 40 percent of the companies that had cut jobs since 1990 experienced any long-term gains in worker productivity. Only 45 percent of those companies saw any long-term increase in operating profits, and their profit growth over time was no better than those companies with rising expenses (Koretz, 1996).

If your data collecting is to pay off, it is crucial to go beyond first impressions. Leaders need to examine data carefully enough to diagnose where problems in organizational fit actually exist and what general level of change it will take to resolve them.

The Importance of Participation in Designing Solutions

Recall the health care company whose CEO spent almost two years working with outside consultants, thinking and pondering and studying the issues facing the health care industry and his company. At the end of that period he came to the conclusion that radical change was unavoidable. He gathered his top executives at a weekend meeting away from the office, explained to them what he had learned and the conclusions he had reached, and then presented them with a dazzling plan for reshaping the company. He assumed that on Monday morning they would come back to work charged up and ready to turn his vision into reality.

It didn't happen that way. Even though the CEO did a first-class job of laying out his plan, he was totally unsuccessful in winning his senior team's support. The outside consultants then advised him that the real problem lay with the senior team, which obviously had to be replaced. When the CEO asked Delta Consulting what might have gone wrong, however, we suggested it wasn't his senior team that was the problem: it was the process. After all, I asked him, "What made you think that they were so much smarter than you that what you took two years to get, they would get in a weekend?"

It seems obvious enough, but I'll say it again: the most frequent mistake top executives make in leading change is to overlook the importance of participation in the earliest stages. I'm talking about genuine active participation, not after-the-fact window dressing. Yet time after time, I've seen CEOs struggle alone through the recognition phase of the change cycle, intent on figuring it all out on their own.

There's usually a pattern to all of this. It starts with the fact that most CEOs tend to be intuitive rather than methodical, analytical thinkers. At some point during recognition—frequently right after being personally exposed to issues from which they are normally shielded—leaders suddenly make an intuitive leap; they experience the "aha!" phenomenon, when everything suddenly becomes clear, sometimes accompanied by an overpowering conviction they sometimes compare to a religious conversion.

At that point they forget the intellectual turmoil and emotional uncertainty they endured during their forty years in the wilderness; now that the answer is obvious to them, it should be just as obvious to everyone else. Having reached their epiphany through an arduous, painstaking, and ultimately gut-level understanding of a complex situation, they somehow believe they can quickly impart that insight to their colleagues—and have them accept it with the same fervor—through a brief, passive intellectual process. Big surprise: it doesn't work that way. Having spent two years becoming emotionally and intellectually prepared for his or her own religious conversion, a CEO can't expect other people to dunk themselves in the river just because the CEO assures them it's a nifty idea.

(To be honest, I experienced precisely the same problem some time ago within my own consulting firm. Concerned at the time about the prospect of losing some of our talented senior directors to larger, well-established firms, I devised what I thought was an ingenious plan to restructure the firm, enlarge some consultants' responsibilities, and enhance their incentive programs. I proudly presented this marvelous plan to the senior team members who, metaphorically speaking, threw up all over it. They hated it. So trust me on this; I know exactly how frustrating the process can be.)

The process I've been describing creates a serious dilemma for CEOs. On one hand, presenting the senior group with a fait accompli doesn't work. On the other, no CEO wants to raise the destabilizing specter of radical change without being reasonably certain that drastic steps are imminent. Nor does the CEO want to make that announcement without simultaneously offering some clear direction about what kind of change will be involved and where the organization is headed. Without that vision, the senior executives would start wondering, "Is anybody in charge here? Doesn't somebody have some idea where this place is going?"

This isn't a hypothetical situation. My colleagues and I recently worked with the newly appointed president of a major corporation who made it clear from the outset that he intended to involve the entire senior team in setting a new course for the troubled company. The reaction was decidedly mixed; people were downright ambivalent. On one hand, feeling disenfranchised by the autocratic style of the past two presidents, top managers said they were delighted by the chance to be involved; but on the other hand, in the next breath they would make it clear that "he's the president now, it's up to him to come up with the strategy and vision."

The CEO, like all change leaders, had to balance the conflicting needs that all of us—even senior managers—tend to have: we want a chance to be active participants in shaping our own future, but we also crave strong leadership. Considerable research indicates that the most effective leaders are those who are absolutely clear, directive, and nonparticipative about outcomes yet tremendously open and participative about how the group (or the organization) gets there. So the solution to the participation problem is not for the CEO to stand up and tell people: "I don't have a clear vision. I don't know where we're going. Let's work together and develop a vision by committee." That will lead only to fear, uncertainty, stress, anxiety, and a loss of confidence in top leadership.

Instead, the effective CEOs say to their people, "Let me tell you what my vision is. Let me tell you what kind of company I want to build. Let me explain to you how I reached that conclusion. Now I want to work with all of you on figuring out how we get there." That is an approach that works. I've seen it happen again and again.

What comes next in successful organizations is a process sometimes called *guided discovery*. At this point the senior team members have to be given the opportunity to walk through some replication of the inquiry and discovery process the CEO experienced alone on the mountain top. Not only that, they must also be afforded the opportunity to influence the outcome of the process. If the CEO has been diligent in constructing a vision of change, the odds are good that he or she and the top people will arrive at approximately the same conclusions. In most cases I've seen, the team's involvement actually made the plan better than the CEO's original idea. (And in the interest of honesty, I have to admit that my own reorganization plan for the consulting firm was much improved after two lengthy meetings in which I hashed it out with my senior team.)

By the way, the story about the health care company CEO and the problems he encountered when presenting a new strategy to his senior team has a happy ending. After my colleagues and I reviewed what went wrong the first time around, the CEO recycled the recognition and diagnosis process, but this time with the involvement of the senior team. The outcome was in many ways a better strategy. Even more important, the team members feel a sense of ownership toward the new strategy; they are personally committed to it, and they will provide the core of support that will make it work throughout the organization. It is a classic example of *appropriate participation*—giving the senior team the chance to buy into the change with their intellectual and emotional equity. It is an opportunity every senior team must have. Consider whether what I've said to more than one CEO applies for you: "You trust people making $50,000 to run your stores and deal with your customers. Don't you think your top executives who make five or ten times that much deserve at least the same degree of trust?"

Of course, appropriate participation isn't limited to the CEO's executive team. What complicates participation is that the same phenomenon must be repeated at each level of the organization. Once the executive team members are on board, their inclination is to spoon-feed their revelation to the next level, and just like the CEO, they're surprised and disheartened when those managers "don't get it." So it's essential to find ways for people to experience their own process of discovery. The stakes cannot remain the same. Not every part of the plan can continue to be up for grabs, nor can every piece of competitive or proprietary information be put on the table, but one way or another everyone's got to be given the chance to participate in the process of learning what the change is about and why it's essential.

At Xerox, for instance, a videotape was produced and shown throughout the organization. It had the feel of cinéma vérité and was scripted as an interview with a Xerox "tech rep" talking about the frustrations of his job. We learn that his father was the owner of a small machine shop who had always taught him the importance of getting a job done right. Now he's trying to do the right thing for his Xerox customers, but his own company seems to be conspiring against him at every turn. When he goes out on a service call to fix someone's machine, he doesn't want to leave until it's really fixed, but his bosses are more concerned about the number of service calls he logs each day. All he wants to do is please his customers; all his bosses want him to do is make the response-time statistics look good. (That may answer some questions for some of you who had Xerox machines in your offices back in the 1970s and '80s and wondered why the machine kept breaking down the day after the repairman was there.)

As Xerox launched its Leadership Through Quality initiative, the film was shown to all employees, in small workshop settings. It was then used as the starting point for a discussion and mini-diagnosis of what was going wrong at Xerox, and why the new emphasis on quality was so important. The film helped focus everyone's attention on the issue that to improve quality for the customer, practically everything about the way the company did business was going to have to change. The film, accompanied by important company data and market information, gave each employee the chance to be involved and independently reach the conclusion that quality-based change was essential.

Interestingly, such guided discovery is most important at the higher levels of the organization. As illustrated by the Xerox film, nonmanagerial employees—particularly those closest to the product or the customer—know most of this stuff already. When told about poor quality and the need for change, their response often is, "Gee, no kidding. Somebody upstairs finally woke up."

Example of the Process

Let me conclude by giving you a quick snapshot example of how the principles discussed in this chapter might help a leader diagnose his or her organizational problems. This is the process Delta Consulting has refined for using the congruence model to help top executives make sense of information that's been gathered and then use it to launch themselves on their path of guided discovery.

Let's assume that much of the data has already been collected—market research, internal financial data, surveys, and employee interviews. My colleagues and I typically begin by collating the results of interviews with dozens of carefully selected employees. We extrapolate the key phrases—there might be up to 1,500 of them in a good-sized sample. Then (using software we have designed) we categorize the interview comments according to key phrases—between 80 and 120 general categories, perhaps. We analyze them and distill each one into a simple declarative sentence—for example, "The poor quality of our products is creating major problems with customers" or "Salespeople know almost nothing about the equipment they're supposed to sell."

Then we apply those statements to the organizational congruence model. We literally write the statements in the appropriate boxes or along the corresponding fit lines on a diagram of the model. Next we add important facts gleaned from hard data and market research, again writing those facts where appropriate on the model. What emerges is an extremely graphic depiction of where the organization is experiencing problems and what kind. Before we show the diagram to the CEO, however, we ask him or her to read the same raw interview data from employees from which we drew our distilled statements. Often CEOs object and say they don't have the time; almost always, once they start, they tend to stay up all night reading the material. There's something tremendously compelling about reading these interviews in employees' own words, and the exercise invariably deepens the CEO's involvement in the process.

The next meeting might be described as a mini guided discovery session. We ask the CEO to describe his or her reactions to the employee interviews, and we lead the CEO through a discussion of what he or she thinks the implications are for changing the organization. After the CEO has had this chance to work through the model personally, we then show the one we've prepared and pursue the discussion in much more substantive terms.

The next stage is where appropriate participation comes into play. We repeat the process with the executive team members, giving them the same chance the CEO had to read all the raw data and start drawing their own conclusions from it. After they've finished working through it, we then take the model back to some of the people originally interviewed and ask them if the analysis of the situation in terms of the model is a correct reading of what they were telling us. That process starts to build participation and support throughout the organization. It also creates some expectations;

now that those people upstairs are aware of all these problems, people assume—or at least hope—maybe now they'll start doing something about them. So before taking that final step, we always warn the CEO and the executive team: "Don't do this unless you really plan to act. Once this result is out there, there's no going back."

At the end of the process, people throughout the top levels of the organization should be reaching some shared understandings about where change ought to occur. And the top leaders should be preparing to move on to the second phase of change, as described in the next chapter: clarifying their vision for the future and building the coalition of support necessary to make that vision a reality.

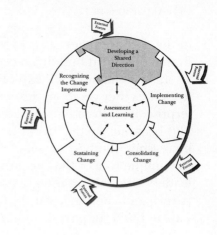

Chapter Seven

Waging the Great Campaign

Developing a Shared Direction

Organizational change, when you get right down to it, boils down to persuading massive numbers of people to stop doing what they've been doing for years and to start doing something they probably don't want to do—at least not at first.

Recognizing the necessity of change and diagnosing the organizational elements are crucial first steps. If done well, the very processes used during that first phase of the change cycle will start building the critical nucleus of support for change. Now, as leaders enter the second phase of the change cycle, they have to broaden support by *developing a shared direction* for the change to come.

I made the case earlier that organizations are first and foremost political organisms. It would be ineffective—and downright foolhardy—to undertake any stage of the change process without thinking through the political ramifications. Early on, that means identifying the key groups and individuals whose support for change will be essential to its success and winning them over. At the same time, leaders must figure out whose opposition has the potential to derail the effort, and then forge a strategy to overcome their resistance. Obviously, that political concern was the subtext of my insistence in the last chapter on the need for participation in the earliest stages of recognition and diagnosis. Those are the first steps toward building a coalition of support.

In this chapter we'll explore three important avenues open to leaders as they go about developing a shared direction for the enterprise. In each case the underlying theme is how to build broader and broader participation in the change, and how to get ever-increasing numbers of people engaged and involved. I start with the unique role of the executive team. Then I describe how some leaders assemble an integrated change agenda to further expand participation and sharpen the focus on change. Finally, I talk about ways to build support throughout the rest of the organization.

Reshaping the Executive Team

As the organization progresses from the initial recognition phase into the work of developing a shared direction for change, the relationship between the CEO and the executive team becomes paramount. Even in a moderately complex organization, no CEO can design and implement a successful change strategy without help; it just can't happen. There's just too much work to be done, not the least of which is winning the support of large numbers of people. Moreover, there are different kinds of work to do, and no CEO is good at everything; it's unlikely that a visionary leader who can make the intuitive leaps required to envision a radically different organization far in the future will be quite as adept at piecing together a methodical, step-by-step plan for managing the transition. Consequently, an important part of the diagnostic work the CEO faces is a realistic assessment of his or her own strengths and weaknesses, with an eye toward fashioning an executive team that complements the CEO's own talents and shortcomings.

Building an executive team is a delicate, complicated task under the best of conditions. But for the CEO committed to radical change, the task is infinitely tougher. There's usually a team already in place. And people have won a position on that elite team, generally speaking, by excelling in a structure and a culture that the CEO now wants to turn inside out. As a result, the people who must play the most crucial role in envisioning a new organization are the very people who have the greatest emotional investment in keeping things just the way they are.

Not surprisingly, a CEO—whether a newcomer brought in for the express purpose of initiating change or an incumbent who has recently realized that change is essential—often faces initial skepticism and tacit resistance from the senior group. "Getting our senior executives aligned around the need for change was difficult," Pepsi-Co's Craig Weatherup noted. "The resistance was a genuine question of, 'Why do it?' They had successfully mastered the current system and had turned in a number of strong years, performance-wise. Convincing them of the threat was difficult in that they were both the architects and beneficiaries of the current organization"(Nadler, Shaw, Walton, and Associates, 1994, p. 254).

Jamie Houghton recalls his early dealings with executives as the newly appointed chairman of Corning similarly: "I think people—especially the five people reporting to me—were testing. I think they were cynical themselves. Their attitude was, 'Who's this new guy? Let's see what he does.' This was a pretty tough group just sitting there waiting to see what happened. I didn't have their immense devotion, I'll tell you that" (Nadler, Shaw, Walton, and Associates, 1994, p. 253).

One of the harsh but unavoidable realities of change in this phase (and continuing for some time) is that it's almost always necessary to remove some senior people who are clearly intractable in their opposition to change. People need to be given ample opportunity to weigh the new evidence, change their minds, and get on board. But in some cases that just isn't going to happen. And in those cases the CEO must be prepared to act swiftly and decisively.

Shortly after retiring from Xerox, David Kearns accepted an invitation to visit Delta and talk with us in unusual depth about his experience as a CEO. Reviewing his leadership of the Xerox change effort, Kearns told us: "Looking back, if there's one thing I wish I could have done differently as CEO, it would have been to have acted more quickly on people we knew weren't going to make it. I kept thinking that either there was hope for them, or else I had an expectation of myself that somehow I could help them change so they would work out—that I could fix it, I could help them. It was unrealistic. By leaving them in place I hurt the company, I hurt myself, and I didn't help them at all."

Of course, throwing people out of the company is more easily said than done, as Kearns would be the first to admit. The truth is that looking another adult straight in the eye and telling that person that his or her services are no longer needed is one of the most difficult aspects—if not *the* most difficult—of being a boss. Firings are emotionally wrenching for everyone involved; they violate all the cultural buffers we have put in place over time to maintain civility and prevent loss of face in the workplace. They require executives to deal face to face with anger and unrestrained outpourings of emotion from the other side of the desk, as well as with their own feelings of guilt and remorse, whether justified or not.

Over time most organizations develop cultural rituals designed to maintain interpersonal working relationships on a relatively pleasant unemotional basis—or if not pleasant then at least nonconfrontational. All those cultural devices come crashing down during the act of dismissal. Many executives who have no trouble whatsoever ordering their subordinates to terminate huge numbers of faceless workers find it almost physically impossible to personally fire anyone. (An interesting case might be made that final decisions about massive terminations or layoffs should never be made by someone who has never had the experience of personally firing someone.)

Several years ago, while doing some work with a financial services firm, I became acquainted with an executive who had a reputation as one of the toughest s.o.b.'s in the company—someone who had ordered thousands of layoffs, a fellow who inspired true fear in his subordinates. When I finally got him to agree that he had to fire one of his direct reports, he invited me to his office, where he proceeded to ask me to help him get ready by roleplaying the termination session with him. Puzzled, I asked him why he needed my help in preparing for what must have become a fairly routine procedure by that point in his career. That was when he admitted that he himself had never fired a single person. "I tried to fire a secretary once," he said, "but she started crying and I let her stay." That experience is not uncommon; one newspaper executive's subordinates, for example, had to conspire to keep him away from any termination meetings at all after an editor went into the executive office to be fired and left with the promise of a promotion, a new assistant, and an extra week of vacation.

CEOs are no different from these other executives; in fact, taken as a group, they are temperamentally less suited to firing people than most managers. For one thing, a common characteristic of most CEOs is a strong need to be liked and admired. They also have unusual faith in their own ability to teach, cajole, or persuade other people to come around to their point of view and thus to magically transform subordinates into people they're really not.

Moreover, it's one thing to fire an employee for some heinous act such as theft, sexual harassment, or industrial sabotage. It's quite another to hand a pink slip, even when it's cushioned by generous settlement terms, to someone who has been a loyal and successful executive but at this stage in his or her career finds it impossible to do things differently or disagrees vehemently with the company's new direction. Even when there is no question that they need to be removed for the sake of the organization, that doesn't make the experience any easier.

Nevertheless, the fact remains that I have yet to see a major organizational change in which some members of the executive team didn't have to be replaced. Every successful CEO with whom I've worked either made substantial changes in the executive team as the change process moved into high gear or later expressed deep regret for having failed to do so. Looking back on his experience at KPMG, Jon Madonna says, "If I were to do it again, it would be: 'You're either on the team, or you're off.' I'd have a tight team, and if you don't want to play, you wouldn't sit there very long. You just wouldn't. I'd just get you out." Madonna likes to offer one other bit of advice, which he attributes to his second in command at KPMG, James Brocksmith. "Never leave the wounded on the battlefield," Madonna says, "or they may come back to kill you." In other words don't demote dissidents and leave them somewhere in the organization where they can become martyrs for the opposition. If they have to go, then get them out.

Compare the situations at IBM and Westinghouse. In each case the board recruited a new CEO from the outside to make drastic changes. The two CEOs—both former management consultants—took dramatically different approaches, however. At IBM, on one hand, in one tumultuous fifteen-month period in 1993–94, Lou Gerstner recruited thirty-six top executives from the outside to fill many of IBM's senior posts. There were so many of these new, unknown executives swarming in at one point that in some circles they became known as the "wild ducks" (as in, What kind of duck are you?). Without question, they played a large part in helping Gerstner engineer IBM's remarkable resurgence in the mid-1990s.

At Westinghouse, on the other hand, CEO Michael H. Jordan was still complaining two years after his arrival about the entrenched resistance to change and his inability to transform the corporate culture of the sluggish industrial giant. Guess what: during those first two years, Jordan hadn't removed a single one of the senior executives who were in place when he joined the company. In the end he gave up on trying to change the company and basically swapped it for another by acquiring CBS, then attempting to spin off all of Westinghouse's nonbroadcast holdings.

The importance of removing even a single top executive goes far beyond the termination of one problematic employee. At the senior level, executives are influential thought leaders, people fully capable of becoming lightning rods for resistance to change and a rallying point for diehards who want to believe that change will somehow evaporate, the wrong-headed CEO will come to his or her senses, and the organization will return to business as usual. The removal of even one senior person who is resisting change packs the powerful symbolic message that change is real and that resistance to it is a "career-limiting move."

Finally, letting firmly entrenched top managers go opens up important opportunities to bring in new people with fresh attitudes and unorthodox backgrounds. At Eli Lilly, Randy Tobias ended up building a senior team of more than a dozen top executives, only three of whom were in their roles when he arrived as CEO. Some new team members were Lilly managers who Tobias felt could handle more responsibility. Others had been working at other pharmaceutical companies. And some—including executives from companies as diverse as General Motors, MasterCard, and Reebok—were brought in, Tobias says, specifically "to bring experiences and perspectives that were very new to this business."

"You've got to get yourself surrounded by people you can count on as quickly as you can do it," Tobias comments. "This whole notion of getting the new team identified and in place is incredibly important."

Once the right people are in place, the CEO can begin the arduous but essential task of building a truly functioning team. In Jamie Houghton's case the process began after he removed one of the senior players and then, instead of naming a president as everyone expected, appointed a small management committee including himself, two executive vice presidents, and three group presidents. "I wanted to get my arms around the business and I didn't want to have anybody in between," he explained. "I got them on board because I was very clear about my expectations. I started to say, 'Okay, guys. We are the quality improvement team for the corporation. We are going to set the example. We are going to meet together 20 percent of our time'" (Nadler, Shaw, Walton, and Associates, 1994, p. 253).

"That's a lot [of time]," Houghton acknowledged, "and they were not happy about that either. I said, 'Occasionally I have to make the final decision, but ninety times out of a hundred, I want it to be a group decision. I want to have meetings that are talking about issues and then we will come to a consensus.' We just spent a lot of time together, in Corning and at off-site meetings. We had some of our most creative discussions late in the evening over red wine, just yelling like hell. It was great, great stuff—and molded us together as a team" (p. 254).

The makeup and dynamics of the executive team, and its relationship to the CEO, has to be addressed by every chief executive, particularly in redirecting and overhauling situations. At Kaiser Permanente, David Lawrence found that the first executive team he put together was too large, too unwieldy, and in some ways too democratic.

"I had not fully appreciated the distinction between dissent, disagreement and consensus-building versus the need to reach decisions and move on," Lawrence says. "My high tolerance for debate was misplaced; the constant dissension began to sap our energy, our focus, and our will to move forward with the kinds of changes we desperately needed." Lawrence came to the conclusion that his team was too big—he reduced it to four from eight—its internal processes were inefficient, and some of its members simply weren't committed to his vision of change.

"I realized I needed a center, an absolute core to this effort, in the form of a team I could depend on without reservation," he says. "I needed a team who would fight the battles even when I was not there, or when we were not all together. I had to know what stands they would take, what language they would use, what changes they would support."

The Agenda for Change

Together, the CEO and the executive team face the task of creating a general vision of change and identifying specific areas of the organization where change is most critical. This vision, which I call the *integrated change agenda,* can take a number of forms and evolve in various ways. But the successful ones all share some important characteristics (see Figure 7.1).

In essence, the integrated change agenda is an umbrella; under it come all the elements of the change effort. Typically, these include the organization's purpose, its strategy, its values, its governance processes, its operating environment, its requirements for

Figure 7.1. Integrated Change Agenda.

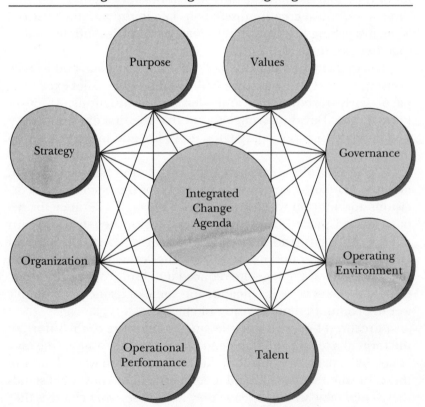

talent and skills, its operational performance, and its organizational structures, processes, and systems. Ideally, these elements are captured in a small number of *high-concept* principles that speak to the strategy, structure, and culture of the emerging organization. Normally, these principles are first communicated through public statements by the CEO, and then, as we'll see shortly, repeated over and over again until they become a kind of corporate mantra.

The integrated change agenda often also includes a fairly specific performance objective, as in the case of Ford's goal of surpassing GM's production and Toyota's quality by early in the twenty-first century.

Think of this agenda as the blueprint for the future state, synthesized into a few key words that form the basis for all discussion of what the organization must become.

To understand more clearly the evolution of this change agenda, let's go back again to Corning and Houghton's intense work with his handful of top executives. Before turning to specific strategic aspects of change, Houghton insisted that senior team members first come to grips with the issue of corporate values. After arriving at what they thought was an inspiring and accurate statement of the company's primary values, they passed their work along to an advisory group composed of the next level of corporate managers. They thought the statement was awful. So it went back to the senior group for a second try. After months of debate back and forth, the two groups finally agreed upon what came to be known as the "seven big V's," Corning's statement of the values that would guide everything the company did. The seven values, communicated in a formal statement to all employees, were—and remain today—quality, integrity, performance, leadership, technology, independence, and the individual. "Strategies will change," Houghton used to say. "These will not change."

The articulation of those values was an important step in the change effort. Houghton explained: "It wasn't an absolutely necessary thing to do—we could have gone along without doing that. But values to me are like buoys in the channel of commerce. In other words, one is changing directions and testing and making strategic decisions all the time, but if one doesn't have values to guide one, there is a disorientation. So, deciding early on, even before you start fooling around with your strategy, what you believe in and what's this company all about, is important" (Nadler, Shaw, Walton, and Associates, 1994, p. 258).

Next came strategy. Because Corning is a conglomerate, the discussion of strategy centered on making sense of the portfolio—determining those businesses in which Corning should be engaged in the future and those that held little promise. What team members came up with was The Wheel—a graphic depiction of the Corning portfolio strategy with technology at the center surrounded by the four key areas that would be the focus of Corning's growth over the next decade: life sciences, communications, specialty materials, and consumer goods. Once they had that road map in place, they were able to move aggressively to reshape the portfolio—selling off some less promising operations, acquiring other companies that helped fill in gaps in The Wheel—all in keeping with the newly developed strategy. Over the next several years, Corning purchased nearly a billion dollars' worth of assets, sold a billion dollars' worth of assets, and reorganized an additional three-quarters of a billion dollars in assets.

Ultimately, Houghton distilled the essence of the change agenda into two major themes—quality and performance—to which he later added a third, diversity. Together with the statement of corporate values, these themes guided the course of change at Corning for the next decade. In important ways those themes and the way they were used illustrate the common characteristics shared by effective agendas in successful change efforts: a limited number of understandable themes, constant repetition of those themes, and a clear relationship between those themes and the change actually going on within the organization.

Developing Critical Themes

Step back for a moment to the first phase of change, recognition and diagnosis. Typically, most senior teams reach the end of that work, look at the to-do list they've put together, and realize in horror that they've diagnosed hundreds of things—in some cases more than a thousand—that have to be done. The list underscores the pressing need to make changes in everything from strategy and structures to staffing, work processes, and the operating environment.

Not even the best teams can effectively change hundreds of core elements in the organization all at once, or within a few months, or even by the end of next year for that matter. Not only that but they have to keep the place running in the mean time— there are goods to produce and distribute, services to maintain, customers to serve, financial goals to meet, employees to supervise. Clearly, the team has to sift through the overall list of necessary changes and set some priorities. Team members have got to agree on the root causes of their organization's problems and then decide on the critical actions that will directly address those fundamental issues.

To do that, the senior team has to develop its *themes for change*. If you're Xerox and your competitors are battering you in the marketplace because customers perceive your products and service as inferior, then improving quality had better be one of your big themes. If you're Corning and your shrinking profit margins are becoming an embarrassment, then financial performance has to be one of your themes. If you're AT&T and you don't even know which of your businesses are making money, then restructuring and cleaning up the organization has got to be a priority. Rather than trying to tackle the full range of pressing problems—a strategy doomed to failure—successful leaders make the tough choices and focus on the vital few.

There's a concept in psychology, described years ago by George Miller (1956), that says most people can absorb only a certain number of pieces of information at the same time. Miller's rule was "seven plus or minus two"—that is, a range between five and nine. My own experience leads me to believe that there is an even more stringent limit to an *organization's* capacity to keep multiple concepts or ideas in its collective consciousness at one time—and that limit is three plus or minus one.

Consequently, organizations with successful change efforts have nearly always dealt with no more than three or four major themes at once, though the list can change and evolve over time. At Corning, it was quality and performance, with diversity added a few years later. At PepsiCo, it was performance and integrity. At Xerox, it was customer satisfaction, market share, and return on assets. Conversely, I worked with another company during an unsuccessful period of change where there were fifteen operating principles and four change strategies and a host of other lists—

and the people who worked there couldn't begin to tell you what was going on.

Interestingly, the cycle of diagnosing problems and clarifying themes is going on once again at Corning. As Roger Ackerman prepared to succeed Jamie Houghton in the spring of 1996, he worked with his own team over a period of nine months to hammer out what would become his own themes as CEO. Today Ackerman is focusing Corning's attention on two areas: growth (a progression from Houghton's theme of performance) and the operating environment (a complicated long-term effort to reshape the "soft" side of the organization in ways that will enable it to achieve its aggressive growth objectives). As Ackerman prepared to take over, I advised him to limit himself to two themes to begin with so that at some point down the road, based on his own experience as CEO, he could add a third theme without running much risk of cluttering his message.

Not all CEOs articulate their basic themes at the outset of the change effort. Some have a sense of what needs to be done, and over time they communicate it to the organization, but not necessarily in the explicit terms I've just described. When Bob Allen unexpectedly became chairman of AT&T in 1988, he immediately sensed the need for change, but gradually moved from one target to the next. A few years later some senior people from Kaiser Permanente visited Allen and asked him to describe his themes for change. (This was before Allen had started thinking seriously about the corporate breakup he engineered in 1995.) He thought it over and said that in retrospect, he'd worked successively on four issues: decentralizing and changing the formal structure; strategic changes in the portfolio; company values; and finally, quality. He'd never announced a change agenda as such, but looking back he could describe exactly what the major themes were.

I would argue in favor of being as clear as possible about themes as early as possible. People are trying desperately to make sense of what the CEO is up to and, ultimately, what it means for them. Even if the situation, like the one Allen inherited at AT&T, is so unbelievably muddled that it's difficult to be specific about the plan for change, people still need general guideposts along the way.

Henry Schacht has been remarkably focused on conveying simple themes and core messages as he's gone about creating Lucent

Technologies. He and Lucent president Rich McGinn are constantly out talking to their people about the new company's vision, mission, and values, and they constantly talk about the "five simultaneous equations" I mentioned in Chapter Four, the set of specific financial targets.

"That's not grand strategy, but it's roughly right," Schacht explains. "We know that in the next three to four years, we've got to do these five things. It's simple, it's declarative, and it's roughly right. Everything else is driven by this; it becomes the unifying theme."

Repeating and Connecting Themes

When Jamie Houghton got up in front of the 1983 annual meeting of top Corning executives and talked about two things— performance and quality—people grumbled, assured each other that this was just another case of a new CEO looking for a new slogan, and went about their business. In 1984, Houghton addressed the same annual gathering, and talked about only two themes: performance and quality. In 1985, the same story: performance and quality. Some of his senior team wanted him to add some new wrinkles, such as innovation, but Houghton wouldn't budge. Not until the late 1980s, well after performance and quality had been drummed into the corporate consciousness, did he add a third theme, diversity.

I can't overemphasize the importance of hammering away at the same central themes over and over and over again. Earlier I related my observation that most people, particularly during periods of stress, have to hear a message at least six times before it starts to sink in. The same principle holds true in communicating the themes for corporate change. It requires untold repetition over significant periods of time before the organization as a whole comes to understand and accept the themes. Because management faddism has been such a rampant problem, employees understandably discount the first announcement of new themes as "the flavor of the month." When the second year starts and they're still hearing the same message, they take it a bit more seriously. By the third time around, if those themes are reinforced by concrete evidence of change in terms of strategy, structure, and human resource practices, then you truly start to get everyone's attention.

Paul O'Neill, who led a tremendously successful turnaround at Alcoa, likes to say that the two most important things to remember when talking about change are "consistency" and "connectivity." The CEO and top management have to be absolutely consistent in the messages they send concerning change. The slightest variation fuels confusion, anxiety, and renewed hope among opponents of change. Beyond that, people need to understand how the major change themes relate to the reality of their organization and their work. And they need to see that the themes themselves are truly interrelated, rather than being this year's "in" idea.

Take the Corning themes, for example. Performance was a serious issue for the entire company when Houghton took over. As an element of the change agenda, he set a performance goal of 10 percent operating profit margin and later set a goal of ranking among the top five corporations in the industry based on return on equity. These goals were consistent with the performance theme. (In 1986, he would set a new ambitious goal—to move from number 70 on *Fortune*'s list of most admired companies to the top 10.) At the same time, attention to quality became one of Corning's highest priorities, consistently supported by an all-out program of quality training, internal quality awards programs, quality management conferences, and so on. The addition of diversity as a third theme reflected both Houghton's personal concern about social issues and a hard-nosed business decision that Corning, located as it is in a remote rural area, would have trouble over time recruiting a qualified workforce unless it undertook dramatic measures to make its working environment much more attractive to women and minorities.

There's another reason why consistency and connectivity are so important. One of the most common complaints during transition periods is administrative overload. I used to hear that regularly from Corning managers: "I have to go to quality training. Then my team has to go to quality team training. Then we do diversity training. Then it's cycle time work. Then I have to do performance reviews. When am I supposed to do my job?"

In normal times, the correct answer should be, "That is your job." Managers who feel they don't have enough time for personal and staff development activities are often the ones who are spending too much time micromanaging the work their people should be doing. And the reality of most organizations is that if people aren't doing some complaining about being overloaded, then management probably isn't pushing hard enough.

But during transition periods, administrative overload is a trickier complaint to handle. On the one hand, if people were not entirely committed to all the CEO's change themes but had the political sense not to come right out and say it, then this would be the politically smart avenue of attack. This is what they would say: "I think the boss's themes are great. I couldn't agree with them more; I'm on board 110 percent. I believe that each of the themes is important, and I want to help him pursue each and every one of them. But doing all of them at once is just impossible. Maybe if we could just take them one at a time, and hold off on the others until we've got this first one under our belts." If you think about it, that's a pretty slick form of resistance.

On the other hand, you have to consider the very real possibility that the complaint is justified. And here's why. The CEO may start out with three clear, concise themes, but the message doesn't stop there. The next level down, in the interests of further focusing those themes, may supplement them with three fairly general performance objectives. At the division level, executives may want to make those goals and objectives relate more specifically to the work they do, so a few more goals get tacked on. Invariably, each level of management feels the need to dress up the CEO's simple themes with its own ruffles and flourishes. At Xerox, I looked into this problem at one point and found that at the regional operations level, the themes of customer satisfaction, market share, and return on assets had somehow exploded into fifty-three objectives. So senior executives and transition managers need to be constantly vigilant about the proliferation of themes, goals, and objectives down through the organization.

Yet the truth is that even without this problem, change takes a lot of work and makes huge demands on the time and energy of managers. They have to keep the operation running today while moving the organization steadily toward the future state.

The trick is to gauge just how far to push, and just how many messages to send, without cluttering the system and bringing people to the point of massive overload. And the key here is connectivity. People can accommodate more tasks and more messages if they can see the point—if they can see that all this added work really is part of an overall plan, rather than one more bright idea shoved down the line by some overly ambitious executive or one more piece of paper demanded by some insecure bureaucrat. Throughout the transition period, it's essential for executives to continually monitor how their themes are being interpreted and amplified down the line.

Building Support

All of this brings us back to the absolute necessity of building a coalition of support for change. It is crucial throughout this process to identify which people fall into each of those four categories I mentioned earlier: those who will make change happen, those who help it happen, those who let it happen, and those who are likely to get in the way. At the same time, it's important to understand the lines of influence running through the organization and to identify the *thought leaders* that others look to for signals on the appropriate response to change. As more and more details of the change become public and people begin to see how values and power relationships are likely to be reshaped, coalitions will begin forming, both in support of and in opposition to the new direction. Traditional animosities that might have been passive features of the landscape in the past may now flare into full-fledged conflicts as the sales or manufacturing or design functions maneuver to win more power.

Almost always, the most intense conflict will center around the question What kind of company are we going to be? The answer requires some hard strategic choices that may lead to deemphasizing—or even completely abandoning—some sector of the business in favor of another. At Harte-Hanks, it meant abandoning the newspaper business in 1997 to focus on direct marketing. For Corning, it has meant walking away from electronics, life sciences, and, most recently, housewares. For Xerox, it meant giving up on personal computers, typewriters, and microelectronics. When companies make those kinds of choices, it is inevitable that some will want to fight to hang onto their portion of the business.

Early on—before any specific aspects of the plan for change have become public—it's important for the senior team to identify these potential pockets of resistance, networks of opposition, and influential leaders, and then develop a specific program for handling them. One way to start is literally to draw a *stakeholder map*—a diagram depicting lines and patterns of influence within the organization—as a means of determining who should be targeted by the first efforts to build a coalition of support.

As is the case with the executive team, it's important to figure out early on which key managers at lower levels are likely to lead resistance to change and to deal with them decisively if necessary. At the outset of change at KPMG Peat Marwick in 1990, Jon Madonna took a close look at the one hundred or so managers of the regional offices. "We got rid of a lot of the ones who were impossible to deal with, which made change a lot easier," Madonna recalls. "The absolute, dyed-in-the-wool resisters, or those who would have been resisters, were shot before they ever saw the new moves. . . . So our guys were either new to the deal, or you could work with them. Otherwise, we shot them—probably a third of them."

The ultimate goal, of course, is to create widespread support throughout the organization at large. But some key groups merit special attention as you go about forging support for change:

The executive team. I've already discussed the importance of winning this group's support. But the members of this team are also essential to winning the support of others, through their formal and informal communication and through their overt and symbolic acts. Recalling the twin concepts of consistency and connectivity, the executive team must speak and act consistently in everything it does in order to present a united front. There cannot be any doubt that top management is in total harmony on the issue of change.

To forge that kind of unity at Lucent Technologies, CEO Henry Schacht devoted an enormous amount of time to getting the senior team totally aligned on the issues of the new corporate vision and values. "We need to get people to sit down," he said in 1996, "and talk through all this in a way that we would have consistency of approach and we're all saying the same thing to each other and to our people, so they see a unified group of 20 people who have come together and created a mission and a value statement for this new corporation."

Executives beyond the executive team. Effective organizations have found ways to broaden the circle of participation beyond the top team as they pursued the early stages of clarifying and formulating their plan for change. At Corning, the corporate management group worked with the executive team, first on the statement of values and then on the formulation of strategy. At PepsiCo, Craig Weatherup estimates that close to two hundred people worked on the design teams that developed the plan for change. At Xerox, following the initial formulation of the plan, change leaders spent nine months working with nearly 125 executives one on one, giving them a chance to understand clearly what was about to happen and why and enlisting their support before the plan was ever made public.

Pockets of support. Any change is likely to have opponents among those who see their power diminished or their values abandoned, but there are just as likely to be others who have been dissatisfied with the status quo and will enthusiastically support the change effort. Again, it's important to determine early on who these people are and to start bringing them into the coalition. David Pockell, who headed up Kaiser Permanente's Northern California Region, identified what he called "the disaffected underclass"—bright young people who felt the company was headed in the wrong direction. He began meeting with groups of these people and giving them encouragement, thereby building pressure from below on middle management while the executive team was driving change from above.

Employees. Every organization can list other important constituencies whose support over time will be crucial to the success of the change effort. At the top of the list should be the employees—the many people who actually perform the work of the organization every day. Essentially, there are two basic ways to gain the support of the workforce at large. First, you have to influence the actions and behavior of their immediate supervisors. I'll deal with this issue at greater length in Chapter Thirteen, when I discuss the role of managers and local change leaders. But in the early stages of change, direct communication from the top is crucial to influencing employees to support senior leaders in their campaign.

"Your ability to communicate and sell is critical," says Jon Madonna. "Communication is really critical. I'm talking about broad, mass communication—speeches, videos, everything. Of course, one-on-one communication is important. But mass communication is critical. It is a campaign to capture the hearts and minds of a whole bunch of people."

Other influential constituencies. It's also important to actively build support among others who feel they have a stake in the organization or who are in a position to influence its performance. For instance, as much as some CEOs dread spending time with Wall Street analysts, regular briefings are a must. Often they help build support among community leaders and policymakers. Many organizations—Lever Brothers comes to mind—have brought key customers and suppliers into the support-building process in the early stages. Depending on the dynamics of the particular situation, it can be particularly beneficial to enlist the support of the unions in the early stages. During that nine-month period of coalition building at Xerox, for example, considerable time was spent informing and educating union leaders, an investment that truly paid off once the time came for implementing the changes. (Clearly, that approach isn't always appropriate. In some situations the working relationship between the company and certain unions may be so poisoned by hostility and mistrust that the effort is impossible.)

The board of directors. Probably the most critical group to get signed on in advance is the board of directors, particularly its most influential members. For Jon Madonna, winning the board's support for his Future Directions change strategy was an essential early step. "You need to have key allies," Madonna later said. "By ourselves, we couldn't have brought about this level of change. I can't sit here in this room and get it done. We had to sell change to the board, and our management team. Both groups had doubts about the need for fundamental change because we had been operating with the same formula forever. And doing quite well, at that. So you have to really understand the organization and how to get things done within it" (Nadler, Shaw, Walton, and Associates, 1994, p. 255). However, as Madonna's changes brought the firm a new level of success, the board became less interested in the idea of continuing change at a rapid pace. Madonna's frustration with winning board support for another round of major change played a major part in his decision in 1996 not to seek a second term as chairman.

At Kaiser Permanente, the board actively sought more involvement in the early stages of change—a new role that David Lawrence ultimately came to appreciate. Over time he reshaped the board through new appointments, shifted its focus from operations to strategic issues, restructured its committees, and stepped up communications and the flow of information.

As a result, he says, "the board is now more aggressive and involved in sharing responsibility for the changes we are experiencing. They have become not only my sounding board, but a crucial source of support in making difficult decisions."

In the end it all gets back to Lawrence's description of large-scale change as a political campaign that's waged simultaneously on a variety of fronts using a wide array of different tactics. The keys to a successful campaign—and to a successful change effort—are first to articulate a clear, compelling vision of change, to continually and consistently communicate a small number of clearly understandable themes, and then to carefully build the nucleus of support among the members of the senior team and have them work together to extend that support throughout the organization.

Up to this point I've been talking about ways to prepare for change and plan for the transition. Chapter Eight turns to the third phase of change: implementation. Because implementation is the core of the change process, I devote the next four chapters to the challenges and techniques of bringing about change within the vital components of the organization as outlined in the congruence model. The logical starting place is how to develop and articulate a new strategy—the topic of Chapter Eight.

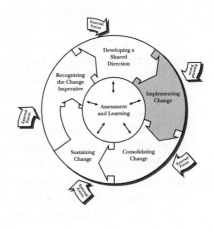

Building a New Strategy

The Strategic Choice Process

We have now arrived at the heart of the change process: *implementation.* In this chapter and the three that follow I deal in turn with each of the four components of implementation. The fact that there are four is no coincidence; each bears a direct relation to the components of the congruence model (Figure 2.4): work, formal organization, informal organization, and people.

In this chapter I explain a process for strategic choice—a way to reshape strategy and, by implication, the work requirements component of the organization. In Chapter Nine I take up the complex issue of organizational design, the process for altering the formal organizational arrangements. Chapter Ten focuses on ways to reshape the operating environment, another way to describe the informal organizational arrangements. And Chapter Eleven takes you through the process of strategic selection, a proven technique for addressing the staffing requirements of the new organization.

As before, I will draw upon my observations and personal experiences with several companies to illustrate the challenges of implementation and some specific techniques for addressing them. In particular I will return in each chapter to the work at Xerox. This is the reason: over a period lasting more than a decade, Xerox has experienced ensuing waves of discontinuous change; it has found itself required to change its strategy, structure, culture, and staffing.

Because the process at Xerox has been so explicit, so carefully managed, and so successful, it provides a classic example of how one organization can effectively weather the most tempestuous competitive environment through a continued commitment to integrated change.

With that background let's go back to 1985, a year when Xerox, in some ways, was a corporation at war with itself.

Historically, Xerox was a producer and distributor of machines that used light and chemicals to reproduce images on pieces of paper. But in 1985, it was much more. Over the years it had gradually expanded into new areas. It was producing printers and electronic typewriters. It was getting involved in the personal computer and workstation businesses. It had a microelectronics operation. In its research labs it was developing an impressive list of innovations in computing hardware and software. It had even branched out into the financial services business.

Xerox was trying to do a staggering number of things at once—and with varying degrees of success. True, it was no longer hovering on the brink of disaster. Financial performance, though unimpressive in comparison with the company's glory days, had stabilized. The program to improve the quality of products and services, after a rocky start, was finally beginning to show results. But priorities were muddled. Every day, seemingly routine decisions over projects, initiatives, staffing, and resources erupted into heated battles that revealed the absence of any underlying consensus about where the company should be headed and how it ought to spend its money. Debates over mundane operating matters became surrogates for more profound but unresolved conflicts over exactly what kind of company Xerox should be.

Fearful that the absence of a clear strategy was literally tearing his company apart, CEO David Kearns launched a process called Xerox 95, with the intention of developing a focused strategic plan for the coming decade. Building upon that strategy, Paul Allaire used the same process five years later in a program called Xerox 2000 to design and implement a radical restructuring of the corporation. Together the two efforts were incredibly successful. As the new, vibrant Xerox emerged as one of America's great business success stories, Wall Street voted its approval by quadrupling the price of the company's stock.

The question, obviously, is how did they do it? And more to the point, can other companies do the same thing?

The truth is that not every organization could or should duplicate the process Xerox pursued as it fashioned a new strategy and then designed a new organizational architecture to fit it. The Xerox process was by far one of the most explicit, formal, and participative processes I've seen. To be sure, it's conceivable that in a much different setting, the same thought processes could occur with three or four people meeting for a week, rather than with more than a dozen people laboring for nine months. It would be simplistic to suggest there is only one way to develop an effective strategic plan or that strategy grows out of a neat linear process that every organization can use. I hope I've made it clear by now that there isn't any aspect of managing human organizations that is that simple or formulaic. The key to developing strategy won't be found in any easy five-step set of rules; instead, the heart of the process is getting the right people in the right room and openly debating the right issues with the requisite degree of clarity, honesty, and discipline. And that is much more easily said than done.

Given that caveat, I'll refer to the Xerox experience throughout this chapter as a way to illustrate the central concepts of strategic choice—a process that involves appropriate participation, the development of viable alternatives, and the rigorous analysis of a wide range of options.

The Elements of Strategy

Let's start by defining the term *strategy*. In this context, strategy describes a clear set of organizational intentions that together present a coherent set of decisions about what businesses the organization is to be in and how to run those businesses. It is a statement of the organization's mission and goals, an outline of its operations, and a summary of the actions it believes will be required to meet its objectives in the context of the competitive environment.

Beyond intentions, strategy also involves concrete action, generally in the realm of resource allocation. In that sense it has been said that "the essence of strategy is denial." A truly effective strategy implicitly involves the rejection of available and often attractive courses of action in order to focus resources on those actions that most closely support the organization's primary objectives. No matter what organization you're talking about, regardless of the circumstances, there are never enough resources to do everything. Consequently, a truly focused strategy involves the full consideration—and then the deliberate rejection—of serious alternatives.

Consider the case of Eli Lilly. When Randy Tobias took over as CEO in 1993, Lilly had slipped from its longtime standing as a leader in the pharmaceutical industry. Its resources were thinly spread over a wide range of health care–related businesses, from drug research to medical instruments. After carefully reviewing the alternatives, Tobias decided to jettison everything except those activities directly related to five categories of diseases and disorders, including cardiovascular, central nervous system, and oncological. Everything else had to go. It wasn't an easy decision; in each of the abandoned areas there were those in Lilly who felt the company was doing important work with potentially far-reaching scientific implications. But as Tobias looked at each area, he decided that if Lilly wasn't likely to become a "world-class player," it was time to get out. Why? Because only by focusing all its resources in a small, well-defined number of arenas could Lilly hope to become a major player everywhere it competed.

Too often that doesn't happen; the senior group keeps revisiting the same menu of options over and over, spends days or weeks wrangling over the pluses and minuses of each course of action, and adjourns without anyone making any clear-cut decisions. I have seen companies where that process went on literally for years. And in the absence of a clear strategy that involved hard choices, the organizations muddled along, continuing to do a poor job of pursuing all the options that were still sitting on the table.

The bottom line is that any successful strategy must combine both intent and the actions to back it up. Strategic intent in the absence of action is a wish list, not a strategy. And a strategy that tries to placate every opposing view is doomed to failure.

Any discussion of strategy must also differentiate between *corporate strategy* and *business strategy*. Corporate strategy, on the one hand, describes complex organizations' efforts to balance and integrate multiple businesses, which may or may not be related, in a strong, profitable, growth-oriented portfolio. AT&T's decision in 1995 to split itself into three separate and independent companies was a classic piece of corporate strategy, designed both to rid the organization of diverse operations it had never truly digested—such as the NCR computer business—and to eliminate the massive and growing conflicts between key operations within the company. New legislation and continuing deregulation made it clear that AT&T was about to become embroiled in an all-out war not only with long-distance services but with nearly all providers of local phone service, including the former regional Bell operating companies. But those same phone service providers were the primary customers of AT&T's network systems operation. Inordinate amounts of time and energy were expended in trying to solve an inherently insoluble problem, and the decision to spin-off the conflicting businesses was clearly the right one.

Business strategy, on the other hand, refers to a set of intentions and actions involving interconnected products and offerings for interconnected markets. AT&T's decision to spin off Lucent Technologies and NCR was a corporate strategy. Lucent's decisions on how best to reorganize its four business units and Bell Labs, how to expand its global market share, how to leverage its assets—those were all matters of business strategy.

A comprehensive business strategy requires an organization to develop answers to four sets of issues:

- Who are our customers, which markets do we want to serve, and precisely what are the needs we intend to satisfy?
- Exactly what is the offering we plan to provide? This means thinking in terms beyond a specific product or service. When people buy a BMW, they're buying more than a car—they're buying the expectation of a certain kind of driving experience, they're buying cachet, they're buying technological innovation, they're buying a quality and style (and cost) of service, they're buying resale value. So how will the complete offering meet customer requirements?
- What are our organizational capabilities? Do we have the right people, the right skills, the right structure, and the necessary operating environment to pursue a given strategy—and if not, what would be involved in reshaping our organizational capabilities?
- How will the strategy provide us with sustainable competitive advantage? Why will the market choose our offerings rather than those of our competitors?

This last concept of sustainable competitive advantage is in the end what a successful strategy is all about. Noted management theorist Michael E. Porter (1985) suggests three bases of competitive advantage for strategists to consider:

Low-cost producer. If you can figure out how to produce your offering for less than it costs your competitors, then you can sell it at a lower price. Gateway and Dell have shown how successful this strategy can be in the personal computer business.

Product differentiation. This strategy requires an organization to produce an offering that is unique in some way and that customers can get only by coming to you—and often by paying a premium price. For years Japanese automakers used quality as a basis for product differentiation. Chrysler fueled its comeback with the minivan, an offering that stood alone in the marketplace for years. Apple succeeded on the basis of its user-friendly Macintosh operating system until Microsoft modified its Windows system to incorporate many of the Mac's most popular features.

Customer focus. This requires an organizational commitment to get so close to customers and to understand them so well that you can meet their needs better than anyone else. In the financial services industry, for instance, there's little advantage to be gained from product differentiation; practically any new financial product can be duplicated by competitors in a matter of days. The successful firms are those that know their customers; understand their lifestyles, financial needs, and methods of doing business; and can reach out to them on a personal basis. In retailing, a parallel might be Paul Stuart, the clothier, which competes not with unique products or competitive prices but by understanding what business executives are looking for both in their clothing and in a shopping experience. In the office, Xerox has become a dominant supplier of services to the pharmaceutical industry because it employs people who understand the FDA drug clearance process and all the documents their customers will need to deal with the government.

One final note on the basic concept of strategy: the essence of an effective strategy is that it provides a flexible framework for daily decision making. Given the rapid rate of change in the business environment, an organization's strategy should delineate the boundaries for appropriate response to unforeseen developments. The strategy is a general game plan, in a sense, which allows the quarterback on the field to call his own plays in response to defensive shifts without having to call a time-out and trot over to the sidelines to ask the coach for a new set of plays. And strategy is most effective by far when the people who have the responsibility for carrying it out understand it, believe in it, and feel they have a personal stake in it.

Flaws in the Strategic Process

All too often the focus of the strategic process is on producing a written document that specifies a detailed strategic plan. But in a business environment where change is the norm, that's a misguided goal. The truth is that by the time the written document is hammered out and distributed, the set of environmental factors it was designed to address will already have begun changing. In this ever-shifting environment the true strength of the strategy is found in the underlying assumptions and the design process from which it emerged. Once again, the greatest value is in the planning, not the plan.

In addition, the strategic process too often results in frustration, confusion, and a sense of disenfranchisement among senior managers—not to mention bad strategy. Over the years I've identified three primary reasons for the frequent failures of this process: inadequate participation, unclear assumptions, and one-off decision making.

Inadequate Participation

Too many strategic plans are put together without the right people in the room. Too often the job is left to strategic planners and outside consultants, who lack both an in-depth understanding of the realities of the business and the responsibility for implementing the strategy once it's adopted. Time and again I've seen impressive strategies devised by outsiders run aground as soon as the key executives get their hands on them. Having been excluded from offering their insights and opinions, they feel no commitment to or ownership for the off-the-shelf plan.

Unclear Assumptions

Unsuccessful strategies tend to evolve from a rush to adopt a pre-ordained solution. In such situations, debates tend to be circular, inconclusive, and unsatisfying because there is no consensus—and often no discussion—of the wide range of underlying assumptions various players hold about the competitive environment and the organization's future. More often than not, the process begins with committed advocates of one strategy or another flailing away at each other, not realizing that their underlying assumptions about markets, customers, offerings, and organizational capabilities are so divergent that they may not even be speaking the same language.

In the summer of 1993, I worked with Bill Marx, then head of AT&T's Network Systems group, on the development of a new business strategy. At that time Network Systems was producing cables, switches, amplifiers, local switching stations, base stations, cell sites, and computer hardware and software for information system providers. Marx brought together the senior team members and told them that if Network Systems was to be able to sell into the environment of the future, they had to know what the environment would look like.

So he had them spend an entire day working in small groups to draw pictures—literally draw pictures—of how they envisioned information services a few years down the road. They taped their pictures to the wall, engaged in some ferocious debates—how would networks be configured, who would control them, would contemporary computers be replaced by "dumb" shells tapping into networks for their software—and then they went back to the drawing board. By the end of the exercise, they had developed what Marx called an "information topography" that embodied a "belief system" about the shape of the future. Whether the picture was right or wrong, it provided a common starting point from which their work could go forward. Every few months they could take out the map, see if it was accurate, make corrections where necessary—and keep everyone operating with the same basic picture in mind.

In debates over strategy—and in many other business situations for that matter—there is an inherent and overwhelming reluctance for participants to raise issues that may be distasteful, irritating, worrisome, or just downright unpleasant to discuss around the table. It may be an issue the boss clearly doesn't like talking about. It may be an issue sure to engender verbal combat, which most people find unsettling. It maybe an issue likely to cause embarrassment to a colleague seated at the table. Management succession, personalities, unsuccessful business initiatives, dysfunctional departments—all those issues and more can be crucial to a senior team's deliberations yet strictly off limits in open discussion.

My longtime colleague Dennis Perkins (1988) describes this phenomenon as "the moose on the table." His point is this: we've all sat through countless meetings where hours were spent on inconsequential discussions of peripheral issues. And yet by tacit agreement no one made any reference to the central problem— what Chris Argyris (1990), a pioneer in the field of organizational behavior, calls "the undiscussables." Perkins says it's just like having a "great, big, ugly, hairy, smelly moose" standing on the conference table. People seated around the table stretch and bend to address each other between the moose's legs, and they are perfectly willing to talk about everything in the world—except the moose. They can sit there talking for hours, but damned if anyone is going to acknowledge the existence of the moose on the table.

It's a useful metaphor. While working with clients, I'll sometimes sit and listen to unproductive discussions that dance around the central issue, and without saying anything, I'll simply place a stuffed toy moose on the table. It doesn't take long before people know exactly what I mean; the appearance of the moose loosens people up and frees them to address the undiscussable. The point is that unless they feel they have explicit permission to bring up "forbidden" topics, most people will continue to avoid some of the most important issues. My colleagues and I have seen this come into play countless times, causing inadequate discussion of differing opinions about underlying strategic assumptions.

One-Off Decision Making

What sometimes passes for strategy is actually a collection of independent decisions involving investments, cost cutting, products, staffing, and work processes rather than a coherent set of interrelated decisions. The truth is that every day, organizations make strategic decisions in the guise of operational decisions. Do we fund this project? Retool that plant? Retrain these people? Expand those stores?

In the absence of strategy, organizations end up making gradual, incremental decisions devoid of context. An opportunity comes along to make an acquisition. Then comes the chance to strengthen the first acquisition by purchasing one of its competitors. The third acquisition looks like a no-brainer. Before you know it, you're knee-deep in a new industry. You've spent hundreds of millions—a few million at a time—to become a player in an industry far afield from your core business.

If the first acquisition had been preceded by the questions, Do we want to be in that industry? and Are we willing to spend $300 million to do it? would the answer have been yes? Maybe, maybe not. If senior managers had understood the real price tag, they might have said forget it. If they were really willing to spend that much money, they might have considered other alternatives, either within the core business or in an entirely different area. Or they might have said, "Yes, that's exactly where we should be, but to do it right we should invest $800 million." But the opportunity for that kind of analysis, assessment, and consideration has been precluded in this case by a series of one-off decisions that resulted in a de facto strategy.

Strategic Choice

Over the years my colleagues and I have developed a process that we call *strategic choice* and that provides some fundamental concepts to address the frequent shortcomings of the strategy-making process. Years of experience have convinced us that in most situations, if you get the right people in the right room, analyzing the right information and openly debating the right issues, you can generally count on them to come up with the right answers. We have no bias toward any particular outcome in the strategic process; to restate my proposition, it is the process itself that is paramount. The fine points of any strategy are likely to be modified over and over again through the years in response to the changing environment. It is the effectiveness of the original strategic process that determines the organization's ability to anticipate, design, and successfully implement those inevitable midcourse corrections.

Let's be clear about one thing: if done well, strategy-making is an inherently messy process. A truly rigorous search for an incisive and meaningful strategy—particularly in the context of redirecting or overhauling—becomes a forum for intensely emotional debates over where the organization is headed and what kind of enterprise it should be. In the end these are issues that have everything to do with people's careers, values, beliefs, professional self-image, and personal goals. Everything is on the line. And the CEO has the most at stake. If the new strategy works, it will become his or her legacy; if it fails, the CEO is unlikely ever to get credit for any of his or her other accomplishments. It's an all or nothing bet.

The strategic choice process, messy as it may be, rests on three underlying concepts that relate to the three main stages of the process (see Figure 8.1):

1. *Focused collaboration on input.* The executive team has got to be actively involved. Their experience, knowledge, judgment, and commitment are vital to the process. Without their full participation, no strategy is likely to succeed. The ultimate decision rests with the CEO, or whoever happens to be the top executive of the business unit going through the strategic process. But it's essential for the CEO to make those decisions with the benefit of the full range of opinions residing within the executive team. The CEO shouldn't necessarily wait for consensus to form; indeed, if the strategic alternatives under discussion are sufficiently bold, varied, and creative, consensus may be impossible. That's all right—this is not intended to be a democratic process, just an inclusive one. What the CEO needs is to hear a wide range of alternatives from people who are thinking originally and looking for the big bets. That kind of thinking won't come from staff planners, who are more inclined to deliver complex analyses of market conditions and linear thinking limited by past strategies and hard numbers. It is the executive team—and the process of engaged interaction among its members—that will provide the CEO with the widest range of exciting and creative alternatives grounded in the judgment and experience of the people who actually run the business.

2. *Identification of driving assumptions.* Productive debate of strategic alternatives is impossible, of course, unless the participants first surface, explore, debate, and reach consensus on an overall outlook for the competitive environment and their organization's

Figure 8.1. The Strategic Choice Process.

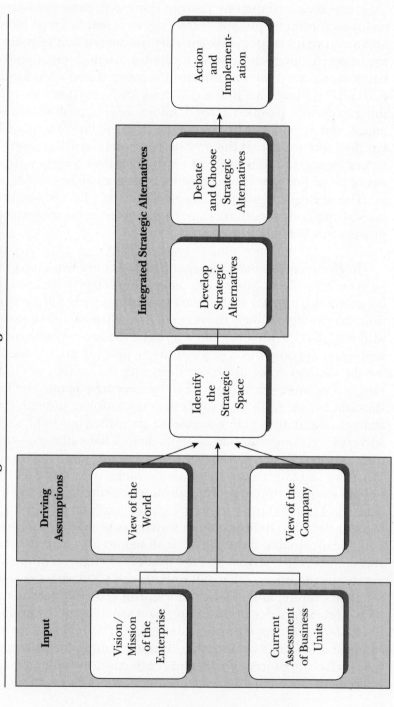

place within it. Without that shared view of the world, discussion is of negligible value.

3. *Integrated strategic alternatives.* The way to avoid random one-off decisions is to employ a process that requires the formulation and consideration of comprehensive options, or integrated strategic alternatives. Each alternative identifies a strategic direction and then spells out what it means in terms of portfolio decisions, resource allocations, restructuring, changes in the operating environment, cash flow, hiring, and capital investment.

That's a very general description of the strategic choice strategy-making process. Now let's turn to the case of Xerox and see how the process actually works in a real competitive situation.

Strategic Choice at Xerox

In 1985, when people at Xerox had radically differing views over where the company should be heading and were badly in need of a focused strategy, what should have been routine deliberations over money, people, products, and technology were turning into major confrontations.

At one extreme were those who believed that with the advent of new information technology, the era of stand-alone copiers was about to end, to be replaced by an era of digitally connected office systems—and that was where Xerox should be. At the other extreme were those who insisted that Xerox had always been a "marks on paper" company. That's what it knew, that's where it enjoyed the highest margins, and that's what it should stick to. After all, this digital stuff was a lot of hype, and who knew how far off in the distant future the new digital world would become a reality.

Those divergent views presented very specific alternatives for spending money. Should Xerox become a workstation company? Should it offer full-office solutions, going head-to-head with industry giants IBM and Digital Equipment Company? Should it expand its electronic typewriter and personal computer operations, and deemphasize its traditional copier business?

David Kearns was convinced that the strategy had to be clarified—maybe even revamped. Beyond that, however, he was increasingly concerned that the rifts within management were so deep that even if he came up with the right strategy, the bloodletting would continue unless the key people were signed on. So he needed not just a strategy but a strategy development process that would have a healing effect on senior management.

At that point Kearns asked me to work with some of his people, including Roger Levien, then the chief strategy officer at Xerox, to design a process through which Kearns and the top leadership could work together to make the fundamental strategic decisions. What emerged was a model for the strategic choice process—a nine-month effort by Kearns and fifteen of his top executives. That group included the executive team members along with a few third-level executives who were clearly destined for senior leadership positions in the future. Together they produced the blueprint for Xerox's future.

A View of the World

It was clear from the outset that members of the strategy team had sharply clashing opinions on almost everything. It also became obvious that it would be pointless to engage in detailed discussions of specific strategy alternatives until all the players were gathered in the same conceptual ballpark. To that end we set about helping them construct something approaching a shared view of the world.

At this early stage in the strategic choice process, much of the work at any organization will fall into three categories (see Figure 8.1):

Input. The collection of all relevant information, including the CEO's guiding vision for the future and a thorough assessment of the performance of the present organization's existing business units

Discussion of driving assumptions. A thorough analysis of the external environment and likely developments in the economy, technology, and government action and among customers, competitors, and suppliers. Using their knowledge, judgment, and experience, team members formulate their best guesses about how the environment will change over time;

Strategic assessment. The team first extrapolates what the organization is likely to look like in the future if it follows its present course, then lays that scenario over the set of driving assumptions about marketplace changes. That process illustrates the *strategic gaps,* the differences between what the organization is likely to become and what it needs to be if it is to compete successfully in the future. The process ideally should identify which elements will require major change—offerings, structures, operating procedures, quality, and workforce training, or internal culture—as it pinpoints particular strengths and competencies that, if properly exploited, could become major sources of competitive advantage.

Once again, don't think of these elements as forming a neat, linear process. The situation at Xerox was fairly typical; all three of these steps were intermingled in the early stages of the process as the team labored to figure out how the world was likely to change and how Xerox could best change with it.

The process had begun with David Kearns presenting his vision and setting some goals, including financial objectives. One exercise that helped set the tone was a movie that described Xerox in 1975, interspersing news reports and Xerox commercials from that year. The point was to show team members that 1995 really wasn't such a long way off; ten years in the future might seem like an eternity, but ten years in the past seemed like only yesterday. The film helped bring not only perspective but a greater sense of urgency to the project.

Still, as I noted earlier, the executives had incredibly divergent views concerning their competitive world and the pace of innovation. Some believed the paperless office would eventually become commonplace; others thought the whole idea was nothing but hype. One group thought new office technology would become pervasive almost any day now; others thought it wasn't anything to worry about in the near future. Many of the executives predicted a slow, gradual shift to digital technology. A few—who turned out to be right—predicted it would take longer than expected for the idea of the digital office to win widespread acceptance, but once it did, the change would happen practically overnight.

Those differing views translated directly into different opinions about the proper strategy for Xerox. Before anyone could start talking about strategy, we had to help the executives construct a worldview they all could accept. We began by meeting with business leaders, such as John Reed of Citicorp, who talked about trends in the workplace and their vision of information and document processing. We talked to industry analysts and consultants, academics and technology experts. Sometimes we had them meet directly with the strategic design team (which met regularly at a conference center outside New York City). In other cases some of us would interview the outside experts and present our findings to the larger group.

With the team awash in data about the company and perspectives on the outside world, it was time to debate and try to reach some consensus on a set of basic assumptions. We tried to lend some structure to that process by presenting the team with a set of eighteen statements, asking them to agree or disagree with each one. Most of the statements had to do with the outside world and the business environment in general, some had to do with customers and the competitive marketplace, and others zeroed in on "the office of the future," specifically addressing uses of paper and processing of business documents. That set of statements helped focus the earliest debates on fundamental issues, before the team had any opportunity to start delving into specific strategies or action steps. And indeed, the group ultimately reached a degree of consensus on how the world of office technology and their marketplace would take shape in the coming decade.

Strategic Alternatives

As the process unfolded it became clear team members had essentially four different views of which path Xerox should follow and what kind of company it should try to become by 1995. Those alternatives embodied the range of views about what was likely to happen in the marketplace and how Xerox's strengths and weaknesses played to those changes. Over time these views emerged as integrated strategic alternatives, each involving not only a general strategic goal but a set of actions designed to move the company in that direction. Then each alternative was named for a company that was known for employing a version of that distinctive alternative in its respective industry. The four alternatives were Boeing, Chrysler, BMW, and Sears.

Boeing. The underlying assumption in the Boeing alternative was that the world wasn't likely to change as fast as some people believed. For the foreseeable future there would continue to be tremendous demand for paper document production in the workplace, particularly in high-volume data centers and production units. This strategy proposed that Xerox should concentrate its development and distribution on big, high-volume copiers and printers, the areas where it already enjoyed its highest margins. The plan was to dominate the high-volume end of the business and forget about small printers and copiers, typewriters, personal computers, workstations, and anything but the giant workhorse machines. The sources of competitive advantage would be an extension of the already-strong market position in the high-volume business, economies of scale involved in focusing resources on a smaller number of products, and a reliance on a technology sector where Xerox was already strong. This strategy was likened to strategy at Boeing, which dominated the market in huge aircraft (at the time there was no real competitor for the Boeing 747) and ignored the entire market for small private jets.

Chrysler. The advocates of the Chrysler strategy believed that most of the right pieces were already in place. They believed the office revolution was under way and would progress quickly, and they felt Xerox was reasonably well positioned to supply that revolution through its involvement in personal computers, workstations, servers, and most of the vital components of digital networks, including the Ethernet software developed at its Palo Alto Research Center. By emphasizing the systems-related operations and making a few acquisitions where necessary—purchasing a computer company, for example—Xerox could position itself as the strong number three to IBM and DEC in the office systems business, much as Chrysler thrived as the strong third player in the U.S. auto industry.

BMW. The BMW view held that the area where Xerox had done reasonably well, but could do considerably better, was technological innovation. In a sense it reflected the widespread frustration felt because the Xerox research operation had developed some of the most innovative advances in office technology—Ethernet, the mouse, the first graphics-oriented monitors, the first laser printer, and the revolutionary graphic user interface that Apple later incorporated into its Lisa and Macintosh computers—but had failed to turn them into successful commercial products. The strategy called for dumping all the "commodity" products, which faced tremendous competition from Japanese producers, and concentrating on technologically innovative products, such as specialized printers, copiers, and workstations. That would mean investing in some new areas, spinning off some old ones, downsizing, and increasing margins. The strategy was likened to strategy at BMW in that this relatively small automaker capitalized on product differentiation to attract devoted customers who were willing to pay high prices for innovative cars.

Sears. Finally, there was a camp that believed the others had it all wrong. We're really not that great at technology, they said, and we can't seem to bring our new ideas to market. We're getting better at quality, but we're still nothing special. Compared with the Japanese, we'll never be the low-cost producer. So what is it we really do well—where is our true competitive strength? Answer: the salesforce. Xerox had tens of thousands of people, generally recognized as one of the best-trained, most effective sales and service forces in America, swarming through the nation's offices each day. So let's figure out what America's offices need and want to buy, and let's provide it, pumping products through the huge distribution pipeline that's already in place. If they want equipment we produce, fine, we'll sell it to them. If we don't make it, we'll outsource it. If they want printers, copiers, typewriters, computers, furniture, supplies—we'll be the place where American business shops. The source of competitive advantage will be customer focus; our salespeople, better than anyone else, know the people who run the country's offices and understand their needs, and we'll sell it all to them. The obvious parallel for this strategy was Sears.

Debating the Alternatives

Given the divergence of these strategies, it wasn't surprising that each alternative had not only passionate supporters but also fierce rivals. From a process standpoint, the challenge was to ensure a full and unencumbered debate. We had to find a way, in essence, to give people permission to speak their minds, unfettered by undiscussables or political considerations. That's terribly difficult to do. When a strategy or idea is identified with a particular champion, discussion of that strategy becomes personalized. If an BMW alternative, for example, is discussed in the context of "Jim's strategy," then Jim's adversaries will look for ways to attack it while his supporters might be reluctant to voice their misgivings. Some participants might be afraid to take Jim on in direct debate; others might shy away from embarrassing him. So it's important to depersonalize the process.

We accomplished this by dividing the team into four groups, each with the responsibility for fleshing out and presenting one of the alternative strategies. Each team included both supporters and opponents of the plan and also some neutrals. By assigning each alternative to a team and making it the plan of everyone on that team, it ceased to be the plan of anyone in particular, thus freeing people to debate the issues divorced from personalities. One team member who was an early champion of his assigned alternative even begin his presentation by saying, "Now, I'm not necessarily in favor of this idea, but . . ." Well, of course he was. But the *process* had made it possible for him to distance himself from the proposal, to hold it at arm's length and offer it up for objective analysis.

In the end, each team was assigned to follow the same format in explaining how its strategy would work and the implications for portfolio moves, capital investment, cash flow, restructuring, human resources, organizational capabilities, and financial performance. (Each team was supposed to limit its report to four pages, though one group managed this only by printing the report in 6 point type, the size most newspapers use to print stock tables. If memory serves, it was the group advocating greater reliance on technological innovation.) The resulting debate was indeed full and open. We attempted to structure it a bit further by asking the full team to assess each alternative on two criteria: achievability and attractiveness. In other words, given the current state of the organization and its access to resources, how doable was each alternative? And even if the strategy was achievable, how attractive was it? Would it result in an organization and a way of doing business with which the team members would feel comfortable?

During this process, people began to change their minds and shift away from their original positions. One executive had favored one of the alternatives for years. But once he had to sit down and figure out what the strategy would actually require in terms of capital and resources and human capabilities, he came to the conclusion that it just wasn't feasible—interesting and attractive, yes, but simply unfeasible. That's the value of this process. It's one thing to sit around the bar at a management offsite and expound on an appealing idea. But only by being forced to buckle down, crunch the numbers, look at the balance sheet, think about the numbers of people involved and the skills they'd need, consider the necessary investments, and analyze the impact on the customer can people fully assess the import of a particular strategy. Executives who had been devoted supporters of particular strategies went through that exercise and then stepped back in dismay and said, "Oh, my God, I had no idea!"

Finally, each team member's assignment was to present his personal strategic recommendations to David Kearns. They had thirty minutes in which to go off and prepare a five-minute presentation, not knowing in what order these presentations would be made. Half an hour later, they returned and, one by one, recommended to Kearns a strategy for the company's future.

Kearns listened attentively; the group adjourned. Kearns met briefly with executive vice president Bill Glavin and myself and then went off to deliberate on his own. The next morning he told the group what he'd decided.

In the end, the Chrysler alternative was viewed as a dream rather than a strategy. The company lacked the resources, skill, and marketing position to be a strong competitor in every sector of information and office technology.

The BMW alternative was seen as placing too big a bet on quickly bringing technological innovation to the marketplace, an area where Xerox had not excelled. Moreover, few in the group liked the idea of scaling down the company, a move that scored low on the attractiveness scale.

The Sears alternative was seen as achievable but unappealing; it was too inconsistent with the history and values of the company and its people. They didn't want to be distributors; they wanted to be technological innovators who changed the way people did business in their offices. In the end the vision offered by the Sears alternative was too limiting, too devoid of an inspirational theme.

So what Kearns announced that final morning was that he had settled upon an alternative he dubbed "wide Boeing." In essence, it combined Boeing and BMW. Kearns agreed with the Boeing strategy of concentrating on the areas where the company was already strong—but his definition of those areas was a bit different. In Xerox terms, the Boeing alternative envisioned a continued reliance on light lens technology, but Kearns believed Xerox had to be a major player both in light lens and digital. Consequently, it needed to be involved in scanning and distributive printing—the exchange of digitized documents throughout the office—and with the full range of equipment, not just the high end. Kearns's focus was on "the document," and his belief was that Xerox would continue its traditional emphasis on document processing but also adapt to new technologies. That focus required the abandonment of businesses he saw as too far removed from the core business, and in the next few years Xerox turned away from typewriters, computers, microelectronics, and financial services.

In truth, Kearns had a general idea of where he was headed before hearing the final recommendations. But his mind was open when the process began nine months earlier, and there's no question the deliberations strongly influenced his thinking. More important, he came out of the experience with a senior team that thoroughly understood the reasoning behind the new strategy and felt a sense of commitment that comes only from having been part of the process.

Incidentally—and not insignificantly—Kearns found that the process also proved a valuable forum for assessing the quality of his management team. Gathered together without their deputies or staff support, they all were playing on a level field. In a sense they all started out "equally dumb," placed in a situation where they all were presented with the same situation at the same time and then asked to analyze, respond, and build on it. Some executives excelled; others proved to be disappointments. One in particular, who had a reputation as one of the more articulate executives in the company, proved to be nearly incoherent when forced to speak without a prepared text.

Additionally, as Kearns prepared to implement the new strategy, the strategic choice process gave him a clear picture of which executives were truly on board and whom he could rely upon for total commitment in the difficult days ahead. Paul Allaire emerged from the process as the leading champion of the new strategy favored by Kearns and was named president in late 1986. Allaire's job was to implement the strategy, beginning with the corporate-level portfolio moves, including divestitures and acquisitions, essential to sharpening the new corporate focus as "the document processing company." (The better known tag line The Document Company would follow a few years later.)

Before long, Allaire would come to the conclusion that the new strategy required similarly dramatic changes within the company, and soon launched his own round of change. In terms of the organizational model, that meant working three leverage points for change:

1. *Redesigning the hardware.* Changing the structural groupings, processes, and systems that make up the formal organizational arrangements
2. *Rewriting the software.* Altering the values, beliefs, and operating environment that make up the informal organization
3. *Restaffing.* Figuring out how to place the right people in the right roles to pursue the new strategy.

These, then, are the issues I take up in the next three chapters as we continue our look at the implementation phase of integrated change.

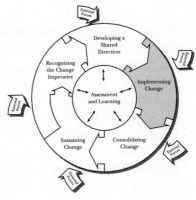

Chapter Nine

Redesigning the Organizational "Hardware"

The Keys to Strategic Design

Our story picks up again with Xerox. It's now 1991, and five years have passed since David Kearns led the strategic shift that produced "The Document Company." Kearns has retired from the company and gone on to become deputy secretary of education in the Bush administration. As expected, Paul Allaire has succeeded him as CEO. Now Xerox is working hard to truly become the kind of company that was envisioned during the Xerox 95 process. Allaire has followed up with Xerox 2000, a second round of focused strategic thinking, refined to reflect technological realities of the 1990s. Still, serious problems remain.

Allaire realized in 1991 that he stood at the head of a worldwide enterprise of 100,000 people, enormous resources, and a well thought out strategy—but Xerox still wasn't getting the job done. It had a strategy that required it to develop new technology, go into new markets, become more accountable, and focus more sharply on customer needs. That was the goal. But the reality was far different. Despite everything, the company was still much too slow—slow to develop products, slow to get them to market, slow to respond to competition. No one seemed to be accountable for pursuing the strategic initiatives. New products and ideas were being

173

ignored. And the organization still seemed unable to focus sharply enough on customers' needs.

Allaire finally became convinced that the strategy Xerox had developed was the right one—but one that Xerox could never hope to execute as long as it remained a traditional functional organization. Clearly, the time had come for a radical redesign of the entire formal organization—a process Allaire launched under the name Future Architecture. By the time Allaire and the design teams he appointed had finished their work nearly a year and a half later, they had drawn the blueprints and planned the construction of a new organizational architecture that would reshape Xerox in ways more dramatic and profound than anyone had imagined.

Though the process was far more structured and intensive than what you would find at most companies, Allaire was following in a time-honored business tradition. When everything is said and done, organization design—reshaping the organization's formal structure, processes, and systems—is one of a very few tools CEOs can use to effectively translate strategy into performance.

The CEO really has only two major alternatives. The first can be described as strategic initiatives. These include portfolio changes at the corporate level, such as spinning off old businesses and investing in new ones, and strategic business initiatives, such as investing in new programs and products. The second alternative consists of actions that actually change behavior within a business by leveraging the components of the congruence model. And as described in Chapter Eight, these actions form an extremely limited list: redesigning the hardware, or the formal organizational arrangements; rewriting the software, or the informal culture; and restaffing the organization.

In many ways, *hardware redesign* is the most appealing and readily achievable of the alternatives. This chapter examines its value and usefulness, outlines the essential elements of organizational design, and illustrates how the redesign process was carried out at Xerox (see also Nadler and Tushman, 1997, which offers a book-length discussion of the redesign concepts in this chapter). As I'll explain in Chapter Ten, reshaping the corporate culture, or operating environment, is a complex task that requires lots of time; consequently, that's not the place to look for immediate results.

Moreover, culture changes can be deeply unsettling and divisive. Restaffing is easier in some ways, but it's another button that can't be pushed over and over again within a limited time. Wide-scale staffing changes always evoke anxiety and instability, and managers must also provide periods of relative calm in which people get a fighting chance to learn and master new jobs. Moreover, staffing the organization with large numbers of people from the outside, though important and beneficial in many ways, can also be disruptive and risky. Experience suggests that at best, only about a quarter of outside hires at the senior level live up to original expectations.

Redesigning hardware, however, means making major changes in the formal organizational arrangements—the structure, processes, and systems—that dictate how work is grouped, controlled, and coordinated. Such structural redesign is attractive because it's one of the few levers senior managers can pull and then experience the satisfaction of actually seeing something happen. These shake-ups, if handled correctly, send sharp, swift signals about what kind of organization the CEO and senior team want the company to be, underscore and support the new strategy, and reinforce concepts of change in real and observable ways.

Moreover, restructuring is a potentially powerful tool for breathing life into low-profile activities. When Jamie Houghton restructured Corning in the early 1980s, he elevated two of the company's relatively minor operations—life sciences and communications—into full-fledged business units. By focusing attention, resources, and a degree of autonomy on those activities, Corning transformed those two units into the engines that drove much of the company's success through the decade of the 1980s, when some of Corning's mature businesses were experiencing less than dramatic growth. (By the mid-1990s, market conditions had changed again, and Corning chose a portfolio change for its next strategic move, spinning off the life sciences operations as two new businesses, Quest Diagnostics and Covance.)

Similarly, Xerox's radical restructuring in 1992 took the struggling Business Services operation, which provided and operated entire document processing centers for Xerox customers, and turned it into one of the nine new "end-to-end" business units, encompassing everything from product design to marketing. An executive with a solid record of performance was named president of Business Services and given the task of essentially creating a new business—he had to find the right products, develop a new customer base and distribution system, and fashion the right marketing strategy. By giving a previously ignored operation its own mission, resources, and the freedom to build a new business without internal obstacles thrown in its way by more established segments of the company, Xerox turned Business Services into one of the fastest-growing units in the corporation.

Redesign can also be used to change business processes so they align more clearly with strategic objectives. Shortly after its spin-off from Corning, for example, Quest Diagnostics reorganized itself into three distinct areas—commercial, operations, and science—and named an executive to head up each group and report directly to the president. Before the spin-off from Corning, the local units had been headed by general managers with operations backgrounds. Quest's restructuring underscored the new emphasis on sales and marketing and on scientific innovation and created new reporting relationships that established individual accountability for performance in each of those areas.

Yet like any radical change, structural redesign is risky. As a management tool, it is powerful but imprecise; in the wrong hands, it can be a machete rather than a scalpel. The changes you get from your redesign aren't always the ones you want. And redesign is so seductively easy that organizations tend to overdo it, to seize upon restructuring as a quick and dirty solution to more complex problems. I have seen troubled organizations announce major restructurings every eighteen months or so, with limited results. In too many cases, what passes for redesign amounts simply to a rearrangement of the boxes on the table of organization—superficial tinkering cloaked in the rhetoric of radical change.

Indeed, Xerox went through four episodes of ineffective redesign in the 1980s alone before truly digging in and redesigning the organization's architecture through the process I describe later in this chapter. I clearly remember one episode during the early days of that process, as we were exposing the design team to successful models of reorganization at other companies. "I just realized," said one member of the Xerox team, "that we've restructured this company half a dozen times since I've been here, but we keep running it the same way. We haven't changed the governance, the architecture. What we've got to do this time is really change it."

One reason reorganizations so often fail to achieve their desired goals is that their restructurings are done so badly. Too many organizational charts sketched on the backs of cocktail napkins during after-hours bull sessions somehow show up as impressive-looking overhead transparencies and then take on a life of their own. Too often the ground rules for reorganization have nothing to do with strategic objectives. I once heard some executives who were thinking about restructuring explain that the final plan had to include five major units because there were five senior executives and each had to have equal responsibilities when the dust settled. That's dumb—but frighteningly common. Another mistake companies make is to hand over the redesign task to outside consultants. It just doesn't work. Just as the senior team won't feel any commitment to a strategy devised by outsiders, they will similarly rebel against a restructuring plan dreamed up by people outside the organization who won't share in the responsibility for making it work.

What's more, executives thinking about restructuring often forget that successful organizational redesign is part and parcel of the overall concept of integrated change. The redesign must be internally integrated. Restructuring doesn't happen in a vacuum; if it is to succeed, it must take a form that fits not only with the strategy but also with the people, work processes, and informal organizational culture. That's where the General Motors restructuring of the mid-1980s ran into such horrendous problems; with the aggressive participation of outside consultants, senior executives far removed from the company's daily operations tried to rearrange structural boxes that had been in place so long they had been superseded by informal processes and relationships. By focusing on changing the outdated table of organization, the company inadvertently shattered the informal shadow structures and processes through which the work actually got done (Keller, 1989). Hardware and software were no longer compatible.

That's not to say that informal relationships are inviolable or must serve as the cornerstone of the new structure; to the contrary, it's sometimes more important to reshape those relationships than the formal ones, particularly when they reinforce resistance to substantive change in the status quo. Changes in the formal and informal organizational patterns must be considered and developed in concert with one another. It is in this way that organizational redesign offers a potent leverage point for dismantling the old organization—the current state—and reassembling it in an integrated pattern that will enhance the chances for good fit in the future state.

Organizational Architecture: An Overview

Senior executives engaged in the task of redesigning formal structures, or hardware, need to view their job in the larger perspective of organizational architecture. Their assignment is just one aspect of the overall process that begins with defining the organization's purpose—the process of strategic choice. That process, as I described in Chapter Eight, requires the CEO and executive team to develop not only a general direction for the organization but also an analysis and diagnosis of how the organization must change in order to start moving toward its new objectives.

Later in this chapter I describe each step in the redesign process in much greater detail. Generally speaking, however, following the analysis and diagnosis, the process (Figure 9.1) begins with a clear statement of what the redesign is intended to accomplish—more specifically, criteria for how work will be grouped to best achieve the goals of the overall strategic plan. The next step is the development of a range of alternative structures, each of which is assessed in the context of the stated design goals. Then comes the work of developing the linking mechanisms essential to coordinating the work of disparate groups with interrelated activities. Once an overall structural design has been selected, the design team moves on to the details of operational design—work units, staffing, resource deployment. Next comes an examination of the actual operational and managerial processes required to produce the organization's core functions (it is in this limited context that the concept of process reengineering can prove beneficial). Finally, the design team must turn its attention to the systems that support those processes.

The design process is rarely as neat and methodical in practice as it looks in Figure 9.1. Nor is it quick if done properly. The Xerox design teams spent nearly a year and a half on the process. At

**Figure 9.1. The Logic of the Strategic
Organizational Design Process.**

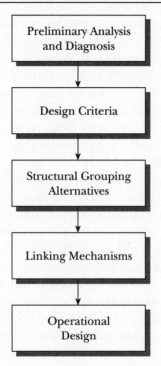

Preliminary Analysis
and Diagnosis

Design Criteria

Structural Grouping
Alternatives

Linking Mechanisms

Operational
Design

PepsiCo more than two hundred people were involved in a three-month process. And AT&T's move to a new business unit structure in late 1988–89 took close to nine months.

Moreover, just as architects must stay attuned to the design opportunities created by new structural materials, so must executives engaged in the redesign process be sensitive to some new developments that have drastically expanded the alternatives for organizational design. The traditional approach to structure has been the venerable *machine bureaucracy,* an organizational model based upon traditional scientific management. In practice, that concept of management gave rise to the functional organization, a pyramid-shaped hierarchy that rigidly controlled the work of employees contained within rigidly compartmentalized functional silos.

Today that model flies in the face of everything we know about the changing workforce, new competitive demands, advances in information technology, and the inherent advantages of well-managed teams. The old organizational model is rooted in the days when workers were by and large uneducated and immobile and were viewed as interchangeable human components in an industrial machine, trained to do a single task over and over again. Education, mobility, and the disappearance of lifetime job guarantees, along with people's widespread desire for empowerment, intellectual fulfillment, and career opportunity, have changed all that.

Indeed, the very nature of the work most companies do has changed dramatically. The key to success now lies in the swift transfer and processing of information. The requirements of information processing and the new technologies that make it more efficient than ever before have fundamentally changed nearly every organization's work requirements. Greater demands for shared information have shattered the walls that traditionally separated functional departments, and increasingly require structures that employ teams of people working across functions and disciplines to achieve shared goals. At the same time, large corporations have sought ways to capitalize on the benefits of scale while they also free internal business units to become more entrepreneurial in developing new markets and sources of competitive advantage.

In broad brush strokes, those are the major forces that have come together to produce entirely new forms of organizational architecture in recent years. They provide the overall context for the ensuing discussion of how to actually go about redesigning the formal structures and processes of an organization in the midst of large-scale change.

The Elements of Design

Now let's consider the basic concepts of organizational design as they appear in the light of architectural design. Any organization's formal arrangements—its hardware—have three basic elements:

- *Structure*—the relatively stable arrangements that define roles and relationships within the organization
- *Processes*—the sets of sequenced activities involved in performing the organization's work

- *Systems*—the electronic and mechanical systems, largely for information processing, that aid individuals and units in performing their work

Beyond these three basic building blocks of organizational design are three important concepts essential to this book's perspective on design. They concern information processing, grouping, and linking.

Information Processing

One way to think about an organization's structure is to view it as a mechanism for generating, transmitting, analyzing, and using *information*. If you think about the work that goes on at just about any organization, there is only one thing that moves from one end of the enterprise to the other and that is needed and shared by every aspect of its operation: information. The core work of an auto company, for instance, is to manufacture and sell autos. But armies of people engaged in a multitude of processes ranging from research and development to design, procurement, marketing, distribution, and consumer financing are also engaged in important activities far from the factory floor. The only commodity each and every one of them uses in his or her daily work is information—information involving design specifications, supply requirements, market conditions, production output, and every other aspect of the complex business of designing, building, distributing, selling, financing, and servicing vehicles.

In short, *structure is the way organizations process information* about their direction, requirements, operations, output, performance, and environment. When we look at it this way, structure performs three vital functions: it directs, motivates, and constrains behavior, both on an individual and organizational level. It tells people and organizations what to do, it energizes them, and it keeps them from doing the wrong things. In this sense, it is the key managerial tool for carrying out the vital functions of coordination and control.

Grouping

We need to ask, then, in the context of a given strategy, what organizational structure will best channel the right information to the right people in the right sequence? The key to our answer will be *grouping*—organizing jobs and processes along the lines of established criteria. In essence, grouping interrelates some jobs and erects boundaries between others. Among the jobs and people situated within a given set of boundaries, information processing is optimized; conversely, it becomes harder to process information back and forth across those boundaries. Within each aggregation of jobs grouped within a given set of boundaries, people tend to create their own language system, task orientation, common supervision, and shared resources. Grouping orients them toward coordinating their activities and performing their jobs in ways specific to the group and possibly not found in any other group within the same organization. Grouping makes it easier for people within the group to work with each other but at the same time impedes their formal and informal dealings with individuals and units outside their group.

When Alex Trotman became Ford's CEO in 1993, for example, he set a goal of becoming the world's leading automaker, in terms of both quantity and quality. And in recent years, Ford had clearly made great strides. The quality of its products and manufacturing processes had improved dramatically. It cut costs significantly. Its breakthrough styling and quality had made the original Taurus a resounding success, and Ford's light trucks and sport utility vehicles continued to lead industry sales year after year. Yet Ford couldn't seem to fully leverage its assets as a worldwide automaker; when it first produced the Escort, its vaunted World Car, the fact remained that only one part was the same in every Escort produced in Ford plants around the world. The World Car was more dream than reality and was likely to remain so as long as Ford operations were geographically segregated.

So Ford underwent a comprehensive redesign process—modeled, in part, on what Xerox did in 1991—and restructured into five worldwide vehicle program centers based on *platforms,* such as light trucks and small front-wheel-drive cars. Each platform—essentially a chassis—then became the basis for multiple lines of vehicles. At the same time, the redesign blurred the traditional lines between auto design and engineering in order to slash the amount of time it took to get a new vehicle from the drawing boards to the showroom. The restructuring accomplished many things, but at its root it rearranged the boundaries—both geo-graphically and functionally—for sharing information about products and processes. Just two years later, after gaining hands-on experience with the new design, Ford went through a second, much less dramatic redesign which it described as a "refinement," consolidating the five program centers into three.

There really are only three fundamentally different ways of grouping people and their jobs:

Grouping by activity. In this structure, people are grouped by the kind of work they do, defined by skill, discipline, or function. At a typical newspaper, for example, the journalists who produce the editorial content are in one department, the advertising sales-people are in another, the people engaged in physically producing the paper are in a third, and the people who sell and deliver the newspapers are in a fourth. That way of grouping newspaper work seems obvious only because that's the way it's always been done. Some newspapers—notably the *Minneapolis Star-Tribune*—are experimenting with grouping the editorial and circulation departments under a single executive responsible for "reader customers," based on the assumption that both departments are supposed to attract and retain the same customers. A different executive is responsible for "advertising customers."

Grouping by output. This structure groups people on the basis of the product or service they're engaged in producing, regardless of their specific job. The Ford restructuring just mentioned is a classic output grouping, replacing a geographic grouping aimed primarily at customers.

Grouping by user or customer. This structure organizes people and their work on the basis of who will be the end-users of their product or service. If you think back to AT&T Network System's strategic choice process, you'll recall that the managers constructed an information topography to describe their emerging competitive environment. What they finally decided was that their traditional grouping by output, with each unit focused on producing specific components of communication networks, was incapable of meeting the new competitive demands. In the new environment, what their customers really wanted were entire systems, someone to install them, and sometimes someone to operate and service them.

So Network Systems restructured into customer business units, some aimed at geographic areas, others aimed at particular kinds of business, such as cable operators. The old business units responsible for producing the elements of the systems continued to produce them—but then provided them to the customer business units, which assembled, delivered, and installed complete systems. The new structure proved enormously successful: for example, allowing Network Systems to sell an entire $11 billion phone system to Saudi Arabia.

It's also interesting to consider these three groupings in light of our earlier look at Michael Porter's thoughts (1985) on the sources of competitive advantage. Clearly, there is some correlation between structural groupings and the kind of strategy to which each is best suited:

- If your strategic intent is to beat the competition by becoming the low-cost producer, then activity-based grouping will probably be most effective because it controls costs by avoiding duplicative operations and providing economies of scale.
- If your strategy is based on product differentiation, then grouping based on output makes the most sense because it focuses information and resources on product innovation.
- If your strategy involves getting closer to the customer than the competition does, then customer-based grouping obviously makes the most sense.

Of course, this is a very general correlation. The truth is that most organizations use a variety of grouping patterns. For years Xerox was grouped at the top by output—copiers, printers, typewriters, and so on—and then groupings at the next level, or cut, were based on function—manufacturing, marketing, sales, research. The next cut in some groups was on the basis of geography. In addition there are variations on the three grouping categories, such as matrix groupings that involve multiple reporting structures: for example, a bank executive in Paris might report both to his company's head of French banking operations and to a chief of institutional banking at company headquarters back in New York.

Each decision about grouping is important, but the first cut—the selection of a grouping method for the very top of the organization—is clearly the most crucial because it dictates where the flow of information will be facilitated and where it will be impeded at each successive level of the organization.

Linking

The third important concept in structural redesign is *linking,* the construction of devices connecting separate groups that have to coordinate their work. Regardless of the overall grouping patterns, groups within organizations must have some way to share and act upon essential information. Information and coordination needs vary drastically from one organization to another, but they're always present in some form or another. Sometimes organizations are made up of semiautonomous operations that need to share only back-office support services and administrative oversight; that's true, for example, of many branch banking operations and of newspaper groups that regard each of their individual newspapers as self-contained operations. In other situations groups need to share information sequentially, as in the design, production, and distribution of hard goods; each group along the way is totally dependent on information from the group that preceded it in the process. Today more and more organizations are looking for linkages that provide swift, reciprocal exchange of information. Units such as design, production, marketing, sales, and service, once separated by unscalable functional walls, are beginning to grasp how desperately they need to share information on a continuing basis in order to respond swiftly to fast-changing customer needs and competitive pressures.

Unlike grouping, which has a finite number of variables, linking mechanisms can assume a variety of forms, depending upon both the organizational setting and the availability of individuals suited to particular roles (Galbraith, 1977). Here are some of the more common linking mechanisms that structural redesigners can consider:

Liaison roles. These linking mechanisms are generally taken on by trusted and respected individuals, in addition to their normal duties. This is a fairly informal method of making sure associated groups regularly share appropriate information.

Cross-unit groups. These devices can take the form of standing or ad hoc committees, and they can focus on processes, output, or customers—or any combination of the three. They may deal with specific problems or ongoing situations. Though they involve more time and more people than simple liaison roles, they provide the opportunity for sharing more information on a wider range of issues and offer a needed forum for addressing emergencies or high-priority projects.

Integrator roles or departments. This mechanism introduces general management functions into the linking process. At some point, an individual or a unit must be empowered to facilitate decisions that transcend group boundaries. Though people serving in integrator roles may not directly supervise the participants in a linking process, they are responsible for making sure the process works and that when necessary, those involved in the process stand by the decisions that are made. Consequently, these individuals derive their authority from their knowledge, expertise, objectivity, and the respect they have earned from their colleagues rather than from their explicit power to make binding decisions.

Matrix structures. These devices are hybrids of grouping and linkage, and they represent the most extreme form of both. At times, for example, an organization's strategy might place equal emphasis on close interrelationships between people working with customers and those working with products, making it essential to remove as many information barriers as possible between the two groups. This will involve a complex set of reporting relationships for managers, one difficult to sustain over time. For this structure to work, managers' two primary responsibilities must be evenly weighted; neither boss nor area of responsibility can take precedence over the other.

Futuretech: Redesigning Xerox

With those general principles in mind, let's return now to the Xerox redesign process of the early 1990s. Much as it had a few years earlier with Xerox 95, the company made the hard choice to use a deliberate, participative process to come up with a fundamental redesign of its organizational structure. Having come to the conclusion that the disadvantages of the process were far outweighed by both the quality of the outcome and the personal commitment it evoked, Allaire chose to follow Kearns's example and pursue major change through a process of education, deliberation, and participation.

However, participation is a bit trickier when it comes to structural redesign. Though the members of the executive team must be involved in the strategy work, they are not necessarily the people you want to have directly involved in the initial stages of redesign. Instead, I strongly recommend the appointment of a special design team composed of managers three and four levels below the CEO, which acts as a working committee to develop alternatives and present recommendations to the executive team. There are several reasons for this.

To begin with, the lower-level managers are much closer to the real work of the organization and possess the depth of current information essential to making informed recommendations about how work should be organized. Second, they are in closer touch with the complexities and nuances of the informal organization, which should play a role in any deliberations. Third, members of this team can go on to become an important source of support; they emerge from the process as committed zealots, proselytizing on behalf of the new structure throughout the organization.

So rather than inviting his executive team to the table, Allaire reached down three and four levels in October 1990 and appointed seventeen executives to a design team he called Future Architecture (and which the team quickly nicknamed Futuretech). They came from every part of Xerox, people who had demonstrated both creative thinking and the ability to get things done. Their assignment was to completely rethink the architecture of Xerox and to present Allaire and his executive team with a range of restructuring alternatives.

Design Criteria

The first step in the redesign process after analysis and diagnosis (see Figure 9.1) is to develop a set of design criteria to help guide the process. At Xerox, my colleagues and I began by educating the design team about the fundamentals of organizational design. We looked at other companies and engaged in some rigorous benchmarking. We exposed team members to the thinking of some of the leading theorists in the field, taking the entire team, for example, to spend time with Edward Lawler and Jay Galbraith at the University of Southern California's Center for Effective Organizations. Then we got to work on design criteria, starting with an exercise that required them to complete a set of statements beginning, "The new design should . . ." For example, "The new design should make specific people accountable for guiding new products from development to the marketplace," or, "The new design should push more decision making out of headquarters and into the field."

In general terms, the goal at this stage in the process is to develop as many alternative criteria as possible to focus the team's thinking about possible structures. Their insights on how the current structure might need to change usually come from four sources:

Strategy. If the new strategy focuses on customer needs, product innovation, or rock-bottom costs, then the design criteria must explicitly address those issues. For Xerox, the implications of the strategy Kearns and his senior team had developed and Allaire had endorsed were enormous. Traditionally, Xerox had been a huge product development and manufacturing engine loosely tied to a massive salesforce that viewed itself as the company's heart and soul. The company viewed the world as groups of customers segmented by geography. There was no marketing or business management to speak of. Machines were designed in almost random fashion; not only were some incompatible but some were developed in such isolation that as soon as they came to market they competed with each other. Somehow the new structure had to coordinate technological innovation with customer needs, providing solutions to officewide document processing problems rather than merely churning out a hodgepodge of inconsistent and sometimes obsolete stand-alone machines.

Work. It's essential for design team members to draw upon their own expertise and understanding of the inherent characteristics of the organization's core functions: for instance, the interdependence of sales and service, or in Xerox's case, the need to merge light lens and digital technology.

Diagnosis. Usually, the redesign stage follows the initial diagnosis process, during which key problems have been identified. If the diagnosis surfaced serious delays in developing and bringing new products to market, for example, then redesign criteria should zero in on giving particular units the responsibility and accountability for championing new products.

Aesthetics. This is a general term I use to describe the CEO's and executive team's values and goals concerning management style, the ideas that follow the statement, "This is the way I want to run the company. . . ." At Xerox, Allaire went to the design team early on and told them he wanted the company to get faster, more customer oriented, more accountable. He wanted decisions pushed from the staff to the line, and he wanted Xerox to focus on finding methods to help its customers process documents of all kinds— both paper and electronic—in ways that would make the customers more productive and profitable.

Paramount in Allaire's thinking was the imperative that Xerox had to become a worldwide corporation that operated like a collection of entrepreneurial businesses yet also capitalized on the collective strengths of shared technology and a mammoth salesforce. At one point I walked into a meeting of Allaire's senior team and wrote the word *Xerox* on a wall chart in large letters, with a hammer and sickle through the *o*.

"The organizational model for Xerox is the soviet system," I explained, "with the corporate office filling the role of the central committee. People sit here in the middle and do all the central planning—they plan supply, they plan demand, they plan resource allocation—and then expect the world to follow it." The system was working about as well for Xerox, I told them, as it had for the Soviet Union. It was the old machine model, with a gearbox at the center controlling all the connected parts.

What Allaire wanted from the design team instead was an organic model—one in which a slimmed-down central staff created the most positive working environment possible for all the constituent parts, tried to make sure those parts didn't bump into each other too often, and energized them to go out and run their own businesses. That vision became the guiding "design intent" for the reorganization.

Grouping Alternatives

The Futuretech group's next assignment was to develop four different grouping alternatives. That's harder than it sounds. Most people tend to think in terms of two: the present structure plus one idea they've been walking around with for a while. Allaire told them he wanted four. One would be to take the current structure and fix it. Another would be to restructure as product-related business divisions. And "you've got to think of two more," he told them. In effect, Allaire had just swept the two obvious alternatives off the table, thereby compelling the team to start thinking of entirely new solutions. Then he threw in another twist: no organizational charts. They had to come up with other ways of conceptualizing and then illustrating how their grouping structures would work.

In February 1991, the team presented Allaire with four options:

A modified version of the existing structure

A plan to structure the company by market segments

A worldwide structure based on geography

A collection of independent business units based on a hybrid of products and markets

The team favored the independent business units. (In keeping with Allaire's assignment, they used maps and diagrams, rather than traditional tables of organization, to describe the proposed structures.)

Operational Design

Figure 9.1. shows design of linking processes as the next probable step; however, in the Xerox process, this design element merged into the strategic design.

This strategic design work occupied the spring and summer of 1991, as Allaire worked with his senior team and two or three members of the Futuretech group (that team had been disbanded after presenting its recommendations) to refine the structure based on independent business units. Eventually, a structure emerged with nine business units and three customer operations units, but huge questions remained concerning definitions, boundaries, and operational processes. Where would the line be drawn, for instance, between the printing products unit and the advanced office document products unit? Would each unit have its own product development, manufacturing, and sales operations, or could those functions somehow be shared?

Allaire also faced a major selling job within his own executive team. For a generation of executives who had come up through a traditional functional organization and a geographic customer focus, the concept of semiautonomous business units, with people three or four levels below the CEO empowered to make major decisions traditionally reserved for the corporate office, was sheer heresy.

"I can't conceive of how you would run the company this way," said one top executive after reviewing the plan. "The only way I could do it is if you gave me a lobotomy." He soon left Xerox—but he was far from alone among members of the executive team in his belief that the delegation of crucial decisions to lower-level executives and product teams would eventually destroy the company.

Still, the work progressed. In September 1991, Allaire chartered a second group, the organizational transition board (OTB), to carry out the next step. Consisting of twenty people—fifteen senior executives plus five people from Futuretech and Allaire's staff—the OTB had the responsibility for translating the conceptual notion of independent business units into a working reality—the operational design.

It was important to get three kinds of people on the team: those with thorough knowledge of how the company ran; opinion leaders, people who could walk out of the room at the end of the process and tell people, "I know this is a big change, but it's a good one," and sway large numbers of people to accept the new plan; and a sampling of people who were probable candidates to run key units under the new arrangement, in order to build their personal commitment through involvement.

What Allaire could not have on this team were members of the circle of executives reporting directly to him. His appointment of the OTB was a response to one of the most ticklish political issues inherent in restructuring: although you want the executive team actively involved in every aspect of the change process, you do not want to put them in a situation where they're being asked to design their own jobs. And job redesign is what is being done at this stage. No matter how well intentioned members of your executive team may be, they're only human. Asking them to objectively agree on who gets which jobs, what responsibilities, and how much power is like throwing the Thanksgiving turkey in the middle of the table, handing each of your starving guests a butcher knife, and inviting them all to have at it. The end result will be a lot of bloodshed and a shredded turkey.

So Allaire reached down two and three levels in the organization to find the OTB members. It was made clear to them at the outset that nearly all of them would hold important jobs in the restructured company. Beyond that general reassurance no specific commitments were given—for two reasons. The first was that at that stage, it was impossible to know who might end up in what job. But beyond that, lack of this information was an essential tool for maintaining everyone's objectivity. It's just like dividing the last slab of cake between two kids: the fail-safe method is to tell one child he gets to divide the cake into two slices but his sister gets to choose first. Invariably, the kid with the knife will take painstaking care to make sure the pieces are absolutely equal. That's the same concept that was used with the design team; not knowing who would end up with each piece of the pie, they were scrupulously objective about structuring groups and responsibilities and jobs.

I've used this method in a number of situations, and I can assure you that it works. Of course there comes a time when the team realizes what's going on. At that moment of enlightenment, people say things like, "Oh, that's what you guys are doing—you've rigged it so we have to be impartial!" To which my response is, Bingo—you figured it out. It also happens from time to time that after it starts to become clear who is headed for which job, some team members will alter their original positions and try to make a case for bulking up the job they think they're likely to get—in other words, they want a bigger piece of the pie. At that point their self-interest is obvious to everyone, and I tell them, Sorry—too late.

Nevertheless, these people are being tossed into a political cauldron and are likely to be subjected to immense pressures from all sides. Sometimes a CEO will meet with the design team at the outset and tell them: "Look, you're working for me now. The people you report to today may or may not be the people you report to tomorrow. Therefore, what I want you to do is make the right choice to help me; you've got a corporate hat on now. You're working for the owners now. I don't want you talking to anybody else about this or taking direction from anybody else."

That's not an unfounded concern. Not long ago, I was involved in a restructuring process at a company where one particularly ambitious senior executive was meeting regularly with three of his subordinates—who also happened to be members of the design team—and was giving them self-serving instructions. When we found out what was happening, the CEO took the executive aside and told him in no uncertain terms to back off.

Years ago I had a particularly unnerving episode while I was working through a restructuring process with a New York brokerage house. (This was early in my career, when I was a bit more naive about how these things worked.) We had put together a design team with representatives from each of the firm's functional units—retail, brokerage capital markets, and operations. To shield the team from outside influence, I had them working at a midtown hotel. Each day it seemed that we would make a little progress. But the next morning the team would file back into the meeting room, and everything we'd done the day before would come apart at the seams. It was a maddening process, and the restructuring it produced was of dubious value. It wasn't until much later that I found out what had gone wrong. It turned out that after we'd recessed each night, the team members would disperse to other rooms in the hotel where shadow design teams from their respective departments would debrief them on the day's events and give them marching orders for the next day's session. It certainly helped explain why we never seemed to make much progress.

Going back to Xerox, it was the OTB's task to look at the full range of issues involving groupings, processes, and systems. These team members were the ones who had to draw boxes and arrows and lines, design jobs, figure out how many people should be assigned to each operation, and help flesh out the criteria for staffing. They had to figure out linking mechanisms, devising a way to construct nine independent business operations that would somehow share product development, manufacturing, and customer operations. They had to determine which work processes needed to be rethought and reengineered. They had to think about how the restructuring would change management information systems and human resource activities. They compiled detailed organizational charts and developed carefully staged transition plans.

The OTB started its work in September 1991 and delivered a detailed plan to Allaire in January 1992. The first executive appointments were made at the end of that month, the plan was announced in February, and the new structure began taking effect on June 1 of that year.

The result of the process, in retrospect, was a truly radical restructuring, one that called for similarly dramatic changes in staffing and culture—and resulted in a dramatically different Xerox than the company Allaire inherited from Kearns. In the end Xerox developed an organizational architecture that made it significantly more competitive, more innovative, and more customer focused. Moreover, it had a structure that was inherently flexible, allowing it to add or eliminate new business units at any time, based on changes in market demands, without altering the company's basic design.

Systems and Processes: Final Thoughts

I would be remiss in leaving the subject of structural redesign without adding a cautionary note about systems redesign and a reminder about process reengineering.

Systems Redesign

One problem I can just about guarantee during the course of a major organizational change is the absence of vital information just when it's needed most. Time after time, organizations have rushed to implement new structural designs without first making sure the information systems are in place to report essential data in a form consistent with the new operations. The company decides to organize around business units rather than functions. At the end of the first budget reporting period, out comes the data—based on functional operations, not business units. The business units can't even get finance to give them basic profit and loss statements for the period because the information just wasn't cut that way. What's the result? In the absence of any statistical feedback, the organization doesn't have a clue whether the new structure is taking off or crashing on the runway. To use another metaphor, it's a lot like deciding to drive off in a new car that has everything in place except the instrument panel. Certainly the car will move, but the driver hasn't the faintest idea how fast it's going, how much fuel is left, or whether the engine is about to overheat. It's a dumb way to drive, and an even dumber way to run a major company.

I can't be too emphatic about this point: information systems have to be taken into consideration at the earliest possible stage in the redesign process, not at the tail end as an afterthought. Granted, the full redesign of an entire corporate management information system is a huge, time-consuming job. What I suggest is phasing in the changes but making sure some rudimentary system is in place before the other redesign elements are implemented. Even if the early information is crude and not entirely accurate, it will provide the people running the new organization with some of the indicators they so desperately need concerning results, performance, and problems.

The Cult of Reengineering

As I described earlier, process reengineering is a term that has come to describe the use of sophisticated information management techniques to completely redesign work processes from the ground up rather than altering them incrementally. It is without question a useful technique when used in the proper context, but *reengineering* should not be confused with *restructuring*. It should not be viewed as a restructuring panacea, a magical solution to the multiple challenges of change. Reengineering properly comes *after* all the crucial strategic planning has been completed. It must be carried out in the context of how the reengineered processes will fit into the overall pattern of integrated organizational change.

When we are designing the formal organization, we cannot afford a technocentric focus that fails to take fully into consideration the human aspects of changing work processes and that focuses on costs as a problem rather than as a symptom of larger, more fundamental shortcomings in the organization. Reengineering nearly always seizes upon widespread job elimination as a quick solution rather than forcing managers to wrestle with more complex issues. Yet when we look to our successful foreign competitors for inside tips about managerial shortcuts to fundamental change, the most important lesson is that there aren't any. Change is hard work encompassing a wide range of difficult managerial techniques and executive strategies, and it requires an enduring commitment to the long haul.

In fact, that's a pretty good description of the next phase of large-scale change—the reshaping of the organization's operating environment. More than any other aspect of change, modifying the way people think and behave in support of the organization's strategic objectives requires an enormous investment of time, energy, and persistence. It's incredibly tough—and absolutely critical.

External
Forces

Developing a
Shared
Direction

Recognizing
the Change
Imperative

External
Forces

Implementing
Change

Assessment
and Learning

External
Forces

Sustaining
Change

Consolidating
Change

External
Forces

External
Forces

Chapter Ten

When Worlds Collide

Aligning Strategy and Culture

There's a story they tell in the newsroom of a Knight-Ridder newspaper. Sooner or later it's heard by just about every journalist who joins the staff. Sitting at the city desk one day, a managing editor (now legendary) took a call from an irate reader. He listened patiently for a few minutes, unable to inject more than an occasional "Yes, ma'am" or "No, ma'am." Whatever he was saying wasn't working, because the voice on the other end just got louder and angrier. Finally, the managing editor decided he'd had enough.

"Madam," he thundered, in a voice heard throughout the newsroom, "if you don't stop your incessant caterwauling this instant, I will be forced to cancel your subscription!"

The story is related with gusto to each new recruit. The fact that it is told over and over again speaks volumes about the culture of that newspaper, and of newsrooms in general. It underscores a traditional view of the relationship between journalists and their readers and of the kinds of editors who are regarded as heroes.

It was into that culture that Knight-Ridder's top management marched in the late 1980s with a major initiative called Customer Obsession, an all-out effort to jump on the customer service bandwagon that was sweeping U.S. business. Corporate executives quickly learned it was one thing to develop a passion for serving the customers in the advertising, circulation, and billing departments; it was quite another to extend the philosophy that "the customer is always right" into newsrooms dominated by skeptical iconoclasts raised on the credo "If your mother says she loves you, check it out." The result was an ugly clash between a well-intentioned corporate strategy and a deeply ingrained corporate subculture.

In any large-scale organizational change, maintaining the proper fit between the human dimensions of the enterprise—the *software*—and the new strategy and structure is always the most difficult job. Strategy and structure—even staffing, for that matter—can be changed fairly quickly, if need be, through executive fiat. But reconstructing a new underlying fabric of values, beliefs, and behavior is tough—very tough. When it comes to implementing change, Paul Allaire often says, "the soft stuff is the hard stuff."

In the 1970s and '80s, as U.S. firms struggled desperately to figure out why Japanese companies were becoming global powerhouses, some observers seized upon *culture* as the key ingredient in the Japanese recipe for success. The term took on outsize and ambiguous, almost mystical, connotations. That is why I prefer the term *operating environment*. It is more specific and implies a direct relationship between the way people do their jobs, relate to their coworkers, and interact with their customers on one hand and the organization's overall performance on the other.

That direct relationship is too often overlooked as managers grapple with the monumental challenges of large-scale change. In critical situations there's a tendency for hardware to drive out software. Recall that the work and formal arrangements components of the organizational model are the organizational hardware. They are the microprocessors, the memory chips, the keyboard and monitor and peripherals—all the equipment you can see and touch and which, in the end, produces the output you're after. Then think about the people and the informal organizational arrangements as the software. Without software, without skilled people who know what they're doing, the computer is a useless collection of plastic and silicon.

Nevertheless, experience illustrates that in the face of pressing demands, organizations will focus on the hardware, often to the exclusion of the software. The immediate demands of running the business, responding to customers, complying with legal requirements, meeting immediate financial goals—these demands are so pressing and central to the organization's survival that the needs of people and the operating environment get shoved aside. In a sense that's understandable; survival is the major priority. The danger lies in leaving those matters on the back burner so long that they eventually fade from management's priority list altogether.

Sooner or later every successful company comes to understand that values, beliefs, and behavior are central to its strategic success. One company after another, after failing to meet its objectives, has figured out the hard way that the most sophisticated strategy in the world is doomed to failure if it's inconsistent with the way employees think and behave.

I begin this chapter on aligning strategy with the informal organization by setting the scene in deeper detail, describing three situations in which deeply embedded operating environments presented huge obstacles to leaders intent on implementing new strategies. Next I talk about the elements that merge to create operating environments and make them so resistant to change. Finally, I describe a tool kit of a dozen different techniques that can be used in concert to alter an organization's operating environment.

Roadblocks to Change

Let's start by considering three organizations whose leaders fully understood how desperately they needed to adopt new strategies—and then ran headlong into the massive barriers thrown up by their deeply entrenched operating environments.

Kaiser Foundation Health Plan and Hospitals (Kaiser Permanente)

For more than three decades Kaiser Permanente was a key part of the oligopoly that made up the U.S. health care system. In a stable environment, operating as a not-for-profit organization, it had little competition and less concern over financial performance. Instead, it was tightly focused on its social mission of providing quality health care, serving communities, and extending knowledge about medical treatment and health care delivery.

"We evolved with a mission, culture, structure and set of practices well-attuned to that minimally competitive era of slow, relatively predictable change," says Chairman David Lawrence. Moreover, Kaiser Permanente developed as a confederation of local and regional health systems, each aligned contractually with a local physicians' group. Power was widely dispersed, decisions were reached through consensus, and internal politics were intense.

By the early 1990s, the competitive environment had changed dramatically with the explosion of managed care and intense pressure to lower health care costs. Suddenly, Kaiser Permanente faced countless competitors who were offering comparable care at lower costs, sometimes with better service. It became clear that the organization had to find ways to experiment with new delivery systems, make physicians more accountable for costs, and make tough decisions about where and how to provide the best care at the lowest cost. In short, it had to trim bureaucracy, act faster, be more responsive to customers, and hold employees to rigorous performance standards.

Fair enough. But what was Kaiser's operating environment? In essence, it had no performance standards in terms of financial results or customer satisfaction. Performance and compensation had never been linked. Experimentation and risk taking were discouraged. Dismissals were practically unheard of. And national executives were expected to act in an advisory role, leaving power in the hands of local managers. In short, the organization's competitive requirements clashed with nearly every element of its operating environment.

It wasn't until the mid-1990s that Lawrence began making real headway in his change effort—and none of it came easily. Over time he found that he had to take the lead in developing and articulating a new set of values for the organization; just as important, he had to reshape both his board and his senior team to position them as allies and supporters in his attempts to reshape the operating environment. "At the end of the day," Lawrence found, "changing an organization really means changing people—their values, beliefs, attitudes, behavior, and relationships."

KPMG Peat Marwick

When Jon Madonna was elected chairman and CEO of the worldwide accounting and consulting firm KPMG Peat Marwick in 1990, he quickly realized how desperately the firm needed to slash costs and grow revenues. His first move was to trim the payroll—not a popular move. But the second round of change was even more fundamental, striking at the core of the firm's traditions and culture. Historically, the firm was built around one hundred or so "local franchises," or regional offices, each headed by a powerful managing partner who ruled his fiefdom with relatively little interference from New York. Madonna changed all that. He nationalized the business, organizing people by discipline rather than by territory. Responding to what he saw as his clients' needs, he began offering clients integrated teams of specialists in the areas of accounting, auditing, and consulting. And he moved to place the firm on a more businesslike footing—a major shift in culture.

"We just weren't run as a business," Madonna says. "It's so foreign to the world we live in today, but you have to think of us as a club; don't think of us as a business." As an example, he recalls an episode when he was one of three managing partners in the San Francisco Bay Area. During a visit, his boss acknowledged that the three Bay Area offices really should be consolidated into one; the problem was that the three managing partners were the same age, so the home office couldn't bring itself to put just one of them in charge.

"That consideration far outweighed any business case that said you ought to do it," says Madonna. "What [the boss] was really saying was, 'The worst thing that could happen would be for these partners to be upset with me. So I'd rather take lower earnings, which is what that effectively means, rather than have somebody be upset with me.'"

Beyond that kind of thinking, the firm's traditions led each partner to believe he had an equal voice in charting the firm's direction. "You can stop any partner on the street today and ask him how the business ought to be run and I guarantee you he'll have an opinion," Madonna says. "He's a smart guy. From where he is, he can only see one hind leg of the elephant, but he's still got a strong opinion about where it ought to go."

That democratic tradition is manifested in the firm's governance structure: the chairman is elected by a vote of all the partners every six years, and all the board seats are filled by partners who stand for popular election. More than most CEOs, the firm's chairman has to be a politician who can make difficult decisions without losing his base of power. Sometimes that's impossible. Five years into his term, frustrated by his inability to push change even harder and faster, Madonna decided not to seek reelection. In his first public statement, Madonna's successor announced he was reorganizing the management committee to restore power to the local managing partners.

Lucent Technologies

Having served on AT&T's board since 1981, Henry Schacht wasn't entirely surprised by what he found when he took over as chairman of Lucent Technologies in 1995. His meetings with employees merely reinforced his suspicion that the new company, launched in a torrid competitive environment, urgently needed to replace some of the deeply held values that were the continuing legacy of the Bell System's paternalistic operating environment.

Early on, Schacht evoked gasps of dismay when he talked about the need to focus on customers, leverage technologies, and lower costs in order to sustain superior value for shareholders. "That was a culture shock for this place," Schacht recalled in late 1996. "It was not viewed as proper—the statement that making money was important. It wasn't supposed to be part of the mission."

"And talk about culture—our return on assets is 5 percent, while the benchmark is 12 to 15 percent," Schacht continued. "So we've got a huge return on assets issue to deal with. And that's cultural, because assets haven't really counted in AT&T."

Schacht also encountered other, more subtle issues, such as the employees' interpretation of the AT&T value of "empowerment." At one of the company's early town meetings, an employee stood up and told Schacht, "The fundamental goal of this company is to provide me with a world-class income that is secure. That's your job as a manager."

Schacht's response: "Not in this company." He went on to explain that employee rights flow from responsibilities, and "your responsibility is to contribute in every way you can to making this a company that serves the customer better than the rest. . . . If you don't want to live in that kind of environment, you're in the wrong company."

How did the other employees respond to the exchange? "She got a round of applause from maybe a third of the people," Schacht recalls. "I got dead silence."

Another vestige of AT&T was the sense of a distant corporate bureaucracy at war with its operating units. "The first concept in culture was 'we,'" Schacht explains. "There is no 'they' who is imposing all these silly things on us." At Schacht's first officers' meeting, one of the senior managers complained about a recent directive he had received; he demanded to know, "Why are they doing this?"

Schacht replied, "This company has sixty officers. Every one of us is here in this room. We're all here; there's no other room like this. There's nobody outside this room that tells us what to do. The person who sent that memo is sitting four chairs away from you. Did you go and talk to him?" The answer was no.

"Well," Schacht went on, "why don't you go talk to him. He's not stupid. You're not stupid. Nobody here is trying to be stupid. Why don't you see what the two of *you* can figure out? There is no 'they.'"

Schacht knew full well he had his work cut out for him. His expectation was that changing the operating environment would be a huge undertaking and that it would be four to five years before the change would really start to take hold.

Understanding the Operating Environment

What is it about the operating environment that makes it so hard to change? That's a crucial question; you can't change what you don't understand. A good place to start is with an approach developed by Edgar Schein (1985) of MIT, who looks at culture in terms of three layers (see Figure 10.1).

Three Layers of Operating Environment

The top layer, so to speak, consists of the *artifacts* of culture. If anthropologists were to study the operating environment of your organization, they would be interested in observable behavior and concrete evidence of your underlying culture. At Ford Motor Company, for instance, they would notice right away that top executives park in clearly marked private spaces, wear conservative suits, inhabit spacious offices, and work amazingly long hours. Conversely, at Sun Microsystems they'd see CEO Scott McNealy going off on sales calls to major clients wearing blue jeans and tennis shoes—

Figure 10.1. Three Levels of Operating Environment.

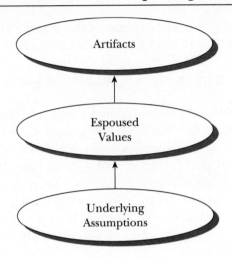

and sometimes a day's growth of beard. On his return he'd park wherever he could find a space in the employee lot and go upstairs to a small, modest office decorated in a style he describes as "early dorm room."

The anthropologists would listen to people's language, noting how it varies when they're speaking with peers, bosses, and subordinates. They'd observe where people eat, and with whom. They'd track work schedules and the pace of activity. They'd record what kinds of stories people tell about the company and whom they look up to as heroes.

The anthropologist would interpret such observable behavior, such artifacts, as overt manifestations of the organization's *values* and *beliefs*. Those are key terms, each with a distinct meaning in this context. Values—integrity, for example—are axiomatically good or bad. You can't prove empirically that integrity is good— either you think it's important or you don't. Beliefs, however, involve cause-and-effect relationships—the belief, for example, that if you treat customers well, they'll keep doing business with you. Every organization possesses values and beliefs that influence its people's behavior and guide their work practices.

There's been so much talk about corporate values in recent years that the concept has become diluted; people tend to roll their eyes as soon as you bring up the subject. Nevertheless, there is a powerful concept at work here. Clearly articulated, universally accepted values show people the way through complex and ambiguous situations. That's what Jamie Houghton had in mind when he described values as "buoys in the channels of commerce."

Here's an example. Back in Chapter One I mentioned the stupefying collection of crises Randy Tobias faced on his first day as CEO of Eli Lilly. By far the worst was the liver failure and subsequent death of several patients involved in clinical tests for a new hepatitis drug. On his first morning, Tobias met with the existing senior team—put together by his recently deposed predecessor—and told these executives he would rely heavily on their guidance in handling the situation. All he wanted to contribute was a single thought: "I wanted to make it very clear that from my point of view, our principal priority in dealing with this issue had to be the welfare of the patients who were involved in these clinical trials and their families. While we shouldn't ignore the potential legal consequences of our actions . . . those could not get in the way of doing the right thing."

"What I subsequently found out," Tobias says, "was that was probably the most important two minutes I could have had. Because what I did was reinforce in their minds the fact that my value system—in terms of why are we ultimately here—was very consistent with theirs."

The fact that everyone in the room embraced the same value—the primacy of the patients' interests over legal exposure or public relations—made the ensuing decisions relatively simple. Imagine how different the situation that day might have been if Tobias and the team had been sharply divided over values; inevitably, there would have been a lengthy, heated debate followed by dissension and recrimination. Instead, there was a common understanding that paved the way for quick decisive action. That's why values are so important.

Values expressed in artifacts can be either espoused or understated. Therefore, the second level of culture consists of an organization's *espoused values*—the public expressions of leadership's interpretations of the commonly held values and beliefs. In recent years, we've all become familiar with statements of corporate values expressing a purportedly deep commitment to quality, integrity, innovation, accountability, diversity, teamwork, customer focus, and so on. These can be important and absolutely accurate statements, or as we all know too well, they can also be aimless exercises in empty rhetoric. (Such statements can be also quite succinct and individual, like Sun Microsystems' "Kick butt; have fun.")

The third level in Schein's model then consists of each organization's *underlying assumptions*—the unstated values and beliefs manifested in the overt behavior, or cultural artifacts. This is where wishful thinking usually collides with reality. In an ideal situation, all three layers—artifacts, espoused values, and underlying assumptions—are neatly lined up and entirely consistent. In the real world, that rarely happens. Typically, the unspoken but widespread underlying assumptions are different, and they—rather than top management's espoused values—truly guide the way people act.

At AT&T, for example, the top leaders worked hard in the late 1980s to reshape the old Ma Bell culture and its rigid command-and-control bureaucracy. They developed a new statement of corporate values, called *Our Common Bond,* which says, among other things, "We communicate frequently and with candor, listening to each other regardless of level or position." Sounds good. But what did you see when you visited an AT&T office? People handed you a business card that identified their rank. People would say, "There's Joan Smith. She's a fifth level" or "Business Systems is sending over three fifth levels to our meeting this afternoon."

Our Common Bond said one thing; language and protocol said quite another: a person's perceived value was directly correlated with his or her assigned grade level. *Our Common Bond* reflected the espoused values; the immense importance people attach to grade levels revealed the underlying assumptions. This clearly illustrates the proposition that culture changes take lots of time and work. If respect for the individual wasn't a core value yesterday, simply sticking it on a new list of core values won't make it one tomorrow.

A similar situation is frequently found at organizations with major problems: a clear lack of consistency between the cultural artifacts, the espoused values, and the underlying values. Too often managers think they can somehow change the operating environment by publicly announcing a new set of values. But it's naive to think a few memos and speeches reverse a complex pattern of behaviors and beliefs.

As a result, indications of a misalignment of espoused and underlying values can be a valuable tool for anyone diagnosing an organization's problems.

Basic Sources of the Operating Environment

The durability of operating environments can be traced directly to the powerful sources, or causal factors, that give rise to them. There are three of these factors,(see Figure 10.2), and the first can be described generically as *external forces*—industry sector and geographic location, for instance. Investment banking firms, hospitals, auto plants, and newspapers each have distinctly different cultures. Within each industry, organizations also frequently reflect the cultures of the cities, regions, or countries in which they're located. That was a major consideration for Walter Shipley in the mid-1990s as he considered possible merger partners for Chemical Bank—and one of the reasons he favored a merger with Chase Manhattan over California-based Bank of America.

"In merging with Chase—in fact, in both mergers (including Chemical's earlier merger with Manufacturers Hanover Trust)—one of the things that made the environment more conducive to success was the fact that all three companies were headquartered in New York," Shipley says. "It's culture. Trying to put Bank of America and Chase, or Bank of America and Chemical, together would be tough—the cultural differences between New York and California are big."

The second source that feeds into the operating environment is the organization's history. Watershed events, even those that predate the tenure of current employees, almost always find a place in the collective memory and help shape culture for years to come. Finally, the third source flows directly from *internal forces*—strategic choices; particular leaders and their styles; policies and practices involving hiring, promotion, discipline and reward. Over time all three sources contribute values, beliefs, and practices that are translated into processes and practices.

Figure 10.2. Causal Factors of Operating Environment.

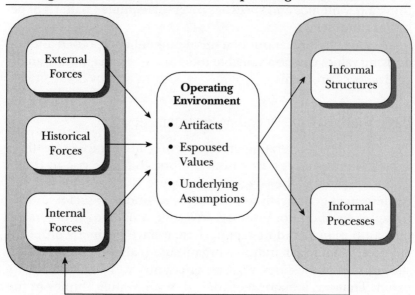

Implications for Leaders of Change

Given all these fundamental elements of culture, or the operating environment—the roadblocks, the difficulties of changing the informal organization, the levels and sources of culture—what are the implications for leaders of large-scale change? I believe they are as follows:

Culture and Performance Are Related

Without question, there is a relationship between operating environment and organizational performance—and more specifically, between operating environment and long-term economic success (Kotter and Heskett, 1992). However, the relationship isn't the one that's commonly assumed: a strong operating environment isn't necessarily a good one.

In fact, not only is a strong operating environment no guarantee of success but as the Success Syndrome illustrates, a strong informal organization based on years of market domination can actually contribute to organizational disaster by blinding the enterprise to crucial changes in its external environment. The only truly successful cultures are those that enable their organizations to anticipate and adapt to environmental change and are associated with superior performance over a significant period of time.

Culture Is Contextual

Culture exists in an organizational context. It is an expensive waste of time to try to change the operating environment in isolation from strategy and from the other components of the organization—work, formal arrangements, and staffing. Remember the organizational model and the concept of congruence. In any organization the culture shapes—and is shaped by—the people, the work they do, and the formal structures and processes that coordinate their efforts. If you change the culture, you will inevitably produce corresponding changes elsewhere in the organization, just as changes in staffing, work requirements, and formal arrangements can't help but change the culture. In short, it's inconceivable that an organization could implement successful, long-lasting organizational change without making the necessary changes in its operating environment. By the same token, changes in the operating environment can't happen in a vacuum; they've got to be tied to the overall business objectives.

A few years ago I was approached by the CEO of a leading insurance company who wanted Delta Consulting to help him overhaul his organization's operating environment. Basically, he wanted a sharper focus on quality and customers. I had just one question for him: "Why?" He hesitated a bit and finally responded that he thought it would be a good thing to do. "Why?" I asked again. When no other answer was forthcoming, I told him I needed to hear a compelling strategic reason, based on hard-nosed business considerations, why he wanted to overhaul his environment. If there isn't one, I said, then don't do it.

"It might be nice to do," I told the CEO, "but the moment something else pressures you, you're going to blink. If you can come back to me and explain with conviction why your business absolutely needs to make these changes in its culture, then we can talk about it." I never heard from him again.

Culture Is Durable

Cultures are resistant to change. Once they take hold they become self-perpetuating. That can be both a strength and a weakness. On the one hand, a deeply entrenched culture can make it difficult for the organization to adapt to changing conditions. On the other hand, a resilient culture can keep an organization on course, even during periods of incompetent leadership. That's what I found while doing some work with the Environmental Protection Agency (EPA) during the Bush administration. Somehow the agency had managed to stay pretty much on course despite a lengthy period of inept and even corrupt leadership. The reason, people there told me, was that the EPA had a tradition as an agency with a mission; people joined it specifically because they were deeply committed, at a very personal level, to its original values and beliefs regarding the government's role in safeguarding the environment. Those values and beliefs were shared so intensely and universally by the vast majority of employees that even overt attempts by their own leaders to thwart the original mission were largely unsuccessful.

What generally happens in most organizations is that a particular culture develops over time because it fits the strategy and the structure, and as it develops, people tend to self-select their membership in it. Most people—particularly managers—who feel uncomfortable in a particular operating environment eventually leave. People who like it stay. And others of like mind are attracted to the organization specifically because of the culture. Over a period of years the organization is populated by employees at nearly every level who have been attracted to the culture, promoted by it, reinforced by it—and who are determined to resist any significant changes to it.

Culture Is Changeable

Despite that, culture change is possible. Major changes have been accomplished at such successful organizations as General Electric, Hewlett-Packard, British Airways, SAS, Xerox, Corning, and Motorola, to name some of the more noteworthy examples. At IBM, Lou Gerstner has made important changes in the environment—opening up communications and eliminating the entitlement culture of lifetime job guarantees, for example. Over time and with coordinated, strategic planning, these companies have inculcated new sets of values and beliefs that demonstrably reshaped their operating environments in areas such as customer service, commitment to quality, technological excellence, competitiveness, and financial performance.

Culture Change Is Inclusive

Successful culture change has an enterprise scope—it starts at the top and spreads from there throughout the entire organization. It's often inaccurate to think of a complex organization as having a single operating environment. Certainly, each unit within the organization will reflect the *enterprise culture*—the culture promoted by the dominant faction within senior management. So when AT&T had a computer operation, it wasn't the same as IBM's or Apple's or Hewlett-Packard's because it was part of AT&T. But just as that enterprise culture is influenced by both external and internal forces, particular operations within an organization can develop distinctly different operating environments based on the kind of work they're doing, where they're located, their unique histories, and their internal leadership and structures.

For example, I've made numerous references to AT&T's enterprise culture and operating environment. But within the old AT&T, people also used to talk about the five distinctly different cultures within the larger organization: the Western Electric, Bell Labs, long lines, general departments, and operating company cultures. Each was marked by a different language system, different unspoken rules for working relationships, and so on. One of the most dramatic examples of an internal culture difference was Xerox's Palo Alto Research Center in the 1970s. Perched on a hillside overlooking the Stanford University campus, it thoroughly reflected the quickly evolving culture of Silicon Valley. The research scientists typically dressed in blue jeans and sandals, wore long hair and shaggy beards, and differentiated themselves in every way possible from the buttoned-down, big-company "Xeroid" culture of the executives in Rochester and Stamford.

Some variations in unit culture are productive, and some aren't. The point is that trying to make *long-lasting* culture change at the unit level—what my colleague Kathy Morris describes as "regime change"—is futile. Consider the new manager of a unit who wants to reshape its operating environment. He gets people excited, creates momentum, wrestles with headquarters for a measure of autonomy, and eventually starts to make things happen. Then, inevitably, that manager moves on and the next boss takes over. More often than not, the new boss is a product of the core culture of the enterprise, and she views the new culture she's inherited as weird, dysfunctional, or downright threatening. She knows that the surest way to score points upstairs is to restore the original culture.

Consequently, unit changes tend to fade away the moment the leadership changes. At that level, the departing manager rarely has the power to select a successor who will sustain the new culture. What's more, managers at the unit level tend to stay in those jobs for relatively short periods of time. At the organizational level, however, CEOs have longer tenures and more time to reshape culture in lasting ways. And CEOs typically play a key role in choosing their own successors, who will almost always be trusted associates who are likely to be the products and perpetuators of the culture the departing CEO helped build. Consequently, changes at the enterprise level are deeper and longer lasting than sporadic, unsupported changes at the unit level.

Leadership Is Crucial

For all these reasons, the single most critical factor in operating environment change is institutional leadership. Virtually every successful CEO with whom I've worked has viewed operating environment change as a top personal priority. Each has poured an immense amount of personal time and energy into articulating values and then communicating and acting in ways that reinforce his vision of what the operating environment ought to be.

"I've probably spent more time on values than any other single subject," says Randy Tobias of Eli Lilly. "I believe that having a shared set of values will, more than anything else, drive the behavior in the business, and the behavior in the business, more than anything else, will determine our success at implementing the strategy we've put in place."

Changing the Operating Environment

Given that basic overview of the principles and dynamics of the operating environment, let's turn our attention to some specific techniques for reshaping values, beliefs, and behavior to support your strategic objectives.

Any serious attempt to change the operating environment of a complex organization requires that leaders consider four basic questions:

- What is the content of the change? What is the leadership's vision of the new operating environment that will support and sustain the organization's strategic objectives?
- Where are the leverage points for creating change? Where in the organization will change offer the greatest opportunity for creating a new operating environment?
- What interventions—specific actions that interrupt the normal flow of business—offer the greatest potential for changing the culture and people's behavior?
- Where and when should leaders introduce specific interventions? What are the tactical choices available to change leaders?

Let's consider each of these in detail.

Content of Change

It is absolutely essential for the CEO and the senior team to determine and communicate in clearly understandable, actionable terms precisely which aspects of the operating environment they want to change, what the new culture will look like, and exactly what that change will require on the part of individual employees. "It's almost like you have to stand in the future and say, 'It's three years from now—what's it like around this place?'" says Patricia Russo, executive vice president of Lucent Technologies.

The changes need to be linked to the core strategy of the enterprise, and top executives must be able to explain why these changes will make a difference in concrete business terms (rather than the nice-to-have terms used by the insurance company CEO mentioned earlier). The senior team has to provide people with a compelling logic to justify such a major change. People need to understand what's wrong with the way they're currently thinking and acting and how bad things are likely to get unless significant changes are made.

The vision of the new operating environment requires two additional elements. The first is a sense of continuity—a reassurance that though some forms of behavior may have to change, certain core values remain intact—though perhaps with a new emphasis. In addition, the vision of the new environment should be expressed in a limited number of easily understandable terms that people can quickly digest.

Consider the situation Corning faced in the early 1990s. In the fall of 1993, the company announced its third-quarter results—and they were horrendous. After years of acceptable growth, the bottom seemed to be falling out of the place. Early in 1994, the company instituted a new effort, called Corning Competes, to trim costs and accelerate growth. The program involved reengineering and substantial downsizing, and it became clear that the new drive for efficiency was clashing with employees' perceptions of the Corning Values (described in Chapter Seven). People began to feel that the company cared more about Wall Street and the bottom line than about its own employees. Delta Consultant Kathy Morris, who has worked with Corning for years, recalls that people were voicing the concern, "If this is where we're headed, this is going to be a very different company."

The result was an effort, driven by then president and now CEO Roger Ackerman, to define and shape an operating environment that would maintain the company's traditional values while supporting the behavior essential to the company's growth. That long-term effort—which is far from complete—is rooted in the development of the Corning Operating Environment, a vision shaped through months of work by groups involving more than one hundred executives and managers. The environment is described in terms of "eight dimensions": customer focused, results oriented, forward looking, entrepreneurial, rigorous, open, engaging, and enabling (see Figure 10.3). Each is amplified in very specific terms

Figure 10.3. Corning Operating Environment Dimensions.

Customer Focused
Our number one priority is to anticipate and respond to the needs of our customers, clients, and patients better than our competitors do. We are determined to bring the best total value as measured by our customers.

Results Oriented
We achieve extraordinary results by focusing on customers and global markets. We have a passion for our businesses and a deep commitment to growth and financial performance. We measure outcomes and the processes that achieve them.

Forward Looking
We are focused on establishing sustainable competitive advantage. Our strategies anticipate where markets, technologies, and customer needs are heading. We are flexible, adaptable, and quick to make positive change.

Entrepreneurial
We encourage appropriate risk-taking through both individual and collective initiative to improve our performance. We provide an environment which fosters creativity. We rely on good judgment to take risks to grow our business. We expect to learn from both our successes and failures.

Rigorous
We insist on well defined processes and standards to provide effective control rather than non value-added bureaucracy. We ensure process reliability and effectiveness through the disciplined application of best practices and continuous improvement.

Open
We create a climate that supports informality and openness. We trust and respect each other. We encourage constructive debate and the expression of different points of view. We believe this results in better decisions that will be actively supported by everyone involved.

Engaging
We share information to gain the active commitment and involvement of everyone. This requires two-way dialogue that provides a common understanding of unit and company-wide issues. We hold leaders accountable for communicating frequently with their employees and listening to their ideas, concerns, and needs.

Enabling
We seek to leverage the diverse backgrounds, experiences, and perspectives of our work force. This requires that all individuals have the opportunity to continually develop their capabilities and contribute to the success of the company. We believe that all people should be recognized and rewarded for their contributions.

Source: Corning Inc.

that describe what the dimension means for the organization as a whole and what specific behavior it requires on the part of individual employees.

The dimensions are part of a comprehensive document that serves as the road map for the change. It articulates the key messages for communications, provides the underlying principles on which to build human resource policies and practices, and lays the groundwork for the training and education required to focus the entire workforce on the desired behavior.

Leverage Points for Change

Assuming the senior team is clear on its vision, then the next issue is identifying the leverage points for culture change—the elements within the organization where change efforts should be focused in order to create the new operating environment. In general, there are four leverage points (see Figure 10.4).

Figure 10.4. Leverage Points for Operating Environment Change.

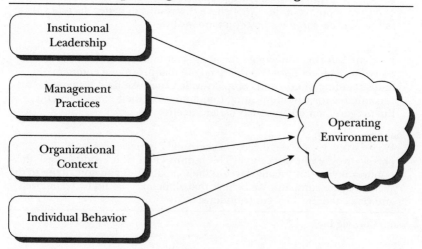

Institutional Leadership

Institutional leadership is a leverage point for change through the words, actions, and behavior of the CEO, the executive team, and a group sometimes referred to as the *colonels*—the senior operating managers in the field. It's not enough to have the generals signed on; change requires active support from the colonels too. In 1987, as my colleagues and I assessed the success of Xerox's quality campaign, we discovered wide disparities in the progress of culture change within different operating units. The key variable was the level of support and involvement by each individual field manager. These managers' actions and behavior along with those of the CEO and senior team are by far the single most important leverage point for culture change.

Executives and managers have the opportunity to influence culture change in several ways. First, they must articulate the new culture and explain what is expected of people. Through their personal actions, they can model the behavior they're expecting of others and perform symbolic acts designed to support the new climate. They can reward behavior consistent with the new cultural objectives and impose sanctions when resistance becomes a problem

I can't overemphasize the importance of the leader's personal behavior in shaping the operating environment. I've rarely seen a CEO who both understands and acts on the principle as well as Henry Schacht. "When you're trying to change culture," he says, "little things count." For Schacht, those little things have included creating a new sense of openness, accessibility, and informality at Lucent. So CEO Schacht and President Rich McGinn make a point of separating at lunch time and eating with other employees rather than with each other. They're seen around the building in shirtsleeves rather than suit jackets. They hold four or five meetings a month with employees at Lucent's various locations.

Another important element in Lucent's new vision was a renewed emphasis on the central role of technological innovation. Because Bell Labs scientists and engineers had been feeling unappreciated in recent years, Schacht and

McGinn make a point of spending half a day every other Monday in the labs, getting briefed on cutting-edge work. Even locating Lucent's headquarters in Murray Hill, New Jersey, was a conscious, symbolic act. "We could have gone anywhere—downtown New York, out in the woods someplace—but we moved in here," Schacht says. "Why? This isn't the most convenient place to be. The offices haven't been updated in years; it's depressing. But we wanted to send a signal to the external world and internally that this was the heart of the place. So we moved right into the headquarters of Bell Labs."

Management Practices

Individual managers below the level of the colonels can help generate culture change through their day-to-day management practices. Whether the emphasis is on open communications, teamwork, customer service, competitiveness, or commitment to quality, these are the people who can teach and sustain the new values and beliefs through their dealings with subordinates, peers, and upper management.

Think about it this way: in large organizations with thousands of people, even tens of thousands, the CEO and the senior team are distant figures. For most people, the corporate statement of values is a piece of paper. The vision is a slogan in the company handbook. For the overwhelming majority, their perception of the company is based entirely upon their relationship with their immediate supervisor. The company may be included on the list of ten best places to work in America; if your boss is a louse, the company stinks. The company's values may include openness and teamwork; if your supervisor manages like a Marine drill sergeant, the values mean nothing to you.

As a leader of change, your ultimate goal in changing culture is to change the day-to-day behavior of the people within your organization. To do that, you have to think in terms of the thousands upon thousands of daily contacts your managers and supervisors have with their people. Those are the most crucial interactions—the ones where people determine which behavior is rewarded or punished, which values are for real and which are empty rhetoric. The challenge to leaders is to find numerous ways, big and small, through training and education, through recruitment and promotion, through assessment and feedback and reward, to shape the daily behavior of the managers and supervisors whose actions will determine the ultimate failure or success of the culture change.

Organizational Context

From the perspective of integrated change, the key to changing the operating environment is to change every aspect of the organization that creates and sustains it. Attempts to change the environment won't last unless they're supported by the formal structures; the business processes; the measurement, appraisal, and reward systems; the selection and staffing practices; and the design of the organization's core work.

Remember that culture shapes and *is shaped by* the rest of the organization. If you want to change the operating environment, one of the most effective techniques is to start with changes elsewhere in the organizational model. The formal organizational arrangements discussed in Chapter Nine, for instance, provide the overall framework within which the culture operates. Changes in the formal structures, processes, and systems, whether intended that way or not, have a huge impact on operating environment.

At Citicorp, John Reed reshaped the cultural perceptions of rank and hierarchy by discontinuing the internal use of any ranks, referring to people instead by functional titles such as group executive.

Jon Madonna felt that the biggest obstacle to change he faced at KPMG was "mind-set," his shorthand for the culture of regionally based, highly independent specialists. By nationalizing the consulting practice, centralizing authority at corporate headquarters, shifting to a customer offering of integrated teams, and revamping the compensation system, Madonna says, "We changed their lives. Your world got turned upside down. We really tore things up. What it meant to them individually was that they had a new boss, they were limited as to what they could work on . . . the reorganization helped a lot. Obviously, what went with the reorganization was the measurement system, so you were now measured by how your line of business did, rather than how your old office used to do. It's how you're organized, how you're measured and how you're rewarded." Over time, the combination of all those changes in formal arrangements began to reshape the way KPMG partners interacted with their colleagues and their customers.

Individual Behavior

Again, the ultimate goal in changing the operating environment is to change the behavior of individual employees. The three leverage points I've discussed so far have involved techniques for indirectly modifying the behavior of large numbers of people. In some situations more direct interventions are required.

During any period of change, including culture change, few things hold everyone's attention—or send such clear signals—as does the treatment of key employees. Employees keep close tabs on who is up and who is down, who is in and who is out. Whenever possible, it's important to publicly recognize and reward those who exemplify the attributes called for by the new culture. By the same token, it's just as important to impose sanctions on influential key employees who visibly resist or ignore the changes.

At one firm where Delta Consulting has been helping to change the operating environment, there is an executive—I'll call him "Frank"—who consistently violates the new emphasis on teamwork, collegiality, and respect for individuals. Nevertheless, Frank keeps getting promoted. His continued success sends dangerously mixed signals. But as is often the case in the real world, getting rid of Frank isn't that simple. In many ways he's one of the most effective executives in the company. He has important ties to vital external constituencies. His departure would certainly hurt the company in substantive ways. Yet at some point top management will have to decide which are the most important signals to send to the rest of the company.

Interventions

Once you've determined what the new environment should look like and how the current environment should change, the next need is to decide exactly what steps to take in order to start the change process. The leverage points indicate where, in terms of the organizational model, specific change efforts can have the greatest impact. Beyond that, specific interventions in the normal flow of business can be employed either to change the culture directly or to change it indirectly by altering some other aspect of the organization.

With those basic principles in mind, my colleagues and I have developed a list of twelve interventions for changing operating environments (see Figure 10.5). I'm not suggesting that all twelve will be equally appropriate in every single situation. Instead, you should think of these interventions as a tool kit. Each organization has to determine which tools—and more important, which combinations of tools—will be useful in its particular situations.

1. *Collaborative culture definition.* This is how Corning began reworking its operating environment: by defining the required environment; constructing its specific dimensions; encouraging broad participation by leadership and other employees; identifying specific behaviors required by the new environment; and defining the relationship of vision, values, and environment to create a clear set of terms for deploying the change.

Figure 10.5. Twelve Interventions for Operating Environment Change.

1. Collaborative culture definition
2. Measurement and gap analysis
3. Stakeholder analysis and engagement
4. Leadership behavior and accountability
5. Communications
6. Large-group engagement processes
7. Education
8. Formal feedback process
9. Structural change
10. Management process redesign
11. Recognition and reward
12. In-depth individual interventions

In Corning's case, this work involved the active engagement of several groups. A task force involving nearly three dozen managers provided the initial input that built momentum for the project. At that point the senior leadership team, involving the corporation's top executives, began fashioning a vision of the new operating environment and defining its dimensions. Their work then went to the hundred-member Corporate Policy Group for further revisions; over time the two groups traded successive versions of the plan back and forth until both were satisfied.

Getting started is sometimes the hardest part. In one early exercise, we showed the Corning group a make-believe cover from *Fortune* magazine. Dated July 1998, it featured a large photo of Roger Ackerman with the huge headline "Corning Triumphs!" We told team members to imagine that when they opened the magazine, they would find a story with the headline "Corning Achieves Victory Through Dramatic Change in Operating Style." Then each would see a picture of himself, accompanied by a quotation that began: "Well, the key thing we did was . . ." It was up to each person and the team to fill in the blanks and answer the question, What was the biggest thing we could have done back in 1995 that would have made the difference?

2. *Measurement and gap analysis.* Throughout the process, it's important for the senior team to assess the current operating environment, compare it with the desired environment, and then identify the gaps between the two. If conducted carefully, this assessment and analysis helps everyone focus on the areas that need the most work. It's also helpful at this stage to identify some outstanding examples of places, both within and outside the organization, that best exemplify the kind of behaviors and practices called for by the new environment; these can then be used as concrete examples for the rest of the organization.

Bear in mind that gap analysis is not a one-time intervention. Once the change effort has begun, the analysis should be repeated periodically in order to assess progress and to determine whether any midcourse corrections are in order.

3. *Stakeholder analysis and engagement.* Early on, it's important to identify the key stakeholders—both inside and outside the organization—who will be affected by the changed operating environment and how they will be affected. It's critical to figure out

where the opposition is likely to come from, what form it might take, how intense it will be. Then it's essential to develop strategies for neutralizing that resistance.

Reflecting on the change effort at Kaiser Permanente and the clash of cultures that ensued, David Lawrence (1996) believes that senior management

> failed to think through a process for winning support and for deal-ing with different responses to change. Some people will gladly rally to the banner. Others, given time, can be persuaded, cajoled, or enticed. But in other situations, you must capture positions from people who are staunchly opposed to what you are doing. You must plan for dealing with pockets of organized resistance. . . . There are some people who are so recalcitrant, who feel they have so much to lose, that no matter what you do you will never win them over. You have to deal with them decisively. Otherwise, they simply will hold you hostage to their never-ending demands.

4. *Leadership behavior and accountability.* I've repeatedly empha-sized the need for senior managers to exhibit both substantive and symbolic behavior that reinforces the new cultural values. In order for that to happen the senior team has got to identify the most crit-ical patterns of behavior, give executives the necessary coaching, monitor how they're doing, and give them lots of feedback.

Ideally, this process starts at the top. In the early 1990s, as AT&T was trying to reshape its culture based on the principles of *Our Common Bond,* Bob Allen spoke to the company's one hundred top executives and told them the problems they were encounter-ing in changing behavior had their roots within that very room. "We are notoriously bad observers of our own behavior," Allen told the executives. Each person in the room was convinced he or she was the only one who was taking the new values to heart. "If only *they* would change, it would all be better," each person believed. Allen explained his belief that the only way any of them could really change would be to receive valid feedback—first from their subordinates and then from their peers and supervisors. He didn't want this change endeavor to turn into one of those all-too-frequent exercises in the top telling the middle what to do to the bottom. Accordingly, he announced, he would be the first person to receive feedback from his team; after that, these executives would receive formal feedback from their teams, and so on.

5. *Communications.* It's essential for the organization to use every means at its disposal to communicate the key messages relating to culture change. All of the company's communication processes—employee meetings, newsletters, video conferences, broadcast e-mail and company Web sites, voice mail, letters from top management mailed to employees' homes, videotapes—the entire arsenal of corporate communication tools should be unleashed in a concerted campaign to hammer the key messages home.

As it was being spun off from Corning in 1996, Quest Diagnostics developed a highly effective process for communicating important news and messages about the new company's values to its eighteen thousand employees in dozens of locations all across the country. At town meetings, employees were shown a videotaped message from CEO Ken Freeman; that video was followed by small-group sessions and then a final session with the entire group. Along with the video, each general manager was supplied with a script for running the meeting, plus key message points and a prepared question-and-answer crib sheet. This process allowed for widespread participation and active engagement by local managers and the reasonably consistent communication of the key messages.

6. *Large-group engagement processes.* It's important to give individuals throughout the organization personal exposure to the purpose and content of the new cultural objectives and, to the extent possible, experience with their own version of guided discovery (discussed in Chapter Six). Sometimes these messages can be conveyed through mass events; personal involvement is easier at the unit or team level. But successful organizations use a variety of venues to ensure the same message about culture is being heard in the same terms by large numbers of people at the same time.

As Corning worked toward instilling a new culture in the 1980s, employees were gathered, hundreds at a time, in annual Quality Progress sessions. Xerox has an annual Teamwork Day, a time when thousands of people participate in sessions at Xerox locations worldwide to celebrate the accomplishments of teams. GE is well known for its Work Out meetings, and Johnson & Johnson sets aside one day each year for the mass meetings it calls Challenge Sessions, in which everyone has the chance to ask top managers whether the company is remaining true to the values embodied in its Credo. Whatever they're called, these all are effective ways to get huge numbers of people involved in talking about their operating environment.

7. *Education.* Beyond these mass meetings, people need to be involved in more highly structured training sessions. Small groups are more conducive to making people aware of the need for change, the dimensions of the new culture, and the specific behavior expected of them. They can be educated about new structures and processes and about how those changes will affect their work. Finally, they can be given training and skill development work in areas essential to the new culture. It doesn't do any good to announce a new team-based structure and to tell people their performance will be assessed on the basis of team performance if they've never had any training in teamwork.

8. *Formal feedback process.* Organizations, teams, and individuals can be expected to sustain behavioral changes only if they receive constant, meaningful feedback. The organization must develop specific behavioral objectives, so that at each level in the organization people can both receive feedback on their own behavior and give worthwhile feedback to others. To give and receive useful feedback, people have to understand precisely what's expected of them—cultural objectives can't be defined in ambiguous "motherhood" and "apple pie" terms.

At Corning, each of the eight dimensions of the new operating environment is supported by specific performance objectives. For example, the term *rigorous* is defined by seven specific requirements—requirements as clear as "communicates performance expectations clearly," "does not tolerate shoddy or incomplete work," and "doesn't allow things to slip through the cracks." Those requirements are then used as a basis for feedback and appraisal, both for individuals and teams.

9. *Structural change.* In terms of the overall change process it's essential to align operational environment change with the structural change addressed in Chapter Nine. This is where the notion of congruence, or organizational fit, truly comes into play. One company after another—Xerox, AT&T, Ford, and Sun Microsystems, to name just a few—has found that you can't expect people to be independent, entrepreneurial, customer focused, and accountable if they're enmeshed in a tightly centralized, functionally

organized environment. Likewise, loosely integrated independent business units don't work if their leaders act like bureaucrats. You can't have the structure without the operating environment, and visa versa.

10. *Management process redesign.* Similarly, management processes such as goal setting, budgeting, and measurement of performance have to be changed to be consistent with the objectives of the new environment. If one of the stated goals is to drive more decision making from the staff to the line, then the budget process has to become a collaborative effort rather than an exercise in micromanagement by corporate staff. Systems for setting goals, measuring performance, and assessing output must all be consistent with the objectives of the new operating environment.

11. *Recognition and reward.* This easily could have been included in the previous step, but it's so important it merits separate attention. One of the frequent obstacles to culture change is that the recognition and reward systems lag behind the announcement that "things are going to change around here." What's the result? Confusion, cynicism, and poor performance. That's how Corning ended up several years ago with employees who were being told that quality was the priority but who were seeing that their performance was measured solely on the number of units they shipped. If the new cultural objectives are to be believed and accepted, then the formal and informal systems for assessing people's work and then recognizing and rewarding appropriate behavior have got to be consistent with the new environment.

12. *In-depth individual interventions.* Provide in-depth coaching and support for those individuals who are willing and able to undertake major personal changes essential to the new cultural dimensions. Conversely, deal decisively with executives and opinion leaders who actively resist. I'm not suggesting that these people be publicly crucified; but at the same time, it is self-defeating to cover up or refuse to acknowledge the reason for the removal or reassignment of an executive who has become a lightning rod for resistance.

As I suggested earlier, each of these twelve interventions will apply differently to each organization. Taken together, however, they provide a powerful portfolio of high-impact actions for reshaping the organization's operating environment.

Tactical Choices

Given this array of possible interventions, the final set of questions involves timing and tactics. Which changes should come first—the hardware or the software? Where does the change effort begin—should it start at the top of the organization, or should it work its way up from the bottom? Should you initiate change at the core of the organization or start on the periphery and work your way to the center? Who should participate, how much, and when?

These are not inconsequential matters. "What has become increasingly apparent to me is how critical timing can be," says David Lawrence (1996). "I have become convinced that the real art of leadership lies in careful pacing. It means moving simultaneously in a variety of areas and keeping each of them progressing so that the combined cadence does not tear the organization apart. I'm positive that nobody gets it 100 percent right. The winners do it less wrong."

His point is well taken. The truth is that you could take the twelve interventions and stage them in any number of ways. Obviously, there is no "right" answer for every situation and every organization.

As a general rule, however, I submit that if you have sufficient time, the most effective approach is a measured, managed effort that starts at the top and addresses the cultural issues at the heart of the organization. That doesn't mean you totally ignore what happens at the bottom of the organization, or that you ignore opportunities to experiment in peripheral units that might be more open to change. In reality, change of the operating environment typically takes place in the context of a larger change involving every aspect of the organization. Rarely is it neatly compartmentalized or clearly sequential. So the scenario I'm about to suggest is just one approach that's appropriate in certain large-scale situations where there's time to carefully manage gradual change.

To begin with, the decision to change the operating environment almost always flows from some precipitating event—a change in strategy or structure or a portfolio change resulting in a merger, acquisition, or spin-off. In the scenario I'm about to present, two initial interventions are crucial at this point: first, defining the culture and, second, assessing the gaps between the current and the desired environments. Frequently, that measurement activity pro-vides the impetus to get the process moving. With everything else they have to worry about during large-scale change, executives tend to put culture last. It's only when they're confronted with solid ev-idence that the culture they have isn't going to get them where they want to go that they move operating environment to the front burner.

At this point there's a major fork in the road. This is the stage at which some companies decide that a major structural reorgani-zation has to accompany the change in the environment. In other situations, that's just not necessary. This is when the leaders have to select a core strategy—top-down or bottom-up, starting from the inside or the periphery. It's also a good time to do the stakeholder analysis because it pinpoints organizational segments where resis-tance to the new culture is likely to be the most obstinate. Consid-ering how difficult this kind of change can be, it doesn't make much sense to launch the initial offensive at the heart of the enemy's defenses. It's infinitely better to start where you're most likely to find a base of support, and then build momentum.

Next come the set of interventions designed to initiate change—leader behavior and modeling, communication, large-group engagements, education, and feedback. Finally come the set of interventions aimed at supporting and sustaining the change—process redesign, rewards, and individual interventions.

Frequently, the kinds of change described in this chapter can be terribly wrenching for the people within the organization. It's one thing to talk about operating environment change; it's quite an-other to live through it. And the unfortunate truth is that not everyone who was successful in the old operating environment will possess the skills, attitude, and experience to excel—or even sur-vive—in the new one. So in Chapter Eleven we will turn to the is-sue of how to find the right people to fill the right jobs in the new organization.

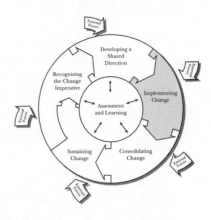

Finding the Right People
A Guide to Strategic Selection

I never cease to be amazed by the number of companies that are willing to go through the hard work, personal sacrifice, and widespread disruption of organizational change, only to obliterate their hard-won gains with haphazard staffing decisions.

In their more introspective moments, most executives readily acknowledge that selecting the right people for the right jobs constitutes one of their most important responsibilities. Few decisions they make will have as direct an impact on every facet of the organization. Yet few other decisions are made in such an illogical, slipshod manner.

The potential costs of bad staffing decisions are practically incalculable. In a large corporation, putting the wrong person in charge of a worldwide business unit can cost the company literally millions—even billions—of dollars over time. Nothing sends clearer messages about management's commitment to implementing change than its decisions about which kinds of executives to place in the most sought-after jobs.

In 1988, when Bob Allen first started talking about a major redirection of AT&T and the creation of a new set of business units, only some people paid attention. Then he revealed that executives generally viewed as "mavericks" had landed many of the top jobs while more traditional stalwarts of the status quo had either been relegated to lesser jobs or were out completely. At that point the entire organization sat up and took notice. People watched as the assignment of choice jobs unfolded, and said to each other, "Hey, there's really something going on here."

Yet despite their crucial importance, these appointments generally are made for all the wrong reasons. They tend to be crude back-of-the-envelope emotional decisions. In one sense it's easy to see why. The assignment of top posts is generally influenced by these three factors:

Analytical perspective. In theory, this means jobs are filled on the basis of a considered analysis of the characteristics required by a particular job and an assessment of a candidate's ability to meet the specified demands. That's the theory. In reality, these decisions typically come down to someone's instinctive belief that a certain candidate has "the right stuff," to borrow Tom Wolfe's phrase (1983). The right stuff can range from appearing calm in a crisis to giving polished board presentations. Whatever it may be, this right stuff is rarely defined or articulated. There just comes a point when people look at a certain individual and say, "Yup, she sure has got the right stuff," or the popular variant, "That guy's really got what it takes."

Emotional perspective. Being only human, it's difficult for any of us to ignore feelings of friendship, loyalty, or guilt as we consider staffing decisions. There's often a sense that people have earned a job merely because they have "paid their dues." Several years ago I watched the board of directors of a major corporation engage in a heated debate over whether to promote a senior executive to fill the job of CEO. Most didn't think he was capable of it, but there was another consideration. "He's played a major role here for thirty-four years," argued one director. "He deserves it." In the end, against their better judgment, the other directors relented and granted the promotion. The CEO's brief tenure was singularly undistinguished.

Naturally, as you deal with staffing decisions, you begin to play out in your mind all the likely scenarios. Everyone does. You try to imagine the range of reactions—anger, betrayal, massive disappointment—you're likely to get from unsuccessful candidates convinced they deserved the job or had earned it or were owed it. I imagine most of us are familiar with situations in which people were promoted solely because managers feared they would "go berserk" if passed over, while another, possibly more qualified candidate, could be counted on to wait patiently for the next opening. Finally, even though all of us are intellectually aware of the dangers of selecting the candidates who are most like ourselves, we often take an emotional perspective and do it anyway.

Political perspectives. It's hard to ignore the consequences of either promoting or passing over candidates who have the support of particular constituencies. Some candidates may have backing from external sources, such as customers, analysts, influential shareholders, or the press. Others may have bases of support within the organization, either on the board of directors or among the workforce at large. In either case, concerns about possible backlash—or, for that matter, potential benefits—from a candidate's supporters often exert a powerful influence on critical staffing decisions.

I've seen this play out more than once on the finance side of public companies, where a particular executive becomes associated with major expense reductions and thus becomes the darling of the analysts. The executive in question may be totally unsuited for a more senior position—or in fact poorly equipped to handle the full range of his or her current responsibilities. That doesn't matter to the analysts; any perceived setback to that executive's career is instantly viewed as management backsliding and an affront to shareholders. The mere thought of scathing analysts' reports and vanishing "buy" recommendations can be awfully chilling to a CEO.

In practice, the emotional and political considerations tend to overshadow the more analytical perspectives—and even so-called analytical considerations usually boil down to the superficial and subjective right stuff characteristics. The right stuff candidates eventually find themselves in a single-elimination playoff. They have the right stuff until the first time they stumble; at that point their bosses and peers decide the candidate has (1) somehow lost his stuff, or (2) never really had the stuff to begin with but had somehow managed to fool everyone into thinking he or she did. Either transgression is unpardonable; at that point the candidate is out of the running. It's just the way things work: those who live by the right stuff die by the right stuff.

As I said before in another context, that's a dumb way to run a business. Considering how incredibly important staffing decisions are to every single organization, it's amazing how many senior executives refuse to invest just a little more time and effort to work through a rational, systematic approach. Particularly during periods of large-scale change, a well thought out process of *strategic selection* should proceed along the same lines as we discussed for strategic choice and strategic design, and at roughly the same time. Simply put, strategic selection provides a logical process for, first, analyzing the requirements of a given job; next, identifying the strengths and weaknesses of the entire pool of potential candidates; and finally, assessing and comparing the candidates from the standpoint of the skills and characteristics the job requires. In plain terms, strategic selection means looking first at the job and its requirements and only then at the potential candidates and their profiles—and then coming up with the best match. It's the reverse of the all-too-common practice of saying, "OK, I've got to find a job for Fred, and there's a new job coming open at his level, so I guess Fred gets it."

A little later in this chapter I turn one last time to Xerox so you can see how an organization that revamped its strategy and totally redesigned its formal organization then went through a similarly exhaustive strategic selection process to find the right people to fill fifty of the top jobs in the company, starting with the executive vice presidents who reported directly to Paul Allaire. The result, as Allaire said, was that Xerox "selected some very nontraditional people based on this approach. People came to the surface who wouldn't have in the old system" (Howard, 1992, p. 116). For example, three of the company's nine business units ended up being led by presidents who had been with Xerox for less than a year. And when the success of the staffing process was assessed two years later, the results, as we'll see, were remarkable.

The Strategic Selection Process

Essentially, strategic selection is a process for staffing jobs in a focused, disciplined way and with a strategic perspective. It is an integral part of remaking strategy and structure because it's impossible to know what kinds of people you want in key jobs unless you know which strategic objectives you want them to achieve, where they will fit in the new organizational framework, and how you want them to behave in the new operating environment. Though I've helped companies use this process primarily in CEO succession planning and in the staffing of the top fifty or so positions within a large organization, it can be easily adapted to filling other jobs as well. In addition, the same principles and methods that make strategic selection an effective tool for filling new or vacant positions also make it a worthwhile device for assessing job performance. Indeed, it's easily adaptable as an instrument for doing annual assessments; because it is tied so directly to the specific components of any given job, it is far superior to the typical fuzzy report cards that have led people on both sides of the desk to detest annual performance reviews.

Strategic selection uses specific criteria and computer-generated profiles for matching prospective candidates with the requirements of the jobs to be filled (see Figure 11.1). Nevertheless, this is not a mechanical process that replaces human judgment with computerized selections. To the contrary, informed discussion and debate are at the heart of the process. Strategic selection doesn't eliminate judgment—it structures judgment along rational lines. It is useful precisely because it provokes discussion at a much deeper level than "she just acts like a leader" or "I think he'll grow into the job if we give him a chance."

The process of rating the relative importance of specific requirements for a particular job, then separately rating the characteristics of the pool of candidates, and finally matching the two sets of profiles doesn't remove human emotion from the final decision—but it does leaven emotion with rational judgment. I recall an instance in which a CEO personally liked one of his subordinates a great deal and desperately wanted to appoint him to an available senior position. So I urged him to sit down and write out a list of all the potential candidates for the job. Then we talked about the job. I asked him to discuss with me in great detail all the dimensions of the job and what it required. Then I asked him to go back and talk about all the candidates in light of the job requirements he'd just outlined. When he finished describing his initial candidate, he paused and said, "You know, I really like this guy, but I just can't put him in this job."

Figure 11.1. Strategic Selection Process.

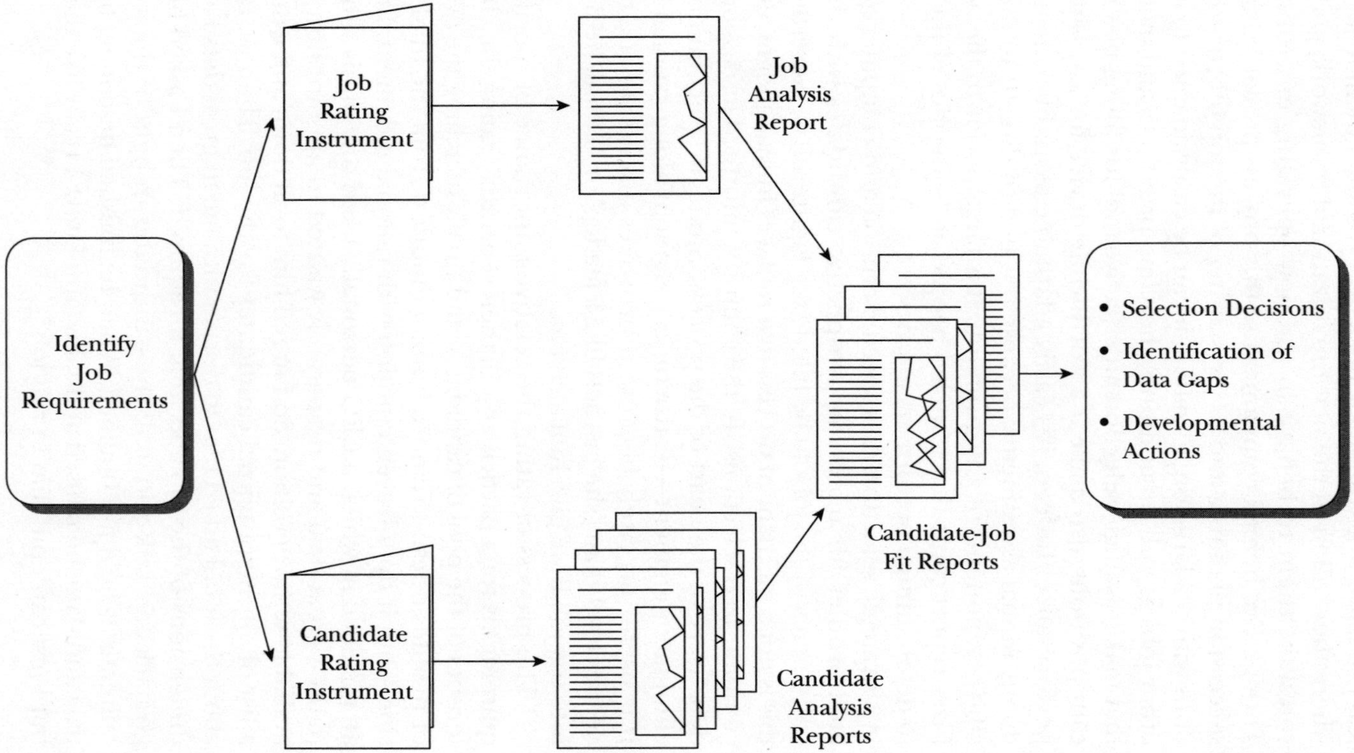

That was a fairly informal process. But even the use of specific numerical ratings, which I'll describe shortly, doesn't eliminate the human factor. Instead, it forces the people making staffing decisions to reexamine their subjective evaluations and try to come up with rational explanations for them—and if they can't, to rethink them. The core of the process remains individual human judgment.

The human dimension of strategic selection was clearly demonstrated by a CEO who used the process to help select his successor. When he'd finished his ratings, the leading contender was the company's general counsel. I was surprised, to put it mildly; despite a recent spate of corporate lawyers getting top jobs, the fact remains that the general counsel's office is rarely the first place you go looking for your next CEO. So I kept asking the CEO why he had rated that individual so highly. The answer finally came from the CEO's wife, who pointed out to him that the general counsel, in terms of background and personality, was more similar to the CEO than any of the other candidates. And indeed, the CEO himself had been general counsel before getting the top job. At that point he stepped back, acknowledged the candidate was "the most like me, and the company doesn't need someone just like me to be its next CEO." Fortunately, he also threw out his first set of ratings and started over again. The episode illustrates why it's so important, whenever possible, to have more than one person involved in the process—even if that person simply forces the decision maker to take a second look at the numbers.

One final purpose of strategic selection is that it provides both a common language for describing job dimensions and performance characteristics and a system for measuring their importance. Universally shared terminology is important in any organizational setting; it's essential in an organization undergoing radical change, when so many long-accepted notions about jobs and performance have gone out the window. If you've redesigned the company and now, for the first time, operations and salespeople have got to work together closely and involve each other in major decisions, the new job requirements include aptitudes for teamwork, collaboration, and conflict resolution, which were largely irrelevant in the old scheme of things. So you have to describe what you're looking for in terms everyone understands.

Rating and Analyzing

Much of the groundwork for strategic selection was laid by Gerstein and Reisman (1983) and Nadler and Gerstein (1992) when they first attempted to develop a rational method for staffing positions in sharply differing strategic settings. Their assumption was that executives would have to demonstrate considerably different strengths in order to succeed in situations as varied as start-ups, turnarounds, liquidations, aggressive growth, and profit maximization. Thus a process was needed to determine which potential candidates would have the best chance of success in a given strategic situation.

As the process developed over time, their focus on the strategic environment became a backdrop for the development of twenty-three specific elements for assessing job requirements. These detailed elements fall into seven broad dimensions that form a helpful framework for pinpointing the specific skills, experience, and requirements essential to any given job:

- Problem solving
- Operations management
- Human resource management
- Strategic management
- Organizational leadership
- Self-management
- General knowledge

Gerstein and Reisman then took the process a step further by outlining six general steps for using those dimensions to make staffing decisions:

- Specify business conditions and strategic direction.
- Confirm or modify the organization structure.
- Develop role descriptions for each key job in the structure.
- Assess key personnel.
- Match individuals with positions.
- Implement selection of candidates.

Based on our work with a variety of clients over the years, my colleagues and I further refined this process. We introduced the use of our own customized computer software to dramatically streamline what had been a time-consuming paper-and-pencil process. Using such software, I've found it possible, by meeting with the staffing team twice a day for two hours, to work through the senior staffing assignments of an entire organization in just three or four days.

From start to finish, the process can be broken down into three phases: rating the job, rating the candidates, and then analyzing that information and making the final decisions. Within those broad stages are thirteen distinct action steps, or tasks (see Figure 11.2).

Rating the Job

1. *Identify jobs or job clusters.* The top executives involved in the staffing process—and it's crucial that they be personally involved, rather than just handing the task to the human resource staff and walking away—define a job, or a category of jobs, as they will exist within the new structure.

2. *Discuss jobs strategically and qualitatively.* In a fairly general and unstructured format the rating team discusses each job in question from a strategic perspective, leading to the identification of major responsibilities and the important requirements the candidates should have to meet.

3. *Review, modify, and add to existing dimensions.* Using Gerstein and Reisman's seven major dimensions and twenty-three specific characteristics as a starting point, the raters decide which of those items are relevant to the job at hand. They are free to alter any of these items, delete them, and add any of their own that the team agrees are important. The result is the Job Rating Instrument, a list of requirements that can be used both to define the job and to assess the candidates.

4. *Rate job requirements, using the Job Rating Instruments.* On a scale of 1 to 7, each person rates the importance of each dimension on their list for each particular job. People are also asked to identify the dimensions they consider the five most important.

5. *Review, discuss, and refine the Job Analysis Report.* The job ratings are combined and averaged to create a single numerical rating for each characteristic; together, all the composite ratings result in a profile called the Job Analysis Report. The profile is discussed and, where necessary, modified by the raters. They also agree upon a set of seven or fewer *key dimensions*.

Figure 11.2. Action Steps of Strategic Selection.

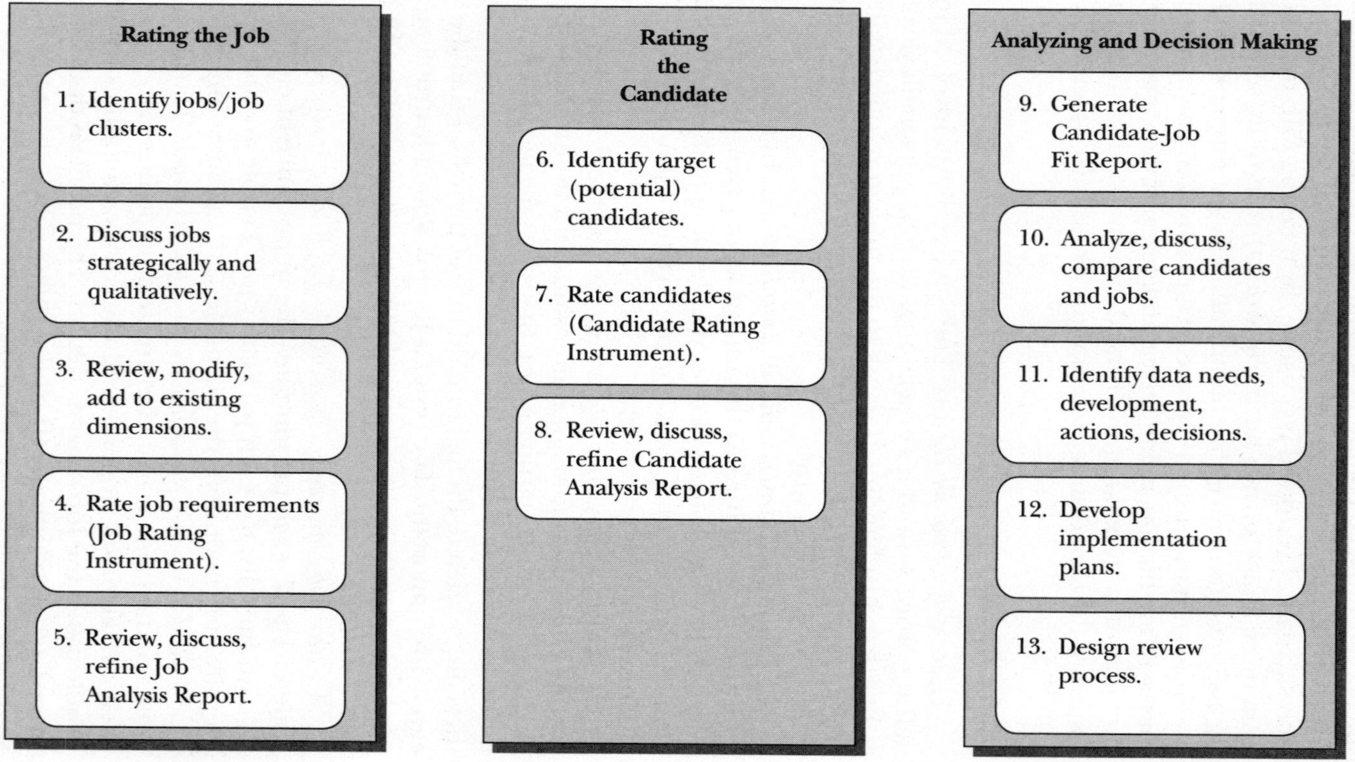

Rating the Job

1. Identify jobs/job clusters.

2. Discuss jobs strategically and qualitatively.

3. Review, modify, add to existing dimensions.

4. Rate job requirements (Job Rating Instrument).

5. Review, discuss, refine Job Analysis Report.

Rating the Candidate

6. Identify target (potential) candidates.

7. Rate candidates (Candidate Rating Instrument).

8. Review, discuss, refine Candidate Analysis Report.

Analyzing and Decision Making

9. Generate Candidate-Job Fit Report.

10. Analyze, discuss, compare candidates and jobs.

11. Identify data needs, development, actions, decisions.

12. Develop implementation plans.

13. Design review process.

Rating the Candidates

6. *Identify potential candidates.* Executives identify a fairly large pool of potential candidates. Their names should be derived from several categories: first, logical successors with high potential; second, benchmark candidates—people who clearly could do the job but for one reason or another are not available for it; still, they can function as benchmarks, yardsticks against which to measure the ratings of the other candidates; and third, deep selections—people with high potential who might not normally be seen as obvious candidates but who might be worth the risk if the raters are willing to gamble.

7. *Rate candidates using the Candidate Rating Instrument.* Using an instrument parallel to the Job Rating Instrument, the candidates receive ratings of 1 to 7 on each required dimension of the job; raters also use a 1 to 7 scale to indicate their level of confidence in each rating, which helps to identify areas in which raters feel they need more candidate information to make accurate judgments.

8. *Review, discuss, and refine Candidate Analysis Report.* As for the job analysis, the numerical ratings are combined to produce a Candidate Analysis Report, a profile graphically illustrating each candidate's composite ratings on each of the characteristics. These are discussed by the group and, where warranted, modified by consensus.

Analyzing and Decision Making

9. *Generate Candidate-Job Fit Report.* The ratings of all the candidates are compared with the job ratings, which results in a report that shows the degree to which all of them fit the required characteristics.

10. *Analyze, discuss, and compare candidates and jobs.* The raters discuss the various options for placement. This discussion also allows them to reflect on the patterns revealed by the data.

11. *Identify data needs, development actions, and decisions.* Job assignments are made; other activities may include providing for training, further assessment, or new assignments.

12. *Develop implementation plans.* Specific plans are drawn up for implementing whatever decisions were made involving assignments or further assessment.

13. *Design review process.* Determine whether the process unearthed any new information or led to any new insights that might have a last-minute impact on any of the placement decisions; also design a review process specifying how soon the performance of new appointees should be assessed (using the same rating instruments) to determine how they're doing in their new jobs and whether any further development activities are called for.

Strategic Selection at Xerox

For a better understanding of how this process can be used in an actual business situation, let's take a closer look at how Xerox employed strategic selection to fill its top jobs in 1992, as the organizational transition board was completing its design of the new structure.

"People may find this hard to believe," Allaire later explained, "but we actually designed the entire organization without any particular individuals in mind. That goes for the key managerial positions in the business divisions. It even goes for my senior management team in the corporate office. We didn't discuss who would occupy those positions until we had decided what kind of structure we needed and wanted. Once we had designed the new organization, however, we tried to be explicit about the type of people we need to operate within it. We started with a clean slate and defined the ideal characteristics of a manager in the new Xerox" (Howard, 1992, p. 115).

As the details of the new organizational structure began emerging from the OTB's work, Allaire and I modified the standard list of seven job dimensions to more closely reflect the new Xerox strategy and structure and the kind of operating environment Allaire was hoping to create. He took that list back to the OTB, and together they engaged in a spirited day-and-a-half–long battle over which characteristics Xerox should use. It was an enormously valuable debate, raising profound questions about what the company was looking for in its top jobs and the people who would fill them.

Consider for a moment how important—and unusual—that process was. Think about situations you've witnessed—or been part of—in which new positions were created without anyone's being certain what the people in those jobs were supposed to do or how they were supposed to act beyond meeting basic business objectives such as growing revenue or cutting costs by a given percentage. How many times have you heard something along the lines of, "Well, since it's a new job, who knows any of the details? We'll just have to let it evolve." Then consider how incredible that situation really is—creating the top job for a multimillion- or perhaps even billion-dollar–plus operation without any specific articulation of the skills, knowledge, operating behavior, and character traits the job requires. By and large, organizations have a much clearer idea and are considerably more specific about the performance requirements and behavior standards for most hourly wage earners than they are for the people who control the company's future.

When Allaire and the OTB debated the job dimensions for a day and a half, Xerox had already decided to create nine new business units and three customer units. Each would have its own president, who was supposed to act as the entrepreneurial head of a semiautonomous business within the larger framework of a global corporation. Fine. But what exactly did that mean in terms of job skills and characteristics? Exactly what were unit presidents supposed to do? How were they supposed to think and act? How were they supposed to relate to their bosses, peers, subordinates, and customers? In relative terms, how important were aggressiveness, innovation, attention to customers, ability to energize employees, and ability to handle crises? How essential was it that they have a detailed knowledge of their unit's core work?

In the end, the team hammered out its own list of twenty-three basic requirements. (That there were twenty-three is totally coincidental. They were not the same as Gerstein and Reisman's original twenty-three dimensions, and as far as I know, there's nothing magical about twenty-three dimensions—it just happened to work out that way in both cases.) Team members then grouped these dimensions into the four categories of strategic leadership, organizational leadership, personal characteristics, and knowledge. Some of the characteristics, they concluded, were essential for any senior management job at Xerox. Others related specifically to the unit president positions.

"We developed a whole new set of criteria for evaluating people," Allaire explained. "Many are things that, frankly, we never thought of as so important before" (Howard, 1992, p. 115). That list included characteristics and skills such as strategic thinking, strategic implementation, teamwork, the ability to delegate, empowering subordinates, integrity, personal courage, and personal consistency.

The first positions to be filled were the handful of executive vice presidents who would report directly to Allaire and, with him, make up the corporate office. Allaire and William Buehler, then head of human resources, went through the process described above; they first rated the importance of each requirement on the list for executive vice presidents, then rated the pool of available candidates on those same requirements, and finally matched the candidate profiles with the job profiles. Once the executive vice presidents had been selected, they then became part of the team that rated jobs and candidates for the unit president positions.

"I sat down with a few top managers, and we rated some forty-five people we thought were candidates for roughly the top twenty-five jobs in the company, including the top position in all the business and customer operations divisions," Allaire said. "First, each of us rated everybody individually. Then we compared and discussed our individual ratings of each candidate and agreed on a common rating. And we did it without regard to particular jobs. It was only afterward that we considered individuals for specific positions" (Howard, 1992, pp. 115–116).

And then the process was rolled out to the next level, with the new presidents using the same system of job and candidate ratings to select their group vice presidents and top support staff. They rated a pool of nearly one hundred candidates to fill approximately fifty top positions.

In the end, how effective was the process at Xerox? On a scale of 1 to 100, with 100 being totally consistent fit between the candidate profile and the profile of job requirements, the average fit score of the people appointed to the top jobs in 1992 was 47. That's not particularly good; at Corning, for instance, the average fit score was 77. However, all of us involved were well aware at the time that Xerox was gambling on some high-potential people who simply hadn't had the opportunity to master and display some of the characteristics Allaire was looking for in the new operating environment.

Two years later we assessed the same group again using the same rating instruments, but with a somewhat different group of raters (which eliminated the concern that the original raters might simply try to justify their earlier evaluations). This time the fit between job requirements and the characteristics displayed by the people holding those jobs averaged in the range of 80 to 85. Those scores strongly suggested that the process had been remarkably successful in helping the company assess both the accomplishments and the potential of a large number of executives. Over time most were able to meet the demanding requirements of their new jobs.

Before leaving this example, let me offer a few final observations on how strategic selection works in practice. First, it's a good idea to avoid asking the identical group of people to rate both job characteristics and a pool of candidates. Whenever possible, each team should have some different members. If the same people do all the ratings, it's conceivable that they might evaluate the relative importance of requirements with specific candidates in mind. However, that's not an insurmountable problem, because any particular rater's predilections will be blunted by the collaborative nature of the process. Each evaluation involves extensive discussion, raters have the opportunity to modify their ratings, and only then is a final rating derived from an average of all the raters' assessments.

The strategic selection process also offers the helpful feature of surfacing emotionally biased opinions that some raters naturally harbor concerning particular candidates. When a full set of ratings is compared, aberrations in the ratings—spikes in the profiles— make it quite evident that certain members of the team have either a "favorite son" candidate or someone they're determined to drown. Sometimes there's good reason for it; in other cases it's merely a gut-level response based on hazy impressions. Either way, structured discussion of widely varying ratings results in the rater either providing valuable information the rest of the team didn't have or acknowledging he or she had insufficient basis for the abnormally high or low rating.

Finally, computer software speeds up the entire selection process. When raters change their minds in the light of discussion and enter a revised rating in the program, a new composite score and candidate profile are available instantly. Profiles are graphically

Figure 11.3. Sample Computer-Generated Comparison of Candidate and Job Profiles.

Organization: Sample Industries Inc.   Candidate-Job Fit Report
Position: Chief Executive Officer   1/1/97

Candidate-Job Fit: Michael Jones

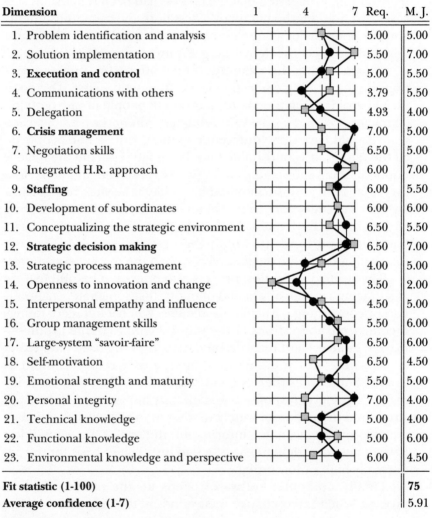

Dimension	1	4	7	Req.	M. J.
1. Problem identification and analysis				5.00	5.00
2. Solution implementation				5.50	7.00
3. **Execution and control**				5.00	5.50
4. Communications with others				3.79	5.50
5. Delegation				4.93	4.00
6. **Crisis management**				7.00	5.00
7. Negotiation skills				6.50	5.00
8. Integrated H.R. approach				6.00	7.00
9. **Staffing**				6.00	5.50
10. Development of subordinates				6.00	6.00
11. Conceptualizing the strategic environment				6.50	5.50
12. **Strategic decision making**				6.50	7.00
13. Strategic process management				4.00	5.00
14. Openness to innovation and change				3.50	2.00
15. Interpersonal empathy and influence				4.50	5.00
16. Group management skills				5.50	6.00
17. Large-system "savoir-faire"				6.50	6.00
18. Self-motivation				6.50	4.50
19. Emotional strength and maturity				5.50	5.00
20. Personal integrity				7.00	4.00
21. Technical knowledge				5.00	4.00
22. Functional knowledge				5.00	6.00
23. Environmental knowledge and perspective				6.00	4.50

Fit statistic (1-100)	**75**
Average confidence (1-7)	5.91

Legend:
Requirements ● Michael Jones ▢

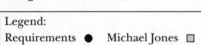

displayed, showing both the strengths and weaknesses of each candidate and the degree to which a personal profile matches or diverges from a job requirements profile (see the example in Figure 11.3). The correlation is also calculated and displayed in numerical terms, but the charted profile is an unusually helpful tool for quickly identifying both consistent patterns and gross mismatches.

Hiring from the Outside

Staffing an organization during periods of radical change also involves one other technique I have seen used by just about every successful organization: hiring from the outside.

As difficult as this may be—and it is difficult, particularly when it means passing over loyal insiders who deeply believe they've earned a promotion—it's often impossible to find internal candidates who can shake off years of experience in the old structure and operating environment. They are the products of the old culture the organization is trying to change; they have been shaped by it, reinforced by it, and in many cases have internalized it. Asking them to be instruments for reshaping that operating environment is in some cases just asking too much.

"Bringing people in from the outside has been a strategy since 1983, 1984," AT&T's Bob Allen said in 1994. "I knew that the people that were here couldn't do it all, not because they weren't good people. We just needed some new thinking—most of 'us' had the same-shaped heads. My obligation to the shareholders subsumed my concern for insiders' promotion opportunities. We had to bring in outsiders" (Nadler, Shaw, Walton, and Associates, 1994, p. 260).

Obviously, hiring from the outside involves serious risks. No matter how rigorous your recruitment and selection process may be, it's simply impossible to assess outside candidates as accurately as you can the people you've worked with for years, so hiring decisions become bigger gambles. In my experience only about one-third of outside hires live up to original expectations. Another third require significant development efforts, and the final third end up washing out.

Still, there are three distinct advantages in hiring from the outside to support strategic, structural, and cultural change:

Skills and experience. People from the outside sometimes have skills and experience people on the inside simply don't possess. There's a good reason why so many of the top positions at Xerox were filled by outsiders in the early 1990s. As a traditionally functional organization with a very narrow pyramid at the top, Xerox had given relatively few of its people experience in general management, and even then they usually did not get this experience until they were in their late forties or early fifties. At a company like Citibank, conversely, people generally got their first general management job in their early thirties and were ready for senior management positions when they were in their middle or late forties. As Xerox adopted a structure requiring a new cadre of executives with senior management experience, it found its pool of internal candidates was surprisingly shallow.

In the early 1980s, the *Wall Street Journal* went through a similar unprecedented binge of outside hiring. The newspaper had traditionally hired promising young journalists with little professional experience and then trained them in the *Journal's* culture, standards, and traditions. But in the early '80s, as the paper began asserting itself as a major national publication rather than a special interest newspaper, it sought out senior journalists from other publications to help supervise coverage of such new areas as social issues and cultural trends and such emerging topics as personal finance and health care. For the first time in its history, the *Journal* began hiring large numbers of editors from daily newspapers and news magazines.

Outside perspective. Radical change sometimes requires a completely new perspective that can be contributed only by people with experience in an entirely different industry. That's what the Times Mirror Company had in mind when it hired an executive with a consumer products background to head its publishing empire. That's why Citibank sought out executives with backgrounds as varied as consumer products and engineering to fill top positions. That's why IBM aggressively pursued the president of Boston Chicken, the enormously successful chain of fast-food stores, to be its senior vice president for strategy. And that's why AT&T, as it tried to reshape itself as a collection of highly competitive business units, recruited executives from PepsiCo, GE, Wang, and DEC. Alex Mandl, who would later be named president and chief operating officer, was hired during that period from Sea-Land, a container shipping company. "Clearly, there are plenty of guys who have a lot more knowledge about the phone business," Mandl commented shortly before his promotion in 1995. "I may bring a broader perspective" (Kirkpatrick, 1995). (Mandl also illustrates one of the risks of hiring from the outside; he stayed for just a couple of years, leaving in the summer of 1996 to accept an extremely lucrative offer to become CEO of a small high-tech start-up company.)

Shake-up factor. Apart from their specific skills and new perspectives, outsiders taking over in visible positions spark change merely by shaking up the chemistry of the organization. Randy Tobias is very explicit in describing the people he brought in to Eli Lilly as he completely reshaped his senior team in the mid-1990s. A few were hired specifically because their expertise strengthened the team in critical areas, and others were brought in from GM, Reebok, and MasterCard to import some fresh perspectives and new ideas.

There's always the risk that the traditional organization, acting much like a living organism, will isolate these outsiders, these foreign bodies, and in time reject them. That's why outsiders who stay—and many decide not to—so often follow one of two patterns; either they give in to the pressures and "go local," taking on the characteristics of the culture they were brought in to change, or they stand outside the culture and continually fight it. By far the most successful strategy is to bring in substantial numbers of outsiders, so they can form their own network; in time this network tends to connect with like-minded insiders who understand the organization's problems, and linked together, these insiders and outsiders become a powerful constituency for change.

It's important to do explicit things to support the outsiders. At Citibank, for instance, during a period of tremendous change, the senior executives met for three days every six months with a group of seventy-five new employees. They would educate each other; the executives would pass along and explain the history and legends that made Citibank what it had become, and the outsiders would explain what they were encountering within the organization and how they understood it from their outside perspective.

At AT&T, Allen believed the problems inherent in bringing in large numbers of outsiders were well worth it. "The final test is how well those people contribute, and whether they are respected," he said in 1994. "I think they have demonstrated their worth and value. In most cases there's been a learning process taking place between so-called insiders and outsiders. It has made both sides stronger, and now we are one" (Nadler, Shaw, Walton, and Associates, 1994, p. 260).

This chapter concludes our look at the implementation phase of large-scale change. You'll recall that I started by describing strategic choice and the process for developing a new strategy. Then I moved on to the organizational hardware and the strategic design process for developing formal structures, processes, and systems. Then I turned to the software, or operating environment, and laid out a dozen techniques for reshaping the way people think and behave. Finally, I proposed a strategic selection process for filling critical jobs with people who demonstrate the skills and personal characteristics required to make the new strategy, structure, and operating environment come together in a new pattern of organizational congruence.

In Chapter Twelve I take up the two final phases of change: consolidating change, or making it an integral part of the way the organization operates, and sustaining change, the challenge of maintaining momentum, avoiding complacence, and searching for signs of the next wave of change.

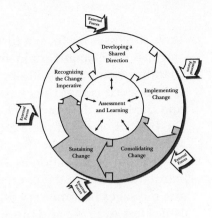

Staying the Course

Consolidating and Sustaining Change

The first three stages of large-scale change—recognition, developing a shared vision, and implementation—require incredible amounts of time and energy. Yet even after implementation is well under way, the change cycle is far from over. In fact, some of the most difficult work still lies ahead in the two final stages: *consolidating* and *sustaining change*.

In most change situations, a disproportionate share of senior management's effort gets packed into the first three stages. The drama reaches its peak with implementation. With much fanfare, leaders have announced new strategies, redesigned business units, and doled out the top jobs. People are well past their initial reaction, whether it was panic or elation. The emotional roller-coaster is definitely slowing down and leveling off.

At this point the real danger is that the hard work of making the change stick becomes an afterthought, a dull postscript to the exciting chapters that came before. If managers let that happen, they risk losing all the benefits in which they've invested so heavily.

Just as design and implementation tend to merge into one another, in actual practice there's a blurry distinction between consolidating and sustaining. Consolidating refers to the period of instability immediately following implementation, when there's a very real danger that if the cart doesn't keep moving ahead, it could easily slide all the way back down the hill. The changes have yet to be baked in to the organization's operations and culture, and their success is far from a foregone conclusion. In the sustaining stage, as the changes gradually take hold, management's fear isn't that the organization will slip back to where it was before; instead, the concern is that the change effort will simply run out of gas and the forward momentum will grind to a halt.

Indeed, many of the executives with whom I've worked have found sustaining to be the most difficult phase, both personally and for the organization as a whole. With each passing day it gets harder to generate the energy it takes to keep working at change; the messages become repetitive, the audiences less excited, the issues less strategic and more mundane. Moreover, although the CEO and the senior team were caught up in leading their internal change, the rest of the world was changing too. As difficult as it might be, just as things seem to be settling into place, the senior team has to revive its external vigilance and start searching the marketplace for new signs of impending threats or unrealized opportunities. Team members have to start thinking about the next wave of change, even as the first wave is still crashing around them.

In this chapter I explore ways to consolidate change and then delve into the specific dangers organizations face as they try to sustain change and avoid the Success Syndrome. I also describe how the typical CEO life cycle makes it all too easy for leaders of change to become obstacles to change.

Consolidating Change

It's important to note a shift in perspective that takes place at this point. Until now I've been emphasizing the central role of senior management and the notion that the leadership of change can't be delegated. Here's the exception. If the organizational change is to succeed over the long haul, it has to be incorporated into the very fiber of the enterprise. And for that to happen, managers outside the senior team have to step up and assume a major portion of the load.

In part that's because the members of the senior team by this point are emotionally ready to move on; having set the change in motion, they're impatient to get back to running the business and more than ready to hand off the change process to their subordinates. Even more important, it's the less senior managers who are best positioned to incorporate the lofty ideas and general themes of change into the organization's operating processes and practices.

With that in mind, there are three basic issues managers have to address during the consolidation stage:

- *Assessment.* Developing systematic ways to monitor the progress of the change and to rigorously measure what is working and what isn't
- *Refinement.* Determining how the change agenda should be fine-tuned to encourage the successes and deal with the failures uncovered by the assessment and to compensate for new shifts in the external environment
- *Baking in.* Incorporating the change into both the formal structures and processes and the informal operating environment, so that over time the once-revolutionary elements of the change agenda are perceived routinely as "the way we do things around here."

From the perspective of top leadership here's another way to frame the issue: How do we inculcate the elements of change into the organization's processes, practices, and behavioral norms? How do we institutionalize an architecture and a culture that until now have existed almost entirely in the imaginations of a few senior people?

Assessment

The consolidating process begins with *assessment.* For months management has been introducing new structures and processes, shifting reporting relationships, emphasizing new practices, articulating new values and operating techniques. Now it's time to measure the success of those initiatives. In quality management terms, this is the time to *check* and *act*—to assess what's already been done and then use that assessment as a guide for fixing what wasn't done right the first time around.

Systematic data collection should be built into this stage of change, the earlier the better. At the very least, an organization should conduct a full-scale assessment within six months of the initiation of major change activities and then every year thereafter.

There are a variety of ways to do this: quantitative performance measures, attitude surveys, focus groups, individual interviews. The best example I've seen was at Xerox in 1987, in the wake of the Leadership Through Quality initiative. At that point change was achieving mixed results; some geographic areas, operating units, and businesses processes were catching on; others weren't. In an effort to figure out why, Xerox launched a huge assessment.

The resulting message was loud and clear: if this big change is all about quality, then why isn't customer service first on the list of new priorities? (Instead, the first priority was increasing the return on assets, and the second was growing market share.) As a direct result of the assessment, management rearranged the priorities and revamped the pay and promotion criteria to reward people for putting quality first.

If people are paying attention, assessment nearly always leads to refinement. The results of assessment can generate an infusion of badly needed energy for reworking the change. In addition, assessment gives management a chance to demonstrate that the change involves more than slogans and pep rallies. In an age when Dilbert has replaced reengineering gurus as the pop symbol of management thinking, you have to assume a forbidding level of cynicism toward each new change effort. That's why it's so essential to assess what's working and what people are thinking, and then to respond in concrete ways that demonstrate the change is more than smoke and mirrors.

Refinement Versus Revolution

In light of that cynicism, one of the biggest challenges during this phase is to readjust and *refine* the original change agenda without creating the impression that the whole idea is being scrapped. Managers have to assume that the immediate reaction to the first round of modification will be, "Here we go again. They blew it the first time, so now they're going to try something else."

That was the situation Ford Motor Company faced in the fall of 1996 as it prepared to alter the structure introduced in 1995 as part of CEO Alex Trotman's Ford 2000 program. Trotman, as we saw in Chapter Nine, fundamentally changed the way Ford designed and produced cars and trucks, breaking down the old functional structures and consolidating a wide range of activities into five vehicle centers and a limited number of platforms used as the basis for eighteen different lines of cars, trucks, and vans. After a year and a half of experience with the new structure, management was ready to modify it to lower costs, simplify processes, and increase speed. But Ford 2000 was still viewed by some—both inside the company and in the financial community—as a somewhat iffy proposition, and many still questioned the company's commitment to the effort. So when it came time to announce the incremental modifications of consolidating five vehicle design centers into three and reducing the vehicle lines to eleven, the company took great pains to describe the move as a "refinement" and a logical next step in the continuing evolution of Ford 2000.

Typically, senior managers share a frame of reference when it comes to such refinements. They understand the big picture; they see the connections, they understand the logic, but sometimes they fail to grasp how their moves will be perceived by the thousands of employees who don't have that same information. That gap is often widened by *path dependence,* a design concept that suggests the most effective route between two stages of organizational development isn't necessarily a straight line. Rather than moving incrementally from Point A to Point B, it's sometimes necessary to let the pendulum swing all the way out to Point C, shattering the existing patterns of work and behavior, before letting it settle back to Point B.

When Xerox reorganized in 1992 into a collection of nine independent business units, each with end-to-end responsibility for designing and marketing products to specific market segments, the massive change was essential to refocusing attention on products and customers. But the design wasn't perfect, and in time cracks appeared. So in early 1996, Xerox modified its structure again, consolidating the nine business units into three. The response was immediate and predictable: people assumed that Xerox was reverting to its old structure. It wasn't. A direct move from the old centralized structure to one with three independent units wouldn't have been sufficiently radical to shatter the old functional loyalties and internal focus. Now that change was consolidating, the three-unit structure looked more feasible.

Which brings us back to the original question: How do you modify change without seeming to abandon your original vision? The answer is to constantly communicate changes in the original plan in terms of continuity and evolution. I often talk to leaders about the need to "connect the dots," to clearly illustrate the path from "there" to "here." It's up to leaders to help people make sense of what's going on, to shape and retell "The Story," and to explain that the core principles driving change remain intact.

Smart executives embark on change with the assumption that no blueprint goes unchanged. They leave room to maneuver. They make the decisions they have to in order to keep the process moving, but they do it with the understanding that they'll go back and fix things when they have more time and better information. Recall Henry Schacht's concept of getting things "roughly right" and his belief that the most common errors involve governance mechanisms and the senior team. "You're either going to devolve too much, or you're going to move too much toward command and control," he says. "You're going to have the wrong people sitting at the table, because your first judgments won't always be right. So leave yourself a little room. Don't make any more commitments than you absolutely have to until you get a firm sense of the place. But don't be afraid to make roughly right decisions rather than putting them off."

There's yet another reason why major change initiatives require refinement. In its initial form the change agenda addresses top management's best guesses about the changing market. These days, however, it's increasingly unlikely that any organization can accurately predict every major development over the next three or four years. Not long ago I ran across the memo I'd written to Bob Allen in the summer of 1994, suggesting that AT&T was facing a period of massive change. In hindsight some of the things I suggested were fairly close to the mark; others missed by a mile, because the telecommunications industry has changed in ways that were unthinkable just a few short years ago.

A final thought about managing refinement: beware of zealots and true believers. In the early stages of consolidation, you desperately need the aggressive support of ideologues who are fiercely committed to the change. As you move into the refinement and modification phase, these same people often become a problem. They get obsessed with the surface manifestations of change—independent business units, total quality, reengineering, and the like—and lose sight of the core intent. They accumulate power by mastering the language systems, metrics, or behavioral symbols of the change agenda, and then guard that power jealously. Belief turns to orthodoxy, and support becomes fanaticism. They become self-righteous, seeing themselves as the true keepers of the flame. They become, in short, a major pain.

As you enter ensuing rounds of change, some of the early adherents will get in the way, just as happens in politics—as movements mature, revolutionaries become marginalized. The single-minded intensity that is so crucial at the birth of a cause becomes a major handicap for those who hope to lead an enterprise, be it political or commercial. It's an important lesson for CEOs to keep in mind as they consider candidates for top positions.

Baking In the Change

Beyond assessment and refinement, the final question in the consolidating phase is this: How do you convert the substance of radical change into business as usual? How do you take the new strategy, structure, processes, standards, and values and permanently *bake them in* to the organization? Up to this point the change has largely been the personal property of a small group of senior people. Now it's time to depersonalize change by institutionalizing it. There are three basic ways to attack the problem.

Communication

The first way to institutionalize change is to employ the whole range of techniques I described in Chapter Eleven for shaping the operating environment. All forms of communication become vital. Public recognition of those who demonstrate the new values and behavior sends important signals. It's essential to create heroes, to transform everyday occurrences into myths and legends that reinforce the vision of the new organization. As Kaiser Permanente's David Lawrence notes, it's the job of the CEO together with the senior team to "aggressively seek out the small victories and subtle successes, draw attention to the people responsible, and celebrate their efforts."

At this stage the ultimate success of the change effort still hangs in the balance; there are still plenty of people who are hoping the initiative will fail and everything will go back to normal. It's essential to seize every available opportunity to communicate how the change is taking hold and making a difference. At KPMG Peat Marwick, Jon Madonna believes achieving and communicating results right from the start was essential to building support.

"You've got to establish and maintain your credibility as you're doing the change," he says. "We would never have gotten as far as we have without the results, because we were able to say, 'Look at the results!' You've got to make sure the good guys win. Make no mistake: this is a battle between the good guys and the bad guys. As long as the good guys have results to prove that what they're doing is right, they're going to win."

Human Resource Practices

The second way to institutionalize change is through the broad set of human resource practices. (I'm setting aside staffing for a moment because it merits separate discussion.) Managers should have at their disposal a variety of policies, procedures, and practices that cultivate the new operating environment leaders hope to create as part of the larger change. These involve systems for measuring and assessing performance, pay systems and rewards, promotion criteria, training and development programs, and socialization techniques for immersing new hires into the changed culture.

In order to succeed organizations have to align these HR practices with the change agenda. In companies where the HR managers have been active players in creating change—and have the required expertise—these practices and policies can have an enormous impact. Unfortunately, human resource management is too often relegated to a distant back seat during the early phases of change; sometimes it doesn't even get to ride on the bus.

That's happening more and more as HR departments increasingly find themselves caught in the crosshairs of corporate cost cutters. Obviously, there are efficient ways to outsource some traditional personnel functions. Too often, however, the knife cuts too deeply, with HR managers relegated to minor maintenance roles. The company pays the price during periods of change, when it desperately needs experienced and influential HR people who know how to support the subtleties of the change agenda. Indeed, my colleagues and I often find that some of our most effective collaborators within client organizations are perceptive HR managers who are in a position to help institutionalize the change.

Staffing

Once the structural changes are in place, the most important and visible decisions management makes involve people—who gets the choice jobs, who gets hired, and inevitably, who gets fired. As discussed in Chapter Seven, there is no easier way to send clear signals—even major shock waves, if that's what's desired—than through major staffing changes at the top of the organization. Promoting people is fairly easy. Getting rid of them is not; but it's essential.

"This may be the most difficult lesson of all for CEOs," says Lawrence (1996). "In separate discussions, I asked both Jack Welch of General Electric and Paul Allaire of Xerox what they would do differently if they had the chance to launch their organizational changes all over again. Interestingly, both said exactly the same thing: they would have removed certain people sooner, because their own procrastination merely forced them to play the opening rounds with a weakened hand. My personal experience was much the same."

Firing people is never easy; forcing out senior people in the midst of turbulent change can be unbelievably tough. These executives often have large followings among various constituencies—employees, customers, or the financial community. In conventional terms, they might be top performers, bringing in important business. If there has already been a good deal of upheaval in the senior ranks, bench strength may be getting thin; there might not be any obvious replacement. In short, you can almost always find reasons not to get rid of someone.

And yet if the individual in question is acting in ways that clearly violate the values important to the new organization, then the CEO has no choice but to act. After all, lack of action also sends a strong message: it tells the rest of the organization, "Top managers aren't credible. You can destroy teamwork, treat subordinates with disrespect, violate all the values they keep talking about—if you bring in the bucks, nothing else matters." And if you want to see change crumble before your eyes, this lack of action is the quickest way to let it happen.

In many cases it makes sense to provide the executive in question with serious coaching and the chance to demonstrate substantive progress within a specified time. If he or she succeeds, terrific. If not—and if the transgressions are sufficiently central to the kind of change you're trying to create—then you have no choice but to get that executive out. Ultimately, executives must ask themselves some basic questions: What are our basic principles? What kind of organization are we trying to create? What are the values that are most important to our long-term success?

I'm not suggesting the answers are easy. I've seen plenty of situations in which long-term success hinged on short-term survival—and without doubt there are times when taking out a particular key player, though ethically satisfying, may border on suicidal. But sooner or later, as David Lawrence (1996), says, "The CEO has to come to grips with the fact that putting off these tough decisions usually has more to do with avoidance than with sensitivity and fair play. In the process, everyone gets hurt. For the employee who sees the writing on the wall but cannot make the required change, it means waiting that much longer for some final resolution to an agonizing situation. For the CEO, it means waiting that much longer to mold an effective, focused senior team. For the organization, it means a delay in the pursuit of the change agenda."

In these difficult periods, I often remind CEOs that not every situation can be fixed. Performance is one thing; personality is another. Skills are coachable; character is not. I've become convinced by years of experience that very few people, in the absence of a major, fundamental life crisis, can change their personalities. So if the problem with a particular manager involves personality, character, and basic values about how to run a business and work with other people, coaching and remediation rarely work.

Another aspect of senior-level dismissals is becoming particularly troublesome today. In the current litigious environment it's almost unheard for a company to announce that someone has been fired. In the absence of an indictable offense or action by government regulators, companies rarely hint at what really happened. You'll never see a memo on the company bulletin board announcing, "Fred Smith was asked to leave because his behavior was inconsistent with our values," or more to the point, "Fred is gone because he screwed up." Instead, you read this: "After years of valued service to Intergalactic Bancorp, Fred Smith has decided to leave at the end of this year to pursue other opportunities. We're grateful to Fred for his many contributions, and all of us join in wishing him and Wilma all the best in their new endeavors."

Yet the impact of mysterious departures can be horrendous. I once observed a situation at a major corporation where one of the president's direct reports—I'll call him "Bob"—began fouling up in a major way. Over the years Bob's mistakes contributed to several hundreds of millions in losses. Year after year the CEO kept giving Bob "one more chance." It wasn't until the CEO had retired and his successor was in place that Bob was finally fired. All too predictably, his departure was announced with the usual ambiguous farewell.

A year later, during a meeting with the CEO and the senior team, the subject of Bob's dismissal surfaced as an obvious point of confusion. So I asked the company's top executives to write down what they thought was the real reason for Bob's dismissal. The result: more than half a dozen wildly different answers, ranging from performance problems to personality clashes to a desire to run for public office.

Think about it. These were the top executives in the corporation, and two-thirds of them had completely mistaken ideas why one of their own colleagues had been fired. If *they* didn't have a clue, just imagine the rumors, conspiracy theories, and misinformed nonsense circulating among the tens of thousands of other employees who'd never laid eyes on Bob. Each one of them was left to create fantasies about what happened to Bob and, as a result, to draw conclusions about what behavior might get him or her in trouble too.

Indeed, even when there's a clear reason to get rid of someone, people tend to be shocked by outright dismissals among senior executives. At KPMG, for instance, Jon Madonna says, "You can take some guy where there's 90 percent agreement that he should not be in the job he's in, and the day you remove him, it's a disaster: 'Oh, my God, the way it was dealt with! Is this the way we're going to treat our partners?' It becomes a huge event—not a one-day event. It just lasts on and on."

The point is that people tend to handle high-profile dismissals badly, particularly during periods of change. They get angry and anxious. Unsure about the new rules of the game, they keep a close watch on the exit, trying to figure out which behavior will earn them a promotion and which will get them shot.

There's no simple solution. When possible, it helps to tie dismissals as closely as possible to specific events—but things rarely work out that neatly. More realistically, it's important to take steps to send precise messages when it comes time to replace those who left. The people who are chosen and the explicit statements top managers make in explaining why those particular people were selected for responsible jobs in the new organization can go a long way toward dispelling ambiguity surrounding departures. New appointments will send important messages as the organization moves from consolidating to the final stage of implementation—sustaining the change initiative.

Sustaining Change

Typically, the consolidation stage lasts somewhere from one to three years. Gradually, in almost imperceptible ways, the change begins to take hold. People have risen to the top who understand and demonstrate the behavior required by the new operating environment. Appraisal and reward systems have been aligned with strategic objectives, supporting people who meet the new performance objectives. Informal processes have grown up to support the new formal structures and systems. Hardly anyone believes it's preferable—or even possible—to go back to the so-called good old days. To use Jon Madonna's term—the good guys have won. Or have they?

The real danger at this point, as I said earlier, is that the change effort could simply run out of gas. Momentum could evaporate. And in the long run that can prove just as deadly as slipping back to the prechange state of affairs. This is a pivotal time for every organization, for one simple reason: success breeds stagnation.

Remember that a need for discontinuous change is often brought on by the Success Syndrome, the dysfunctional behavior of longtime market leaders. Typically, these organizations are characterized by self-satisfaction, an obsession with internal issues, and a lack of external focus. As it turns out, the consolidation stage of change is fertile ground for all those conditions to take root and flourish.

Recall also that discontinuous change is an unnatural state of affairs for most people and organizations. Change typically comes as a response to some stimulus; it is an attempt to remove a source of pain or discomfort or a perceived imminent threat. If the consolidation stage of change has been successful, people feel their pain easing and the threats dissipating. They start to feel satisfied with the new status quo; the last thing they want to think about is more change.

Before joining Lucent, Pat Russo helped lead the turnaround of AT&T's troubled Global and Business Communications Systems unit. In that role she personally experienced the frustration of trying to sustain momentum after people perceive the crisis has passed. "The fear of extinction is a far greater motivator than, 'Let's go grow this business,'" she explains. "Sustainability is a huge issue. How do you keep people charged up? How do you come up with the next innovative thing that will get people more engaged and involved?"

In Jon Madonna's mind, success became the enemy of continued change at KPMG. "Everyone assumes the results are fine, which is a huge problem," he said in 1996, just weeks before a successor was named to the job he had voluntarily relinquished. The results for the previous five years were indeed impressive; annual revenues were up 32 percent, and yearly net income per partner had risen by 58 percent. But Madonna ran into a brick wall when he tried to convince the firm's partners that they should be aiming for another leap of similar proportions rather than settling for growth in the 7 percent range as others favored. "This is a classic, difficult organizational change because of success. What you get into with people is, 'We don't need to change. What's the problem?' Five or six years ago, they were a lot more open to it."

The problem Madonna saw was that though KPMG had switched gears and accelerated its growth, so had its competitors. Despite its progress, KPMG still lagged behind its competitors, just as it had when Madonna first instituted change in 1990. It is a huge—and very common—problem for change leaders, unlike Madonna, to lose sight of the competition as a moving target. The set of competitive demands that a change was originally designed to meet has probably changed considerably in the intervening years. Leaders who fail to take that into consideration quickly become the proverbial generals who are still fighting the last war. Consider some of the companies we've been discussing: in one case after another, the competitive threat their change was designed to address had taken on a new form by the time the change was in place.

AT&T, for example, went through tremendous change in the 1980s as it tried to become an aggressive player in a competitive marketplace. Before it had reached its goal, massive deregulation of the telecommunications industry completely changed the rules of the game. So a wave of change was followed by a historic breakup, which was then followed by another round of change.

At Corning, the emphasis on quality, the diversification of the portfolio, and the restructuring of business units all made sense in the 1980s. Ten years later, the once-effective strategy was causing major headaches. Structural changes in the health care industry and the heavy demands of managing a highly diversified company led the Corning in the 1990s to spin off much of what it had acquired during the previous round of change.

At Xerox, the push for quality and a redesign that focused on customers and products succeeded in overcoming the original threat from Japanese competitors. By the mid-1990s, new competitors were lurking on the horizon, and advances in information technology were changing the way businesses produced, distributed, and stored documents—all of which undermined Xerox's dominance in traditional office technology. As the decade drew to a close, Xerox was once again contemplating a fundamental change in its business.

The Success Syndrome springs from the external environment and attacks organizations it finds napping. The primary defense is vigilance—a commitment on the part of top leaders to maintain, and even intensify, their external focus just when things finally seem to be falling into place. Many of Xerox's most fundamental changes have resulted from the massive environmental scan the company conducts every five years. Not every successful company uses such a formalized process. But whatever form their vigilance takes, leaders of change have to learn to manage "ambidextrously," as my colleague Michael Tushman puts it (Tushman, Anderson, and O'Reilly, 1996). On one hand, they can't abdicate their personal responsibility for change already well started; on the other, they have to begin looking ahead, thinking about what comes next.

What's more, that attention to the future has to be handled deftly. In general, I've been urging leaders to encourage the widest possible participation in each aspect of change. At the same time, there's great danger in sending mixed messages. If top management airs its focus on the future and its concern for changing conditions too publicly, the organization at large can easily interpret this new focus as a signal that the current change is being abandoned. Concerns about the next round of change have to be handled in ways that won't undercut the ongoing work.

The CEO as an Obstacle to Change

Clearly, success—or the perception of success—can sap the organization of its enthusiasm for change. But that's only part of the problem in the final stage. The truth is that large-scale change consumes a huge amount of energy under any circumstances, and organizations are not perpetual motion machines; they're human systems. Science teaches us that systems use up energy, they don't create it. To remain healthy, they must periodically find new infusions of energy, especially when the process of large-scale change can seem to drag on and on.

"It can be a grueling environment," David Lawrence observed around five years into Kaiser Permanente's change process.

> I constantly hear people say, "My God, this is hard stuff." They are right. Not only is it hard—there is no clear end in sight. People tend to become frustrated and depressed; often they lack any sense that we are making progress. It is not surprising. As a society, we like to keep score, declare winners, move on to the next game. But with organizational change, you could watch a long time without seeing any game-winning grand slams. The change process is more like a soccer match; you have to appreciate the seemingly endless positioning that precedes the sporadic scoring" [Lawrence, 1996].

After a while, the excruciatingly hard work of change begins to take its toll on even the most committed and energetic of CEOs. "From a very personal standpoint," says Lawrence, "I have to admit that I was not prepared for how isolating, enervating, and de-energizing the task of leading discontinuous change would be."

That's a common theme that runs through practically all my experiences with CEOs. Even as they maintain an energetic, upbeat public facade, most change leaders privately feel they're paying an incredible personal price. At AT&T, Pat Russo went out of her way to become a lightning rod for opposition to the changes she was making in her unit, publicly encouraging people to confront her with their objections to change. What she quickly learned, she says, is that "you cannot please everybody. In any large organization the fact is that a certain percentage of people will think you're doing the wrong things. And it's very personal, especially when the anonymous letters are addressed to you. To do the things I talk about took an incredible personal toll."

After a while, even the toughest and most energetic CEOs find it harder and harder to keep crashing through walls, changing attitudes, dealing with opposition, and leading one more charge when everyone around them is worn out. David Kearns told me that after leaving Xerox, his immediate and overpowering sensation was that someone had suddenly lifted an enormous burden he'd been carrying on his shoulders twenty-four hours a day, day in and day out, year after year. None of the CEOs I know, if given the chance, would have passed up the experience, and every one of them derived immense satisfaction from the accomplishments. But there's always a price.

"It's rewarding, it's stimulating, it's a great experience, but it's not fun," Madonna said as he concluded his six turbulent years as CEO. "It's at times been extremely frustrating. . . . Whatever pats on the back you get, you've got to give to yourself, because no one else is going to give them to you. You don't get recognized for the good stuff; you get recognized for all the pain. . . . The good things are kind of assumed." After a while, Madonna says, he began to lose patience with people, and his tolerance for opposition narrowed considerably—a symptom exhibited by more than a few CEOs in the latter stages of change. "You get much less patient, and you get much more confident," he says. "You accumulate a wealth of experience. And as the architect of the change, you know what's supposed to happen. . . . You've fought so many battles that when you see things, it's like Boom! It's obvious. This is the answer."

The CEO Life Cycle

Madonna's observation reflects a concept known as the *CEO life cycle* (Nadler and Heilpern, 1997; Hambrick and Fukutomi, 1991). Briefly, Donald Hambrick and Gregory Fukutomi of Columbia University have described what they envision as five distinct "seasons" that punctuate the normal tenure of a CEO. The first three involve a sharp learning curve, openness to new ideas, experimentation, and the development of the "enduring theme" that will characterize the CEO's time in office.

However, it is the fourth and fifth seasons we should be concerned with here. The fourth season—*convergence*—closely parallels the consolidation stage of the change cycle. At this point the CEO is increasingly concerned with incremental changes. He or she has mastered the basic requirements of the job, to the point where they're now becoming routine. Knowledge is high, interest is starting to sag, and the CEO relies on fewer sources of information, much of it highly filtered. Then comes the final season, which, significantly, Hambrick and Fukutomi have named *dysfunction*. The CEO's views of the business environment have hardened. There's a resistance to change and experimentation, a further narrowing of information sources, and an overall weariness toward the job.

Let's face it: sooner or later even the most challenging work in the world gets boring after you've done it enough times. As I have reminded CEOs, "I know you're about to go out and give your 273rd speech about the importance of quality and teamwork, and you can give this speech in your sleep. But this will be the first and perhaps only time the people at that plant will hear the message from you. And unless you deliver it with enthusiasm and show them your commitment, they're not going to buy it." Gradually, the CEO has to work harder and harder at generating the enthusiasm that once came naturally.

Now consider the consequences for an organization when the CEO's dysfunctional season coincides with the final cycle of change. Not only is the leader running out of energy just at the moment when the rest of the organization badly needs to get its batteries charged, but what's even more critical is that the leader becomes the embodiment of the Success Syndrome. At this stage, CEOs feel they have won the big battles. Now they'd like to spend the rest of their reign savoring the fruits of their triumph, enjoying the perks of office, gradually handing off the tougher chores to subordinates—in general, majestically slipping out to sea on the victory barge. In most cases, the last thing they want is to start thinking about another painful round of change.

These one-time leaders of the revolution have become the defenders of the status quo. The strategy that may no longer address the realities of the marketplace was their strategy. The organizational architecture is the one they designed. The operating environment is the one they worked so long and hard to create. And the people who might not be up to the challenge of leading a new round of change are their people, the ones they groomed, recruited, mentored, and entrusted with great responsibility. The more rigid these CEOs have become in their views, the more any suggestion of massive change starts to look like a repudiation of everything for which they stood.

Succession Planning for Change

As if that weren't enough of a problem, factor in one final element: the increasing rapidity of change. The implication is worrisome: it means that most CEOs, after going through one exhausting and emotionally demanding change, are almost certainly going to have face the prospect of another. At that point there really are only three choices CEOs can make. If they're a Jack Welch or Bob Allen, they decide to take up the challenge, and they muster the energy to do it all over again. If they refuse to acknowledge the need for change, they find themselves enjoying early retirement while their successor wrestles with the issues they left behind. The third alternative is to manage the next round of change through a carefully planned succession.

I firmly believe that succession is an invaluable element in change management. Both at Xerox, where David Kearns was succeeded by Paul Allaire, and at Corning, where Jamie Houghton was succeeded by Roger Ackerman, the succession process was deliberately planned with the full knowledge that the incoming CEO would be responsible not only for continuing the change that had been set in motion but also for planning and implementing the next wave of change that was already in sight. The criteria for selecting the successor and the executive apprenticeship program undertaken to fully prepare the incoming CEO provided models of succession planning that ought to be studied by other companies.

One element both situations had in common—and that played a major role in the success of each—was that both retiring CEOs chose successors who were quite different from themselves, both in terms of personality and management style. Their values were consistent, and that's what was most important. But beyond that, Houghton and Kearns gradually ceded more and more power to their successors, and made it clear they would be free to run the companies in keeping with their own styles. More specifically, each CEO believed it would be to the company's benefit to have a new leader who brought new and different strengths to help meet new challenges.

That leads us to the issue of leaders' skills and styles. What is it, specifically, that enables some people to become successful—and sometimes remarkable—leaders of change? In Chapter Thirteen our discussion moves from organizations to individuals, as we zero in on the lessons successful CEOs can offer on what it takes to become a successful leader of change.

Leading the Charge
The Unique Role of Senior Management

Several years ago Delta Consulting took on a major assignment for one of the nation's best-known financial institutions. The CEO's goal was a complete overhaul; nothing less, he was convinced, would maintain the company's dominant position in a rapidly changing competitive environment where banks, insurance companies, and specialized firms of all kinds seemed to be launching vigorous new assaults practically every day.

So we went to work. It didn't take long to figure out that the CEO was right; everything had to change. We did an extensive diagnosis to identify the worst problems. We did all kinds of benchmarking to measure performance. We helped put together a comprehensive change agenda that dealt with strategy, structures, processes, values, the operating environment—the whole bit. And yet there was still a major stumbling block—the executive team.

Everywhere we turned, we were getting the same message: the group of executives who reported to the CEO just didn't get it. They were so risk averse, their performance standards were so dismal, and they were so disconnected from the marketplace that nobody believed things could change as long as that team was in charge. Armed with overwhelming information, I took up the matter with the CEO—who quickly dismissed it. "I think this is a good group of guys," he told me.

"I don't buy that," I responded. "But given their performance, there really are only two alternatives. Either they're as bad a group as everyone thinks, or they're a good group that's getting poor leadership from you. Unless you either replace them or completely change the way you lead, all the change initiatives, project teams, and consultants in the world aren't going to help you."

He continued to resist making any changes at the top, at which point I told him, "We're wasting our time and your money," and parted company. As things turned out, the company's performance continued to crumble; within two years, the firm had been swallowed up in a huge acquisition.

What's the moral of the story? Here was a company that in terms of change was doing everything right. It was pursuing a deliberate, well-planned strategy that took into account all the elements essential to large-scale change. And yet at the moment of truth, there was a failure of courage—of true leadership—at the very top. The CEO hoped that he could somehow start the change in motion and then leave it to others to make the hard choices and get their hands dirty. It didn't work. As a result, an enterprise comprising thousands of people and billions of dollars in assets ceased to exist as an independent entity.

The lesson was clear: there is no substitute for an active, personally committed CEO who is willing to do the critical things that only a CEO can do during periods of change. Every successful change leader will tell you the same thing. "You can't subcontract it out," says PepsiCo's Craig Weatherup (Nadler, Shaw, Walton, and Associates, 1994, p. 264). The chief executive simply cannot delegate the leadership of change.

What's more, leadership that's "just OK" won't get the job done. The truth—and we all know it—is that many organizations can, and do, get by with less than spectacular leadership at the top during periods of relative stability. But I have yet to find a single example of an organization that successfully underwent discontinuous change without the personal involvement of a chief executive who could do exceptional things in exceptional ways. In episodes of massive change at the enterprise level, CEOs assume a role that transcends their routine chores as head of the organization. These leaders become the psychological focal point for many of their employees; in an almost mystical way they become the personal embodiment of the institution, its values, its beliefs, and its future.

These are the people I describe as *mythic leaders,* a very special group of individuals who combine extraordinary clarity of vision and a single-minded sense of purpose with the ability to excite, energize, and win the loyalty of large groups of people. They create change through their ability to mobilize and sustain activity. They convince people that they are engaged in an important, exciting, and worthwhile mission. They come in all shapes and sizes, use drastically different styles, and sometimes defy conventional notions of the telegenic, central-casting type of executive. What they have in common is their ability to make a personal connection with large numbers of people and to share their confidence and vision in a dynamic, energizing way.

David Kearns, on the one hand, possessed the physical presence most of us normally associate with a mythic leader—classic good looks, a dynamic personality—a man who exuded energy wherever he went. Citibank's Walter Wriston, on the other hand, hardly looked the part—a large, hulking man with a nervous tic and a halting manner of speech. Nonetheless, he traveled the globe to meet and talk with Citibank employees and would leave them feeling they'd been part of a special experience. Somehow Wriston forged a special bond between himself and Citibank people, just as Kearns developed a unique relationship with tens of thousands of people at Xerox.

Despite their many differences, one characteristic shared by most mythic leaders is that they are essentially outsiders (Kotter and Heskett, 1992). Some are recruited from outside the organization for the express purpose of upsetting the traditional scheme of things. So you find David Kearns leading radical change at Xerox after spending much of his career at IBM; George Fisher leaving behind a brilliant career at Motorola to reshape Kodak; Bob Eaton, a lifelong GM employee, leading immensely successful change at Chrysler; and Lou Gerstner overhauling IBM after years with American Express, RJR Nabisco, and McKinsey & Company, Inc.

Two other categories of executives are neither total outsiders or classic insiders. The outside-insiders are the homegrown executives who spent much of their careers somewhere out on the periphery of the organization, far from the core of its operations and the heart of its culture. For example, Paul Allaire and Jamie

Houghton both spent years in their corporations' overseas operations and worked for a relatively short time in the core business before reaching the top. Then there are the inside-outsiders—nonemployees who have had some other affiliation with the organization they're asked to lead. Henry Schacht, for instance, while CEO of Cummins Engine served for more than a decade as an outside director of AT&T before being tapped to head Lucent Technologies. Randy Tobias was an AT&T executive who was an outside director of Eli Lilly for seven years before his fellow directors asked him to become CEO. "I think the view of the board was that I was probably the most 'inside' outsider that any company would ever have," Tobias says.

There are good reasons why it usually takes an outsider to engineer change. As I suggested earlier, people who have spent years in the mainstream of the organization's culture are unlikely to be the architects of its destruction—and that's particularly true for chief executives. At the very least they're bound to find that discontinuous change takes a heavy personal toll as they find themselves forced to behave in ways that run counter to what they've grown up believing—and counter to what their longtime colleagues expect of them. David Lawrence found that to be the case as he kept colliding with Kaiser Permanente's collegial culture—one that favored consensus over command and rarely dismissed underperformers.

"If you are a CEO who, like me, was a product of the organization rather than an outsider," Lawrence (1996) says, "it is difficult suddenly to begin treating people in ways that run counter to the culture that shaped and nurtured you."

But the reluctance to take radical measures involves more than perspective; it's often a problem of simply knowing too much. Executives who personally lived the organization's history, who were around "way back when" and understand why certain structures and processes were developed years ago, find it particularly hard to tear them apart. Moreover, although it's generally laudable to be familiar with your employees' personal situations, their spouses and children, their career aspirations, their dreams and disappointments, that familiarity can be a powerful obstacle to making some of the tough decisions that are unavoidable during periods of unsettling change.

I'm familiar with a publishing executive whose name was in play for the top job at the newspaper company where he had spent much of his career. Returning as the top executive would seem a pretty attractive prospect, but he knew otherwise. "I couldn't do it," he said. "Whoever comes in is going to have to clean house, and these are the people I grew up with. They have to get an outsider to do it." As it turned out, a lifelong insider was chosen for the job, and the long-overdue housecleaning has yet to materialize.

In one case after another "knowing too much" has kept people from taking drastic but necessary measures. It probably had much to do with the failure of Robert Stemple at GM and John Akers at IBM to satisfy their respective boards' demands for change, although either might have been considered a first-class CEO under other circumstances. In each case they were too much a part of the culture they needed to overhaul. In contrast, outsiders enter the fray blessed with ignorance, unburdened by the personal relationships and shared history that can be deterrents to decisive action at critical junctures.

In the remainder of this chapter I look further at the specific elements of mythic leadership that make leaders effective at guiding discontinuous change and also at some leadership traps. I show how mythic leadership is complemented by operational leadership, and finally, I talk about ways to expand the number of people who can take responsibility for leading change throughout the organization.

Mythic Leadership

For years management theorists have attempted to dissect the elements that go into making a *mythic* or *charismatic* or *heroic* leader, or whatever other term is chosen to describe leaders who possess that special combination of characteristics that sets them apart. French and Raven (1959) produced one of the classic pieces of research in this area, arguing that power—the ability to effectively influence others—is derived from five sources:

- *Legitimate power.* When we accept the legitimacy of a social system—be it a company, a club, a school, or a political jurisdiction—we accept the legitimate exercise of power by those to whom the system delegates authority. One of the clearest examples is the military, where individuals are expected to respond immediately to orders given by people they don't know, merely because of the insignia on their sleeves or shoulders.

- *Reward power.* We accept someone's exercise of power when they have the ability to give us something we want.
- *Punishment power.* Conversely, we acknowledge someone's power when they're likely to impose unpleasant sanctions of some kind if we don't,
- *Expert power.* We accept someone's power when we believe their expertise, in some important way, surpasses our own.
- *Referent power.* The leader has the power to influence us when we identify with the leader and want to be like him or her. When John F. Kennedy called upon Americans to start exercising and getting in shape, why did long hikes and touch football suddenly become popular? The president doesn't have the power to make people work out. He couldn't reward or punish us for it. People did it because they wanted to be like Kennedy, to identify with him.

The most effective leaders are those who have the personality and position to combine all five sources of power. Mythic leaders, however, seem to benefit as well from a particularly strong combination of expert and referent power. The two work together to create a multiplicative effect that greatly expands the leader's ability to influence people.

Extroversion

Another ingredient can be factored into the recipe for mythic leadership. These leaders can be smart, focused, energetic, articulate, even visionary—what they can't be is introverted. Indeed, nearly all of them possess some element of extroversion.

I remember a time in 1988 when I had arranged a meeting between the senior teams from Xerox and Corning, both of which were working through some similar organizational changes. David Kearns, Paul Allaire (then the president), three or four other Xerox senior executives, and I were in the airport waiting room before getting on the corporate shuttle between White Plains and

Rochester, and Kearns started working the room like a politician. He walked up to each and every person, introduced himself, and asked why they were going to Rochester that day. He left all the people in the lounge feeling that David Kearns was deeply interested in them and their work.

While Kearns was mingling with the troops, Paul Allaire grabbed a newspaper, sat down, and buried himself in it until it was time to board the plane. The contrast between the two men couldn't have been sharper.

A few years later when Allaire became CEO, I reminded him of that episode and suggested that although the number two could get by with that behavior, the CEO couldn't. Intellectually, Allaire was well aware of that. He also knew that even though it wasn't in his basic nature to walk up to strangers and strike up a conversation, he'd have to start working on it. So his personal assistant began structuring his appearances so that he had no choice but to interact with people and gradually grow more comfortable with his new role.

There's no doubt that some of the most successful mythic leaders have an innate dramatic flair—and more than a little touch of ham. Lee Iacocca is an obvious example, but many mythic leaders have an instinct for the inspirational speech, the memorable gesture, the unforgettable symbol. To those who witnessed it, one of the more remarkable examples was delivered by Norman Pearlstine in 1984, early in his tenure as top editor of the *Wall Street Journal*. (He later became editor-in-chief of Time Inc.)

At that time the *Journal*'s top editors and a few executives from its parent company, Dow Jones, would meet each year at a three- or four-day off-site management meeting, which traditionally concluded with the managing editor's annual address. The 1983 meeting was Pearlstine's first as managing editor, a position he'd reached as a classic outside-insider by virtue of his many years working outside New York. That first year he set forth his vision of change in an astounding three-and-a-half-hour extemporaneous talk. Insiders instantly dubbed it the Castro Speech, a derisive reference to the Cuban dictator's interminable stem-winders. A year later, as the managers gathered again, everyone was speculating on what Pearlstine would do for an encore to the Castro Speech.

In keeping with tradition, the final night of the meeting was celebrated with a raucous marathon party. At one point in the evening—or perhaps it was the early morning—Pearlstine performed a trick he'd been doing at parties for years: he removed his shoes and socks and proceeded to peel a banana with his toes, an astounding act of dexterity and a telling trademark for an executive who clearly wasn't cut from the traditional mold of *Journal* editors.

The next morning, the hung-over and bleary-eyed managers straggled into the auditorium for the managing editor's speech, but Pearlstine was nowhere in sight. As people began wondering whether Pearlstine was in any shape to make an appearance, martial music suddenly began blaring from loudspeakers. The rear doors swung open, and Pearlstine—dressed in Castro-style military fatigues and wearing a fake beard—strode to the podium, and the hall was suddenly alive with cheers. He climbed the stairs to the stage, marched to the podium, and held his arms aloft to accept the applause. Finally, the room quieted down. Pearlstine gazed around the room, stroked his fake beard, reached into his tunic.

Slowly, he pulled out a banana, held it up for the crowd to see, and then placed it on the lectern.

The place went wild.

Without saying a word—in fact, few who were there can remember anything about his subsequent speech—Pearlstine had crossed the invisible boundary into the realm of mythic leadership with a marvelous display of self-confidence, theatricality, and self-effacing humor. It was a stunning bit of stagecraft, the kind of grand gesture of which some leaders are capable and some just are not.

And yet—and this is what's so intriguing about mythic leaders—on the other end of the continuum you find a Paul Allaire. No one has ever accused him of being flashy or extroverted. In fact, *Fortune* magazine in 1996 went so far as to include Allaire on a list of twelve CEOs who were notable for their lack of charisma (Sellers, 1996). Nonetheless, Allaire engineered and led some of the most fundamental change any major corporation has seen in recent decades. Clearly, matters of style and personality are only the roughest indicators of a leader's capacity to produce change on a grand scale.

Shared Characteristics

Given their range of personalities, styles, and backgrounds, what exactly is it that mythic leaders do that makes them so effective? Over the years I've closely examined the CEOs with whom I've worked and carefully observed many others, searching for patterns. What I found was that their shared characteristics seem to fall into three broad categories (see Figure 13.1).

Envisioning

Mythic leaders share an ability to articulate a compelling vision, one that excites and captures the imagination of their people. At Corning, Jamie Houghton painted an engrossing picture of a future in which Corning would be one of the most competent, profitable, and respected corporations in the entire world. Scott McNealy successfully portrayed Sun Microsystems to his employees as "the guys with the white hats," the champions of an information world where people would be free to choose from a range of vendors rather than held captive by a single, all-powerful megacorporation. (In case you missed it, that's Microsoft McNealy's talking about.) Often the vision these leaders articulate includes extremely high expectations, so high they often seem unattainable.

Figure 13.1. Shared Characteristics of Mythic Leadership.

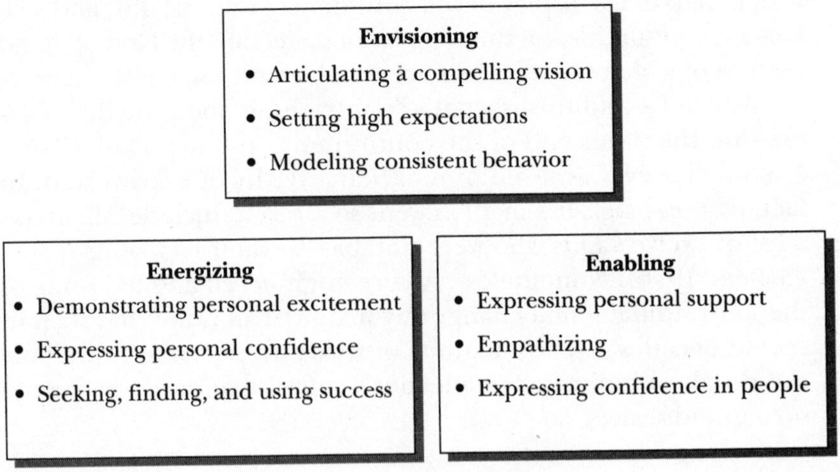

Envisioning
- Articulating a compelling vision
- Setting high expectations
- Modeling consistent behavior

Energizing
- Demonstrating personal excitement
- Expressing personal confidence
- Seeking, finding, and using success

Enabling
- Expressing personal support
- Empathizing
- Expressing confidence in people

And yet those are the expectations and goals that truly energize their people. Finally, their actions are consistent with their words. If their vision includes unparalleled attention to customer needs, then they spend a huge amount of their own time with customers. If their vision involves empowerment and teamwork, then they find ways to let their senior teams make important decisions in their absence.

Energizing

Almost universally these leaders energize their followers by demonstrating their own personal sense of excitement. I once accompanied David Kearns on a trip to Japan, and on the flight back I had to get up and switch seats with him several times. Why? Because whenever Kearns got excited—and he saw things on that trip that had fully engaged his excitement and enthusiasm—he couldn't stop himself from continually jabbing his listener's shoulder as he made his points. "We've gotta go back and do that!" he'd say, jabbing for emphasis. There was no way one shoulder could take that outpouring of excitement for an entire thirteen-hour flight.

Bob Lipp demonstrated a similar level of excitement while he headed up Chemical Bank's consumer banking operation in the early 1980s. He'd get up in front of his managers and talk about taking on giant competitor Citibank on the battleground of neighborhood banks. "It's gonna be fun!" he'd exhort his bank executives. "It's gonna be fun! And we're gonna win!"

In addition, mythic leaders typically energize their people by constantly expressing personal confidence in ultimate success, rarely—if ever—allowing any hint that they harbor doubts. That's tremendously important. During periods of upheaval and uncertainty, everyone is constantly looking to the leader for reassurance, asking themselves, If he's not confident about how this is going to turn out, why should I be? And the fact is that successful change leaders, after going through a period of questioning and soul searching, finally decide upon a course of action and commit themselves to it without the slightest reservation. They have the ability, once they've decided to follow a path, never to look back.

Finally, mythic leaders energize people by endlessly seeking, finding, and using instances of success. Bob Lipp used to say, "I'm going to look for upticks." If he found a branch bank that had done something—anything—particularly well, he'd be on his way out there to throw a party for the employees. Like other leaders of his type, he constantly looked for ways to celebrate and display people's successes as a way to build their confidence and sense of accomplishment.

Enabling

In addition to showing people where they ought to be going and energizing them to start the journey, mythic leaders also help them along the way. They do this in a number of ways: expressing their personal support, demonstrating confidence in the organization's ability to reach its goals, and empathizing with people during the difficult times. Sometimes that means telling people, "I understand what you're up against. I know you're out there and competing against outfits that have more money and more people than you do. But I believe in you. I know you can do this." Enabling can't end with empathy, however; when it's warranted and possible, leaders also find ways to give people the resources they need to do what the leaders have asked.

Henry Schacht is a great believer in this leadership role. "You can't just say 'do it harder' without telling people why you think it's possible," Schacht says. "Exhortation only gets you so far. . . . What happens in so many situations where people have tried to bring about change through exhortation is that the exhorter is in a very different position from the person hearing the exhortation. And if the person who's hearing it doesn't have a clue what to do, then the person who's using exhortation as a leadership mechanism isn't likely to be very effective."

At the same time leaders are urging people to do better, Schacht believes, they have to help people figure out how to do it by asking, "What are your alternatives? What's in the way? What's blocking you? How can I help?"

Traps of Mythic Leadership

Having explained why mythic leaders are essential to successful change, now I have to balance out the picture. Mythic leadership almost inevitably creates its own set of special problems.

Unrealistic expectations. People frequently imbue the mythic leader with powers and capabilities that are just unreasonable. Though the leader's public persona may take on heroic proportions, the fact is that he or she is still quite human and fully capable of making occasional mistakes. Given enough time, even a Lee Iacocca demonstrates an inability to leap tall buildings in a single bound.

Misdirected psychological responses. Mythic leaders stimulate a response known in psychological terms as *transference*. People within the organization often transfer to the leader their personal feelings about authority figures, sometimes replicating their childhood relationships with parents, teachers, or other authority figures. This transference generally take one of two forms, reflecting the tenor of those personal feelings: some people become overly dependent upon the leader, unable to act without his or her perceived permission or direct orders; others become *counterdependent,* irrationally resisting the power of the authority figure.

Stifled dissent. People desperately seeking leaders' approval are reluctant to disagree with them or give them bad news. It's not really a question of fearing punishment or harmful repercussions; rather they just don't want to risk introducing any negative elements into the relationship. They simply want leaders to like them and feel comfortable with them.

Growing expectations. The leader who captivates the organization with seemingly magical accomplishments gets caught in the trap of having to create more and more magic. After a while, the organizational audience becomes jaded, in effect telling the leader, "I saw that trick already. Do something new." After a while that becomes a tall order for any executive to fill.

Feelings of betrayal. One of mythic leaders' great strengths lies in their ability to convince people of their absolute conviction that if others follow the course the leader has set, things will get better. The moment things go wrong, then, feelings of anger and betrayal begin to surface. People who believed in the leader's vision and promises react bitterly. David Kearns used to say, "When things go well, I'm not the hero people think I am—I'm not that smart—and when things go wrong, I'm not as bad as they think I am."

Disenfranchisement of management. As the mythic leader's regime starts taking on the overtones of a personality cult, other managers begin to feel their power draining away. I recall a session with Corning executives where the universal complaint was that they felt like go-betweens, not managers. Nothing they did seemed to carry any weight unless people believed the instructions were coming directly from Jamie Houghton.

Operational Leadership

Given enough time, mythic leadership in any organization will inevitably create some combination of these traps. Consequently, in successful change situations, after a while a second form of leader emerges. This is the *operational* leader (sometimes titled the chief operating officer), a person who generally serve as the mythic leader's number two. While the mythic leader focuses on generating and sustaining excitement, the operational leader shapes an environment that motivates people to work and behave in ways that support the change agenda. The operational leader's priority is to oversee processes and systems that make it clear to everyone that the required behavior is also instrumental to achieving their personal goals.

The work of operational leaders falls into three basic categories. First, they create structures, build processes, and monitor the systems essential to the organization's performing its work. Second, they make sure the reward systems are effectively reinforcing the desired behavior and performance. Finally, they direct the essential control functions, constantly monitoring organizational performance in relation to the articulated objectives.

Together, the mythic and operational leaders complement each other. Both are endowed with power by virtue of their formal positions in the organization—that is, they have legitimate power. In addition, however, mythic leaders derive much of their influence from expert power and referent power, the desire of others to emulate and be associated with them, whereas operational leaders' influence is strongly reinforced by their power to reward and punish. Mythic leaders, as a general rule, don't spend much time on those functions, in large part because they'd much rather be out giving speeches, connecting with employees and customers, and extending their influence in direct and personal ways.

It's possible for these two forms of leadership to emerge sequentially: a mythic leader initiates change, then is succeeded by an operational leader who consolidates it. In the most effective situations, the operational leader emerges in the number two role a year or two after change has begun, and both leaders remain in place simultaneously for a period of time. Strong operational leaders leverage the strengths of mythic leaders, allowing them to spend the bulk of their time on the things they do best—envisioning change, articulating goals, and energizing people to achieve those goals.

Moreover, there are certain things mythic leaders generally don't do well, such as dealing face-to-face with people in unpleasant situations. Most mythic leaders are narcissistic, sometimes to extreme degrees. It's why they love getting up in front of crowds and basking in the applause. It's why they feel compelled to win people over and to want everyone to like them. It also accounts for their frequent ineptitude at firing people or giving them bad news in person. In the worst cases this behavior results in a backlash and a sense of mistrust. Word gets around that people leave the leader's office feeling great, only to find that someone else has been assigned to follow behind and perform the unpleasant deed. With good reason, people start to feel betrayed. In those situations it's better for everyone to have the operational leader handle the unpleasant tasks right up front.

In short, both kinds of leaders are essential to the success of any large-scale change. Nearly all the changes I've discussed in this book have involved this kind of partnership—Jamie Houghton and Roger Ackerman at Corning, David Kearns and Paul Allaire at Xerox, Randy Tobias and Sydney Taurel at Eli Lilly.

For mythic leaders at some point, the issue of managing change becomes the question of succession. Assuming they want their operational second in command to follow them into the top post, they need to help that person work on developing some of the character traits exemplified by the mythic leader. The good news is that it can be done. For example, despite some of the introverted tendencies he displayed as president, Paul Allaire as CEO has proven to be as strong a leader as Kearns was in terms of his personal connection with the people at Xerox.

Extended Leadership

Organizations with an effective combination of leaders in the top two positions will still have a leadership problem, however, if power is effectively concentrated only in those two people. The mythic leader is limited by the need to make personal contact. People at Citibank may well have been energized by their meetings with Walt Wriston, but they might have seen him only once every year and a half. People loved meeting and shaking hands with Jamie Houghton, but he was out on the road visiting forty to fifty Corning locations around the world each year. By the same token, the operational leader is limited by the need to observe and control behavior. In a large complex organization it's physically impossible for him or her to observe everything and everyone.

So it becomes imperative for the top team to construct human and structural extensions of their leadership (Figure 13.2 compares mythic leadership, operational leadership, and extended leadership). They have to find ways to institutionalize their vision, objectives, standards, and operating policies. Here are three ways in which effective organizations have extended their leadership, and some specific techniques for accomplishing each.

Figure 13.2. Leadership of Change.

Mythic Leadership	Envisioning	Energizing	Enabling
Operational Leadership	Structuring	Rewarding	Controlling
Extended Leadership	Leveraging the Senior Team	Broadening Senior Management	Developing Leadership in the Organization

Leverage the Executive Team

If the top leaders have reached the conclusion that they need to reduce the organization's dependence on them as individuals, then they have to develop an effective, visible, and dynamic executive team, consisting of the people who report directly to the CEO and the chief operating officer, to assume some of the leadership roles. Here are six techniques for doing that.

1. *Visible empowerment.* The top leaders have to find ways to let others see the top team making important decisions in their absence. For example, the team might perform periodic operations reviews without the CEO or COO in the room. At a company where major internal announcements were in the form of videotaped announcements by the CEO played at regional staff meetings, our firm encouraged the CEO to periodically substitute videos featuring two or three executive team members, without any visible involvement by the CEO.

2. *Staffing.* The CEO makes sure the executive team consists of people who are widely perceived to be valued and trusted by him or her.

3. *Individual development.* Each member of the team is given specific opportunities to develop his or her leadership skills. One way is to give each an assignment that allows that person to be the internal champion of some aspect of the change.

4. *Strategic planning.* The executive team is made the focal point for strategic planning. When asked how Corning does its strategy work, Roger Ackerman says, "We have no strategy staff, no strategy office. The management committee is the strategy office."

5. *Collective learning.* The leaders use the executive team as a tool for organizational learning, actively involving team members in activities that constantly sharpen their external focus.

6. *Focus on team consequences.* Leaders turn their teams into cohesive units by structuring rewards on the basis of collective rather than individual performance. Corning did this in the 1980s by developing a performance bonus that paid handsomely if the entire company met its goals for stock performance and return on equity. And those potential bonuses far outweighed any rewards team members could hope for based on their particular unit's

performance and that led to new behavior. I clearly recall an off-site planning session when the Corning senior team was sitting around after Jamie Houghton had gone to bed, discussing the problems at its most troubled unit. (That in itself marked a sharp departure from the days when these executives wouldn't have dreamed of openly discussing their internal problems.) John Loose, then in charge of Corning's television unit, spoke up and offered to transfer two of his people to the troubled unit. "How can you do that?" asked the executive he was addressing. "Those are two of your best guys."

"I know," Loose said. "But I can get by."

"But why would you be willing to lose two of your best people?" he was asked.

"Look," Loose explained. "I love Nantucket. We've been going up there for a long time, and we've got this little house. Now I've got an option on a beautiful piece of property that I want to build a house on. The only way I can do that is if the bonus plan pays off. I want that house. You can have the guys."

The underlying concept was clear: it was much more important for the entire organization to meet its goals than for one unit to look good in relation to the others. The epilogue to the story is that the company met its goals, huge bonuses were paid, and today there's a gorgeous new house on Nantucket called Loose Ends.

Broaden Senior Management

As I described earlier, I've been in situations where executives earning several hundred thousand dollars a year, people with thousands of employees reporting to them, would couch their complaints in such terms as, "They're doing this to us," or, "They just don't understand." My reaction was, "Who is *they* ? I thought *you* were senior management." There's no way top leaders can expect executives who are feeling disenfranchised to that degree to effectively lead others.

If you could get everyone in your organization out into the parking lot and then ask all those in senior management to raise their hands, typically you'd see only three or four people respond. Ideally, in a large organization you'd like to see one hundred or two hundred people who sincerely believe, "I'm part of the leadership here. I understand what's happening. I'm signed on. My job is to lead people rather than to sit here and worry about whether I'm going to be the next victim."

So the task of top leadership is to bring these people into the fold by extending senior management out to the next circle—and possible two circles—beyond the CEO's direct reports. Corning, for instance, had a management committee of eight people. Then it formed the Corporate Policy Group with thirty people who met four or five times a year for several days at a time. Then Houghton appointed the Corporate Management Group of more than two hundred people who met once a year. The members of this large group began to feel they were indeed a part of top management, that they were in the know and privy to the important things going on in the organization. In effect they became the human extensions of Houghton's leadership.

These are some techniques for broadening the senior management group:

- Create clearly defined senior management groups beyond the existing senior team (such as those used by Corning).
- Celebrate rites of passage; turn appointments to the senior groups into major events.
- Get the members of these management groups actively involved in planning organizational change. (It was these groups Houghton used to develop the list of Corning's core values for example.)
- Communicate with the groups regularly and intensively; make sure they have more information than the organization at large and make sure the communication goes both ways—make them active participants rather than just passive listeners.
- Involve the groups in important processes such as making strategy, dealing with human resources, and budgeting.
- If necessary, flatten the organizational structure to include more people in senior management.

Develop Leadership Within the Organization

Think about Corning or Xerox or AT&T or any large organization where there are literally thousands of managers, each supervising his or her own team or department. To the employees who report to them, those managers *are* Corning and Xerox and AT&T. Certainly, they know that Houghton or Allaire or Allen or some executive is in charge of the entire operation. But in terms of their daily interrelationship with the organization, leadership is embodied in their immediate bosses. And if you ask them a question like, How is Corning treating you? the answer you get back will reveal their attitude toward their manager, not their CEO.

So if the vision, enthusiasm, and standards of the top leaders are truly to become embedded in the mind and the soul of the organization, then managers at every level must understand and embrace the essence of the new enterprise. They need to understand where it is headed strategically, how work will be structured, what they as managers will be expected to do and how they'll be expected to behave, and how they can earn rewards and career advancement.

However, in a typical change situation you have to assume also that the old processes and systems that guide and control behavior are still in place. Existing managers are creatures of the old organization; you can't expect them to be the spawning grounds for an entirely new style of management. Indeed, you need to find new managers and, when possible, reeducate those already in place so they know how to replace antiquated processes. Again, there are several ways to accomplish this (see Figure 13.2).

1. *Define managerial competence in new ways.* More specifically, define it in terms of the new strategy, structure, and culture that top management is trying to implement. This is exactly what Xerox did when it developed its list of twenty-three characteristics essential for anyone filling a management position. For example, one factor that used to be one of the most accurate predictors of managerial success at Xerox was "personal drive." Now the best predictor is a high rating for "cross-unit cooperation and teamwork," an important indication that the company has substantively altered its definition of managerial competence.

2. *Seek out managerial talent.* Because most of the obvious candidates for management positions during the early stages of change will have been trained and nurtured in accordance with the old ways of developing leaders, it's almost always necessary to look for managerial talent in new and different places, both within

and outside the organization. In many situations there's just not enough time to meet all the needs for management talent by growing managers inside; it becomes both essential and advantageous to bring in talent from other places. Moreover, once appropriate outsiders and nontraditional insiders have been identified, recall that it's important to seed them strategically throughout the organization in places where they can have the greatest impact. Frequently, that means having enough of them concentrated together so that they not only support each other against the traditional forces resisting change but join forces to create a critical mass of energy and support for the top leaders and their change agenda.

3. *Provide socialization.* It's always important for organizations to socialize new managers brought in from the outside, to expose them to the norms, values, and practices of their new workplace. For managers brought in during change episodes, that socialization process has to be even more explicit than usual; they have to fully understand the culture they've been hired to create. That's particularly important because there will be so much pressure on them to accept and adapt to the old culture that will still be much in evidence. In these cases recall that the socialization process gets tricky; you want the new managers to fit in, but you don't want them to fit in so well that they lose their value as agents of change.

4. *Provide management education.* All managers must be given ample opportunity to gain the new understanding, knowledge, and skills necessary to succeed in the new organization. I'm not talking about one or two seminars. Management education requires sustained activities of different kinds over a period of time. First, there should be specific activities to help people understand the new strategy, environment, and management model. They also need lots of constant feedback, so they know to what extent they're succeeding. One particularly effective effort I've observed was at Citibank; there, with the help of Forum Corporation of Boston, the company took a close look at its most effective managers and extrapolated a list of twenty-six practices that seemed to characterize them. Then every manager went through training on those twenty-six points, with periodic feedback from subordinates. At the same time, managers were attending seminars on marketing, growth, systems technology, and other vital issues. In effect, these managers were bombarded with continual learning.

5. *Provide new career management.* Although specific education and training events are important, much of a manager's most important learning comes from experience. In organizations undergoing discontinuous change the old career paths typically fail to provide managers with the range of experiences they'll need to be effective—and personally successful—in the new environment. So it's crucial during these transition periods for top management to expose managers as widely as possible to the fullest range of managerial assignments in different settings, such as teams, task forces, and cross-functional groups, rather than just funneling managers through the traditional succession of incrementally more responsible but otherwise similar jobs.

The ultimate goal, then, is to project ever-expanding concentric circles of leadership that spread and sustain a consistent message of change to every corner of the organization. The true test of leaders is not their ability to generate a short burst of excitement or to generate intense loyalty among a small number of devoted followers. Instead, their long-term effectiveness is measured by their ability to create lasting change by developing legions of leaders at all levels who understand, internalize, and communicate a shared vision of the changed organization.

Chapter Fourteen

Learning to Lead Change
The New Principles for CEOs and Companies

No organization I've ever seen has started out, from day one, doing major change just right. It's impossible. There are too many variables, too many moving targets, too much information to collect and digest, too many techniques to try out and refine. There's just a lot to learn.

By the same token, no CEO, business unit president, division chief, department head—you name it—has ever moved up to a more responsible job and started work the first morning with a full understanding of the concepts and a total grasp of the techniques required to do the new job. There's a reason people always talk about the learning curve faced by someone in a new position.

Learning—both individual and organizational—is at the core of leading change. The champions of change I've been talking about throughout this book are people who have opened their minds to learning from every new change experience. Beyond that, they understand the importance of helping the people around them—both individually and collectively—benefit from the same kind of learning. They also understand that learning doesn't just happen; there's nothing automatic about it. Learning, both on the individual and organizational scale, is a deliberate process.

I begin this chapter by talking about individual learning and about the role of managers. Certainly, much of the material I've presented in this book deals with the roles, responsibilities, and actions of those senior executives who have the primary responsibility for driving radical organizational change because I believe those insights are essential to managers at any level who are interested in understanding the dynamics of change. In the process, I've talked about concepts and techniques that can be applied throughout the organization, not just at the very top. At the same time, I hope I've made it clear that elitist, exclusionary change processes won't work in large, complex organizations. There are important decisions to be made and actions to be taken by managers at every level, and I reiterate key ideas from various parts of the book to focus on managerial learning here.

After that, I turn to learning from an organizational perspective. Successful organizations make change work by engaging themselves in a continuous process of collective learning—of experimenting with new ideas, products, and processes; analyzing both successes and failures; and using that new knowledge to reexamine practices and beliefs in order to replicate what worked and avoid repeating what didn't. So I also examine how effective organizations turn collective learning into a source of competitive advantage.

Finally, I demonstrate that most of the concepts in this book revolve around five basic principles that together encapsulate the essence of integrated change. I pull together the threads that are interwoven throughout the book and articulate the principles that can be learned and used as guideposts for change.

Managerial Roles and Learning

If you're among those who entered the workforce more than ten years ago—indeed, even if you started working within the past decade—there's a good chance that your formative notions about work and careers were spawned by a world that no longer exists.

Those traditional expectations all rested upon a presumption of stability. The classic career plan was to find a prosperous company with good prospects, one whose values and beliefs were consistent with your own, where the people and the atmosphere and the pace made you feel comfortable. Then, if you worked hard, performed well, mastered the essentials of office politics, and were loyal to your employer, you could reasonably expect to get your ticket punched in a clearly defined succession of jobs that would bring incremental increases in responsibility, status, and financial rewards.

Now consider that scenario in light of the competitive environment I've been talking about throughout this book. Maybe somewhere out there are isolated enclaves of stability, cut off from the flow of history like the marooned Japanese soldiers who hid in the jungles of the South Pacific long after the conclusion of World War II. Rest assured that if such places exist, it's only a matter of time before the inevitability of change catches up with them.

The only certainty now is uncertainty. Today's market leaders are tomorrow's also-rans. Cutting-edge technology becomes obsolete overnight. Companies are traded back and forth like baseball cards. Changes at the top produce disruption and instability. One restructuring follows another. Jobs are lost. Hierarchies are flattened. Strategies, objectives, and processes are tossed out the window and replaced. New owners and new management bring new values and beliefs, new people, new roles and requirements for managers.

All of us can and should count on all those things happening in our own working lives—and not just once, but two, three, or four times if we stay with the same organization. In the end there is only one guarantee: nothing will stay the same.

For executives running the organization and driving change, the issues are challenging and complex. For managers at every level within organizations buffeted by change, the issues are intensely personal. In their minds the arrival of a new regime or the adoption of sweeping change, by definition, means someone upstairs is questioning the skill, judgment, and effectiveness of the stewards of the status quo. It's only human for managers to react to these upheavals with emotions ranging from anger, resentment, and betrayal to fear, insecurity, and a sense of self-doubt. Their deeply held assumptions of how careers should work has been shattered; their years of loyalty, hard work, and success suddenly count for nothing.

For managers, then, the issue of change involves profound choices. The first major decision is whether to stay or go. There are situations in which the manager finds the new direction, leadership, job requirements, and operating environment so much in conflict with his or her own beliefs that it's in everyone's best interests for that manager to leave, if that's an option. Recall the Xerox executive who, upon hearing for the first time about the plan to massively restructure the company, said, "The only way I could do it [manage in that situation] is if you gave me a lobotomy." Even though the new structure apparently worked, given Xerox's impressive results since it was instituted, that doesn't mean it was the right situation for him to remain in as a senior manager, given his own deeply held ideas about how to manage. From that perspective, his personal decision to leave properly acknowledged the fundamental and irreconcilable clash between his beliefs and those of the company.

In the majority of cases, however, managers probably won't consider the impending changes abhorrent, repugnant, or disastrous—just different, unsettling, and perhaps a little scary. At that point managers must look within themselves and develop their own personal strategies. They must arrive at a firm conclusion about what kind of leadership role they intend to play. They must decide whether to think of themselves as authors, participants, or victims of change.

Obviously, the most effective managers are those who decide to take an active leadership role in implementing the new vision of change. In Beckhard's terms, they are the ones who "make it happen" rather than those who passively "let it happen." And at the managerial level, leading change involves three basic requirements. It's no coincidence that all three match the requirements faced by the ultimate leaders of change, the CEO, and the senior team.

First, the manager should constantly demonstrate behavior consistent with the change. It's not enough to tell other people to spend more time with customers, take risks, or improve their teamwork skills; the manager has to be seen and heard doing those exact same things. The manager, in short, has got to walk the talk.

Second, the manager has got to help other people understand the change. Periods of radical change are characterized by message clutter, leaving everyone confused, anxious, and desperate to get answers to the question, What does this mean for me? An important variant of that is, What do you want from me? People eagerly look for signals telling them how they're supposed to act, what they're supposed to do. It's the manager's job to help them understand how they'll be affected and what their new role should be.

The third element of leadership at the managerial level is rewarding people for demonstrating the new behavior or performance the change requires. Indeed, reinforcing appropriate behavior is even more important than usual in change situations. Not only does it support and energize the person who's rewarded, but it's also one of the most effective ways to send clear signals to others about how to succeed in the new environment.

Change Management Practices

In more concrete terms, managers at all levels can solidify their role as active supporters and drivers of change through a number of day-to-day leadership practices (see Figure 14.1).

Owning

Successful managers do everything possible to publicly demonstrate their active personal involvement in the change process. At all costs they want to avoid conveying the impression to their own people that the change is something "those guys upstairs" have imposed upon the managers against their will. Managers who are perceived as grudgingly carrying out the will of others lose the confidence of their superiors, weaken their own stature among their subordinates, and put themselves in the counterproductive position of passively resisting inevitable change. Instead, they should do everything possible to identify themselves with the change and the executives who are pushing it. This period is crucial; this is when managers must seize the opportunity to become

Figure 14.1. Change Management Practices.

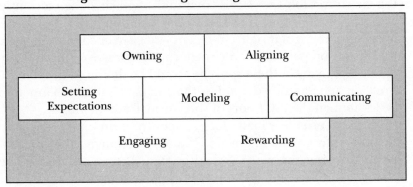

the owners of change, rather than its potential victims. To succeed, they must go through several steps.

To begin with, managers can't own the change if they don't really understand it. So they must first make an investment in learning, committing whatever time and intellectual energy are necessary to fully understand every aspect of the change. That means learning why the status quo was unacceptable, what strategic concepts are at the core of change, how the structure and culture of the organization will have to change. It means undergoing a personal version of guided discovery, replicating the process senior management pursued in its development of the change strategy.

Once managers fully understand the change, then they have to buy in on both an intellectual and emotional level. This is the point at which managers have to decide if they're on board and if they're willing to make a total commitment. I realize this advice may sound suspiciously like the slogans on those motivational posters sold in in-flight magazines, but take my word for it: there's no way successful managers can be disengaged or halfhearted about change. The moment managers demonstrate any hesitation or the slightest sign of skepticism, their ability to lead others is seriously impaired.

Managers have to articulate the essence of the change in a clear, concise, and consistent way. Years ago managers at Xerox used to practice what was then a fairly novel technique: the *elevator speech.* The premise was that if managers found themselves in an elevator with someone who asked, "So what's this quality thing all about, anyway?" they'd have thirty seconds between the lobby and the third floor to explain it in a nutshell. The managers—and top executives too—took this communication challenge seriously, videotaping their practice sessions and critiquing each other's delivery until they got it right. In recent years I've encountered more and more companies that use the term *elevator speech,* but unfortunately, not many of these speeches could be delivered in their entirety on an elevator ride, unless the company's offices happen to be located on the top floors of the World Trade Center.

Finally, effective managers concentrate on expressing and demonstrating personal ownership of the change. They make a point of using the word *we* rather than *they* in discussing the change, and they find appropriate opportunities to express their support for it.

Aligning

As strategic change at the executive level begins filtering down throughout the organization, effective managers make sure there is a clear alignment between their people's work and the new direction. This involves a concept sometimes described as the *golden thread*. In quality management there's an explicit policy deployment process; at each level, managers take the set of general objectives developed at the level above them and then make them specific to their own unit's work. At each successive level, the objectives become narrower and more specific, but if they're done correctly, there's still a direct link to the companywide objectives. When you get down to the end of the process, every employee should still be able to identify the golden thread running directly from the CEO's change agenda to his or her individual objectives. It's the job of managers to direct and energize their own people's work by constantly reinforcing the direct connection between their own efforts and the organization's overall direction.

Setting Expectations

As the new organizational hardware and software take shape, it's up to managers to make them work—and work together. This is the time when managers must clearly articulate new goals for their people, being as explicit as possible. In Chapter Thirteen I devoted considerable attention to the issue of institutionalizing leadership, of extending the CEO's agenda through ever-widening concentric rings of influence. This is where that process fails or succeeds. It's up to each manager to capture, focus, and boost the important signals coming down the line from the executive office. That means setting tough performance objectives that require people to stretch their skills, knowledge, and abilities. It means clarifying expectations of how people are expected to behave in the new operating environment. And in particular it means paying special attention to clarifying expectations for the next level of managers, who need to perform the same functions with their people.

Modeling

As people begin to better understand precisely what kind of behavior is expected of them in the changed organization, it becomes doubly important for managers to exhibit that behavior with absolute consistency. Most important, behavior has to be consistent with the values the organization has identified as the core of the new culture. A manager can't espouse "respect for the individual" as a lofty organizational value and then turn around and treat support staff as second-class citizens. Integrity, customer focus, teamwork—they're all values that managers can and should use as guides to their day-to-day behavior. Managers who do that not only contribute to further embedding those values in the culture of the organization, but they more closely link themselves to the new culture and its leadership. Inconsistency, in contrast, feeds both cultural confusion and cynicism among people, who begin to view managers as hypocrites.

Communicating

Effective managers, particularly during change periods, are effective communicators. They understand that during these turbulent change periods, people are desperate for information. Deprived of it, they will fill the void with rumors, gossip, and horror stories about impending changes that tend to be much worse than anything managers are really considering. Backstairs talk is always inevitable, but the best way to control it is by giving people as much information as possible. Effective managers also understand that what we often think of as communication is really a one-way flow of information, not a back-and-forth exchange that fully engages the interest and ideas of all concerned. Accordingly, they look for ways to develop genuine communication, in which information is traveling in both directions. Finally, managers should keep in mind that it's just as important to communicate up as down, making sure their supervisors are kept fully informed about staff's concerns, triumphs, and expectations.

Engaging

Communication is important but not sufficient. Effective managers look for ways to fully engage their people in shaping their own environment within the framework of the overall change agenda. These managers actively involve people in planning new directions and implementing change at their level. They give their people the freedom and resources to pursue the new objectives. They empower people to act, and give them support and encouragement as they work to develop new skills, acquire new knowledge, and exhibit new behavior.

Rewarding

Effective managers always make it a priority to reward people for demonstrating the desired performance and behavior. That's never more important than during a change situation when people tend to be frustrated, confused, and on the lookout for any positive sign that they're headed in the right direction. Rewards, particularly well-publicized ones, make it clear to people not only what the new requirements are but also that they are achievable and that managers understand and appreciate the effort people are putting forth. At the same time, it's also crucial to monitor activities more closely than usual and impose timely sanctions in cases where people are clearly ignoring or resisting the requirements of change.

The Importance of Managerial Learning

Clearly, managers can't hope to direct, encourage, and sustain their people in all the ways I've just described unless they've personally undergone an individual transformation by learning, understanding, and internalizing what the change is all about. That kind of personal change is enormously difficult and generally involves overcoming some serious obstacles.

The first set of roadblocks can be categorized as external barriers to learning. Breaking these down is the responsibility of the more senior people in the organization. Inadequate training, inconsistent rewards, budgeting processes that undercut the new agenda, leadership models that reinforce old priorities—all these can critically impede a manager's ability to learn and digest new goals, objectives, and ways of behaving.

The second set of obstacles consists of internal barriers to learning—problems such as the following that are within each manager's power to control and overcome:

Knowledge. As I said earlier, it's the manager's responsibility to invest whatever time and effort are necessary to fully understand the change—the changing environment, the implications of not changing, the organizational and cultural characteristics that have to change—and how they must change.

Skills. New strategies, structures, work processes, and operating environments almost always require new managerial skills. In more and more organizations the command-and-control drill sergeant style of management has been discredited and discarded. Now organizations need people who excel at thinking and acting strategically, leading teams, resolving conflicts, and empowering subordinates. Few of us are born knowing how to do those things well; successful managers have to make a conscious effort to learn them.

Emotions. Managers naturally have strong emotional ties to the vanishing organization. It's likely that they were initially attracted to and then nurtured by a set of organizational values and beliefs, which they probably internalized over time. The decision to become fully engaged in the changed organization involves an implicit decision to become emotionally detached from the old one.

Inertia. Management, like most human behavior, becomes a matter of habit. With the passage of time, people simply get used to managing in certain ways. Consequently, managers mastering a dramatically different management style must not only learn new knowledge and skills and make emotional adjustments—they must break old habits. This fact was addressed in a particularly touching way in the film shown to all Xerox employees as the company launched its quality-based change in the mid-1980s. Earlier I mentioned the service technician who was seen in the film explaining how he wanted to do a good job for customers but his supervisor's priorities were getting in the way. Another scene then showed the service tech's supervisor at home over the weekend, tinkering with his motorcycle and talking about the changes going on at work. He says it's finally dawning on him that he's going to have to start doing some things differently, and he doesn't know if he can because he's managed people the same way throughout his entire career. "I'm going to try," he says, "but I don't know if I can do it." It's a particularly poignant scene, and one that struck a responsive chord among many of the managers who viewed it.

Consider Sydney Taurel, chief operating officer of Eli Lilly. A classic operational leader, Taurel came to understand that his penchant for what some considered micromanaging was inconsistent with changing management styles at the company. So he arose at a meeting of the company's managers to make it clear that he had gotten the message—that he had to change the way he did things. "I'm going to get less detail-oriented," he announced, prompting an outpouring of cheers and applause from the managers—extremely strong feedback, you could say.

All that's fine, but if you're Syd Taurel, how do you suddenly change after a lifetime of managing in one particular way? Change and learning are inseparable concepts. Change is impossible without learning; effective learning invariably results in change. To summarize, then, these are the steps managers need to go through in aggressively engaging themselves in the change process:

- Understand the change.
- Be open to change.
- Make both a personal and public commitment to the change.
- Observe others, learn from role models.
- Experiment with new behaviors.
- Gain feedback.
- Use that new learning to make continuous improvement.

Another way of describing that process is the learning cycle, a concept refined by David Kolb (1984) into these steps:

- *Active experimentation.* Based on available knowledge, skills, information, values, and beliefs, the individual attempts a new process or form of behavior.
- *Observation and feedback.* The individual actively seeks all available forms of assessment of the initial activity.
- *Reflection.* The individual analyzes the results of the experiment and the relative feedback, analyzing what went well and what didn't.
- *Insight and planning new actions.* In the light of feedback, analysis, and reflection, the individual plans how to incorporate what has been learned into the next experiment.
- *Experiment again.*

As the next section illustrates, organizations—successful ones, at any rate—go through a very similar learning cycle as large numbers of people collectively prepare themselves for organizational change and then go about mastering the new skills and requirements they're expected to learn.

Organizational Learning

To a great extent I've been talking about successful change in terms of the roles to be played by certain key individuals. Mythic and operational leaders have to initiate, guide, and propel the change. The senior team must be actively involved in planning and implementing it. Managers up and down the line have to enlist in the cause and carry the banner to the front lines. Beyond that, all of their collective efforts have to be focused on the crucial, never-ending process of organizational learning.

Chapter Six discussed organizational learning from the perspective of scanning the changing environment. In that context I talked primarily about the collection of information, or cognitive learning. That process, once begun, should become a regular practice. Organizations that constantly examine the outside world have the best chance of recognizing and anticipating change early enough to avoid the trauma of radical change in crisis situations.

At the same time, truly effective organizations also learn how to benefit from their own experience. Let's turn to Xerox one last time for a couple of examples.

In the late 1980s, Paul Allaire became intrigued by Xerox's continuing inability to turn technological breakthroughs into successful products. It kept happening over and over again—with the mouse, the bit-mapped screen, the graphic user interface—the list went on and on. So my colleagues and I set up a workshop and created teams of high-potential people with a variety of backgrounds to look at three products from start to finish: The Star workstation; the Interpress 2.1 page description language (which a company formed by Xerox alumni later used as the basis for their successful Adobe Postscript); and the 4045 printer, a technologically advanced product that failed in the marketplace.

Some technical people worked with the teams, helping them review and dissect the history of each product from original conception through its performance in the marketplace. When the process was over, the teams found that even though the three projects were introduced over the span of a full decade, they all suffered from exactly the same failures of marketing and development.

If the failures had occurred only with the Star workstation, that would have been unfortunate. For them to have happened with both Star and Interpress 2.1 was lamentable and upsetting. For the workstation, the software, and the printer all to suffer from the same problems over the course of ten years was tragic and inexcusable. Somehow the company had simply failed to learn from its mistakes—over and over again.

A related experiment looked at six projects currently in progress in various parts of the company. Six graduates were each assigned to observe a different project and act, in effect, as an anthropologist, observing and documenting the process, the relationships, the group dynamics, the decision making. What each of them observed was a closed-loop process of persistent, almost mindless repetition of the same mistakes.

Why does that happen—and happen so frequently? If you think about people's behavior, it's generally motivated by two things: knowledge and beliefs. If your underlying belief is that the right technology will produce the required results and if you believe your knowledge includes the necessary technological information, then you feel you're ready to act—to develop a new product for instance. The product is either successful or it's not; let's say it flops. You interpret those outcomes in the context of your beliefs and knowledge. If you continue to believe in the ultimate triumph of the right technology, then obviously your technology wasn't good enough. You go back and try again and do essentially the same thing, making incremental adjustments to your technology.

What's missing in this cycle is reflection, the process of stepping back and analyzing everything learned during the experiment—even if it means questioning the underlying beliefs (see Figure 14.2). It's entirely possible your product was absolutely fine from a technology standpoint. Maybe it was just too hard for customers to use. Maybe it was incompatible with other related products. Maybe it was priced wrong. Maybe it was marketed poorly. Maybe it did a great job of performing a function that's no longer important—or that people won't perceive as important for several years to come. Maybe, in fact, you were spending your time packing first-rate technology into the wrong product at the wrong time for the wrong market.

Reflection is the capacity to go back and analyze—without blame, without attempting to find fault—the elements that contributed to the success or failure of a product or process. Reflection leads to insight, which enables organizations to question their knowledge and beliefs and avoid repeating the same mistakes. It is that collective learning that provides successful organizations with the intellectual capital that becomes a true and unassailable source of competitive advantage. That's precisely how Chemical Bank

Figure 14.2. The Organizational Learning Process.

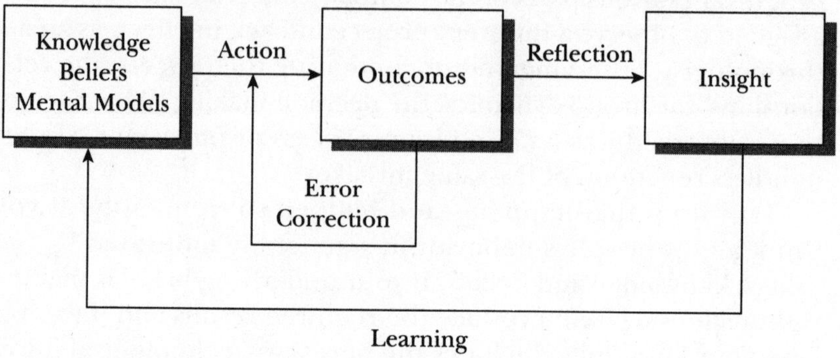

Learning

came to view its successive mergers with other banks; Chemical's management consciously studied what worked and what hadn't as it went about building mergers as a core competency and a source of competitive advantage in a rapidly consolidating industry.

I often cite two quotations to illustrate the concept of collective learning. The first is from Walter Wriston, who used to tell people, "Good judgment is the product of experience. Experience is the product of bad judgment." It's a succinct way of summarizing the essence of the learning cycle—learning from mistakes.

The other is a somewhat cocky advertising slogan from the past: "We must be doing something right." Remember who used it? National Airlines, which no longer exists. That kind of arrogance—often closely related to the Success Syndrome—and the tendency to make the same mistakes over and over often account for an organization's inability to become or remain a successful innovator. Instead, the successful innovators are those who create explicit ways to reflect upon both their successes and failures, to gain insight from them, and then to disseminate that insightful learning throughout the organization.

Following our two research projects at Xerox, for example, Paul Allaire said, basically, we can't keep doing this. Organizational learning became one of the company's new dimensions for change, and Allaire launched the Presidential Reviews, a formal process through which the company could experiment, reflect, gain insight, and use that new learning to move ahead.

This is how the reviews worked. Four to six times each year, a particular product or process was chosen for review. It might be a printer or copier that was already out in the marketplace. It might be a success story or it might not. The company put together a team that would spend months studying the history of the product—how it was developed, how it got to market—and investigate the root causes that would explain not only what happened but why.

Then a day was set aside for the research team to lead a seminar involving the Xerox senior team and perhaps seventy other people from around the company—managers from marketing and development, the chief engineers on other projects, and managers involved in related work. Allaire would start the meeting by explaining its purpose: "My goal is not to find fault, fix blame, or even fix this product," he would say. "It's to influence you who are out developing products right now."

The sessions focused on identifying specific reasons for failure or success. The goal was collective reflection, a search for answers that went far beyond "we must be doing something right." Organizations often attribute both success and failure to the environment, or they personalize them—as in, "He's a really good guy, and he made it happen." The only learning to come from that is to "be a good guy"—not a particularly helpful insight if your goal is to replicate the good guy's success throughout the organization. The Presidential Reviews, in contrast, identified fundamental causes for success or failure, producing what became an often-heard phrase, "lessons learned." After participating in these seminars, managers would go back to their operations and share these lessons learned, thereby building upon Xerox's store of collective knowledge.

Interestingly, the seminars worked equally well for analyzing processes. The company was able to use them to examine organizational changes involving customer satisfaction, empowerment, and reorganization.

Ideally, you don't need Presidential Reviews to formalize the process of reflection, although they were a useful tool for getting the process started. Japanese companies in particular are constantly reexamining their efforts and looking for ways to learn from experience. The Xerox review process, in fact, was borrowed from its Japanese operation, Fuji Xerox, which had been doing something along those same lines for years.

Final Principles

One final bit of learning is in order.

If you reflect upon the various examples of organizational change discussed in this book, it should become clear that despite differences in companies, personalities, and specific circumstances, some basic themes apply to just about every successful change situation. Now I'd like to pull them all together and offer them as a set of underlying principles for planning and implementing organizational change (see Figure 14.3).

1. Ensure Appropriate Involvement

If one thing is certain about organizational change, it is this: it cannot succeed if top leadership refuses to take the time to actively involve the key people who will bear the responsibility for making the change not only happen but succeed. And yet failing to do this is the most common mistake organizations make. Why?

- Top executives often believe that they can search objectively and find "the right answer" on their own. They fail to realize that to the extent there is one right answer, their chances of

Figure 14.3. Core Principles of Integrated Change.

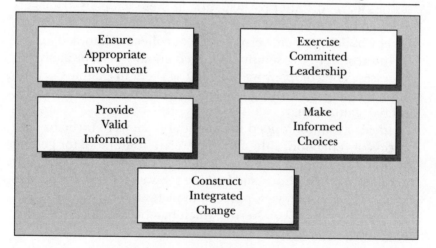

finding it are greatly enhanced by having knowledgeable, experienced people help them with the search. Even more important, the right answer is of little use if the essential people don't understand it, don't feel committed to it, don't feel they personally own it.

- Top leaders often lack an appreciation of how long it takes for true understanding to evolve. Too often people who have undergone a lengthy process of exploration before arriving at an important conclusion forget how long it took them and assume everyone else will understand the conclusion as soon as it's explained to them.

- Top leaders often have an unfounded belief in rationalism. They put what to them is compelling information in front of people and expect those people to passively accept it. In doing this they ignore the deep-seated emotions that are inevitably tied up in decisions about the future course of the organization, and they overlook our basic human need to feel we've had some influence over decisions affecting our lives and careers.

There's no doubt that leaders who are certain they've found the right answer find it frustrating to have to sit and listen to their visions being criticized, questioned, and debated. They have to remember that the payoff, likely to come only years later, will be in having the people who were involved in the original decisions use their shared understanding of the guiding vision behind the change to keep it alive and on course.

2. Exercise Committed Leadership

Leadership is not a chore to be delegated. There is absolutely no substitute for leadership that feels passionately about change and is personally involved in it in an active, aggressive, and energizing way that inspires and excites the entire organization. The best leaders are those who understand the need to articulate a vision and goals that appeal on an emotional level to the basic values and highest aspirations of their people, who deeply believe in the benefits of getting people fully engaged, and who then motivate people to go out and act.

3. Provide Valid Information

Everyone involved in making key decisions about change must have the full range of information that will enable him or her to make the appropriate decisions at each step in the process. That often means casting a wider net for information than most organizations generally feel is necessary. It means looking beyond the normal and obvious information sources, both outside the organization and within. It means validating information, not just accepting what's provided at face value. Because there's generally so little incentive to share bad news with top leaders, everything has to be questioned and confirmed.

The principle of valid information works both ways—it means not only collecting enough useful information but also disseminating that information thoroughly and often in unusual ways. There are times during change when senior management wants to withhold information and times when it wants to make it public. My advice is this: when in doubt, tell the truth. People aren't dumb. They can figure out what's happening. Management buys trust and credibility by sharing information *before* it becomes available from other sources—which it probably will, sooner or later. And the anxiety and uncertainty created by the dissemination of that information is probably far worse than the fear and confusion emanating from the rumors and gossip that are sure to be flying around the hallways and lunchrooms.

4. Make Informed Choices

The best decisions emerge from full and open consideration of the widest possible range of plausible alternatives. It's human nature to seize upon the first available solution that meets our minimal requirements—the concept economist Herbert Simon (1945) describes as *satisficing*. Unfortunately, at that point the search for solutions comes to an abrupt halt, despite the fact that a little searching might turn up much better alternatives. (This is why stores feel secure in advertising that they'll pay the difference if you can find a product for less than you paid at their store; they know that we have an acceptable price in mind, and if their store comes reasonably close to it, our search for a bargain is over.)

Moreover, for all the reasons I've discussed—including Chris Argyris's undiscussables (1990) and Dennis Perkins's moose on the table (1988)—executives tend to shy away from rigorous and probing debate of alternatives. Yet in change situations, organizations just can't afford that implicit conspiracy of silence—they can't allow themselves to satisfice. Whether it's strategy, structure, staffing, or any other aspect of change, it's essential that top managment insist upon and then actively engage in free, open, and informed debate of a wide range of alternatives.

5. Construct Integrated Change

Modern organizations are so resistant to change for the simple reason that they were designed specifically to maintain stability. Asking them to change is kind of like taking draft horses that were bred, one generation after another, to pull heavy loads and then demanding to know why they can't win the Kentucky Derby. The organizational design most of us have grown up with is just as much a product of natural selection—and it was bred to resist change.

Think of it this way. In earlier times organizations were essentially tribes in which the cohesiveness of the group rested upon personal or moral authority. Religious groups controlled adherents through a shared belief in a higher being or moral code; military and commercial organizations centered around loyalty to a leader. That was largely true through the end of the nineteenth century, when Max Weber (1947) developed the concept of an organization based on rules; it divorced ownership from management, employed a set of rules that applied to everyone, and created formal roles and operating procedures. Weber called the concept bureaucracy, and Bismarck was his most avid student, applying the concept first to the German civil service and then to the military. It was tested and came of age on the battlegrounds of World War I, when the sprawling feudal Russian army was outmaneuvered and outfought by a much smaller bureaucratic German army that operated with standard procedures, rules, promotion requirements, and lines of communication—all the accouterments of a modern organization.

Why the history lesson? Because so many organizations undergoing change today are the direct descendants of Weber and

Bismarck. They represent decades of experience and practice in developing complex organisms designed specifically to promote their own stability and buffer themselves from changes in the outside world. Consequently, the leaders of organizational change are challenging immense forces arrayed in defense of the status quo. From that perspective there's no reason to think any one point of attack will bring about radical change.

Challenging those multiple forces of tradition is what integrated change is all about. It is based on the principle that if you hope to change complex human organizations, you have to consider every aspect of the enterprise, every possible leverage point. It demands a disciplined assessment of every component of the congruence model—strategy, structure, people, processes, and operating environment—and an appreciation that isolated change anywhere in the system will falter and eventually fail if unsupported by a full arsenal of related initiatives.

There is no place in the change process for fragmented actions and one-off decisions. Ignore the web of relationships that make up the organization, and you can fail in a hundred ways. You can fail like Dynacorp (the Chapter Two case study), which tried to refocus its strategy and structure but ignored the importance of its operating environment. You can fail like so many companies that hope a weekend in the wilderness doing trust and problem-solving exercises will build teamwork, only to see the bonding dissolve because the formal structures and reward systems thwart the notion of teamwork at every turn.

There's no doubt about it: integrated change is hard, demanding work that requires energy, courage, vision, and commitment. There are always setbacks and moments of doubt. Every single company discussed in this book, even those that have engineered the most successful changes, ran into problems along the way. They made false starts and wrong turns, went through periods when the momentum seemed to vanish and change was dead in the water.

In each case, change progressed, however, because its creators and defenders returned to these five underlying principles. I've intentionally avoided presenting them as some kind of a simplified five-step how-to guide to change. Human organizations are too complex, too varied, and too much the creatures of their unique characteristics to lend themselves to mass-produced, off-the-shelf solutions. Instead, I offer these principles as a conceptual road map. They won't provide you with all the right answers or a neat set of specific solutions; but in moments of doubt, when you reach the most perplexing forks in the road, they will help point you in the right direction. Time and time again, they have proved their worth as the guiding principles of the champions of change.

References

Argyris, C. *Overcoming Organizational Defenses*. Needham Heights, Mass.: Allyn & Bacon, 1990.

Beckhard, R. *Organizational Development: Strategies and Models*. Reading, Mass.: Addison Wesley Longman, 1969.

Beckhard, R., and Harris, R. *Organizational Transitions: Managing Complex Change*. Reading, Mass.: Addison Wesley Longman, 1977.

Delta Consulting Group. *Dynacorp*. (Case study). New York: Delta Consulting Group, 1980.

French, J.R.P., and Raven, B. H. "The Base of Social Power." In D. Cartwright (ed.), *Studies in Social Power*. Ann Arbor: University of Michigan, 1959.

Galbraith, J. R. *Organization Design*. Reading, Mass.: Addison Wesley Longman, 1977.

Gerstein, M., and Reisman, H. "Strategic Selection: Matching Executives to Business Conditions." *Sloan Management Review*, 1983, *24*(2), 33–49.

Hambrick, D. C., and Fukutomi, G. D. "The Seasons of a CEO's Tenure." *Academy of Management Review*, 1991, *16*, 719–742.

Howard, R. "The CEO as Organizational Architect: An Interview with Xerox's Paul Allaire." *Harvard Business Review*, 1992, *70*(5), 106–121.

Hutton, C. "America's Most Admired Corporations. *Fortune*, Jan. 6, 1986, p. 16.

Katz, D., and Kahn, R. *The Social Psychology of Organizations*. New York: Wiley, 1966.

Kearns, D. T., and Nadler, D. A. *Prophets in the Dark: How Xerox Reinvented Itself and Drove Back the Japanese*. New York: Harper Business, 1992.

Keller, M. *Rude Awakenings*. New York: Morrow, 1989.

Kirkpatrick, D. "AT&T Has the Plan." *Fortune*, Oct. 16, 1995, pp. 84–89.

Kolb, D. A. *Experiential Learning: Experience as the Source of Learning and Development*. Upper Saddle River, N.J.: Prentice Hall, 1984.

Koretz, G. "An Update on Downsizing . . . : Job-Cutters Turn into Job Creators." *Business Week*, Nov. 25, 1996, p. 3.

Kotter, J. P. *A Force for Change: How Leadership Differs from Management.* New York: Free Press, 1990.

Kotter, J. P., and Heskett, J. L. *Corporate Culture and Performance.* New York: Free Press, 1992.

Lawrence, D. M. "Market Leading Performance and Social Purpose: The Future for Kaiser Permanente Health Plans and Hospitals." Paper presented at the Senior Leadership and Corporate Transformation Conference, Harriman, N.Y., Apr. 1996.

Lorsch, J. W., and Sheldon, A. "The Individual in the Organization: A Systems View." In J. W. Lorsch and P. R. Lawrence (eds.), *Managing Group and Intergroup Relations.* Homewood, Ill.: Business One Irwin, 1972.

Miller, G. A. "The Magical Number Seven, Plus or Minus Two: Some Limits of Our Capacity for Processing Information." *Psychological Review,* 1956, *63,* 81–97.

Mintzberg, H. *The Rise and Fall of Strategic Planning.* New York: Free Press, 1994.

Nadler, D. A., and Gerstein, M. "Designing High Performance Work Systems." In D. A. Nadler, M. C. Gerstein, Robert B. Shaw, and Associates, *Organizational Architecture: Designs for Changing Organizations.* San Francisco: Jossey-Bass, 1992.

Nadler, D. A., and Heilpern, J. "The CEO in the Context of Discontinuous Change." In D. C. Hambrick, M. L. Tushman, and D. A. Nadler (eds.), *Navigating Change: CEOs, Top Management Teams, and Boards in Turbulent Times.* Boston: Harvard Business School Press, 1997.

Nadler, D. A., and Tushman, M. L., *Competing by Design.* New York: Oxford University Press, 1997.

Nadler, D. A., Shaw, R. B., Walton, A. E., and Associates. *Discontinuous Change: Leading Organizational Transformation.* San Francisco: Jossey-Bass, 1994.

Perkins, D.N.T. *Ghosts in the Executive Suite: Every Business Is a Family Business.* Branford, Conn.: Syncretics Group, 1988.

Porter, M. E. *Competitive Advantage: Creating and Sustaining Superior Performance.* New York: Free Press, 1985.

Schein, E. H. *Organizational Culture and Leadership.* San Francisco: Jossey-Bass, 1985.

Seiler, J. A. *Systems Analysis in Organizational Behavior.* Homewood, Ill.: Business One Irwin, 1967.

Sellers, P. "What Exactly Is Charisma?" *Fortune,* Jan. 15, 1996.

Shaw, R. B., and Nadler, D. A. "Capacity to Act." *Human Resource Planning,* 1991, *14,* 289–300.

Simon, H. *Administrative Behavior.* New York: Free Press, 1945.

Teece, D. J. "Profiting from Technological Innovation." In D. Teece (ed.), *Competitive Challenge.* New York: HarperCollins, 1987.

Tushman, M. L., Anderson, P. C., and O'Reilly, C. "Technology Cycles, Innovation Streams, and Ambidextrous Organizations: Organization Renewal Through Innovation Streams and Strategic Change." In M. L. Tushman and P. C. Anderson (eds.), *Managing Strategic Innovation and Change.* New York: Oxford University Press, 1996.

Weber, M. *The Theory of Social and Economic Organization.* New York: Free Press, 1947.

Wolfe, T. *The Right Stuff.* New York: Farrar, Straus & Giroux, 1983.

Index

A

Ackerman, R., 78, 142, 214, 222, 266–267, 281, 283
Ackoff, R., 37
Aesthetics, in strategic design, 189
Akers, J., 73, 272
Alcoa, 144
Aligning, by managers, 295
Allaire, P., 63–64, 66, 152, 172, 173–174, 187–192, 194, 198, 232, 240–242, 257, 266–267, 270–271, 273–274, 275, 281, 286, 300, 302–303
Allen, R., 8–9, 51, 52, 77, 142, 223, 229–230, 245, 248, 254, 266, 286
Allied Signal, 68–69
American Express, 68–69, 270
American Management Association, 124
Anderson, P. C., 262
Anxiety, in transition state, 88–90, 99–105
Apple Computer: and change realities, 10, 11; and environment, 40; and strategic choice, 74, 156, 168
Architecture. See Strategic design
Argyris, C., 159, 307
Arrogance, in Success Syndrome, 71
Artifacts, of culture, 203–205
Assessment: for consolidation, 251–252; of culture gaps, 222; of senior team, 171–172; in strategic choice, 164–165
AT&T: and change realities, 1, 5, 8–9; and consolidation, 254; culture at, 206, 211, 223, 225; dis-

continuous change at, 51, 52, 67, 77; and leadership, 271, 285–286; and recognition stage, 117, 118–119, 123; resources of, 29; shared direction at, 141, 142; strategic choice at, 154–155, 158; strategic design at, 179, 183–184; strategic selection at, 229–230, 245, 246–247, 248; sustaining change at, 261, 262, 263–264; transition state at, 90

B

Banc One, 37
Bank of America, 207
Bankers Trust, 56
Beckhard, R., 86, 94, 292
Beliefs. See Values
Bell Laboratories, 1, 155, 211, 217–218
Bell System, 8, 51, 89, 202
Benchmarking: of current state, 100; for diagnosis, 120; for strategic design, 188
Betrayal, and mythic leaders, 279
Bismarck, O. von, 307
Blinder, S., 99
Bliss, D., 20
BMW, 167–168, 170, 171
Board of directors, and shared direction, 149–150
Boeing, 167, 171
Boston Chicken, 246
Braddock, R., 57
British Airways, 210
Bristol-Myers Squibb, 5

Brocksmith, J., 135
Brzezinski, Z., 117
Buehler, W., 242
Bureaucracy: machine, 179–180; tradition of, 307–308
Bush, G., 10–11, 173, 210
Business Roundtable, 114

C

Candidates, rating, 238–239, 243, 246
Canon, 18
Capacity to act, in Success Syndrome, 72
Castro, F., 274–275
Celebration, by leaders, 278, 285
Change: adapting, 53, 56; anticipatory, 52, 59; background on, 1–3, 44–45; baking in, 255–260; certainty of, 291; champions of, 5–8; characteristics of, 62; charting, 45–49; and competitive advantage, 16–19; consolidation of, 250–260; cycle of, 75–82; demand for, 8–9, 14–16; dimensions of, 44–62; dynamics of, 43, 44–62; failures of, 10; human dimension of, 4, 81; imperative for, 75–77, 109–130; implementing, 151–248; incremental or continuous, 49–50, 59; integrated, 12–14, 20, 138–143, 307–308; intensity and complexity of, 59–61; learning to lead, 289–309; magnitude of, 65; motivation for, 99–105; multiple and concurrent, 66; and organizational model, 21–43; overhauling, 54, 58; political dynamics of, 92–99; principles of, 304–309; process of, 299; radical or discontinuous, 49–52, 59, 63–82; reactive, 52–53, 59; readiness for, 100; realities of, 1–20; redirecting, 54, 56–58; resistance to, overcoming, 83–108; responses to, 53–58, 94; S-curve of, 46–47, 68; scope of, 50–52; success of, 10–12; succession planning for, 266–267; sustaining, 260–267; timing of, 48–49, 52–53; in transition state, 85–108; truth about, 3–5; tuning, 53, 55–56; types of, 49–53; zones of, 59–61
Chase Manhattan, 5, 84, 99, 207
Chemical Bank: adapting change at, 56; and culture, 207; and industry analysts, 116; and leadership, 277; and learning, 301–302; and transition state, 99, 107
Chief executive officers (CEOs): alternatives for, 174, 266; centrality of, 6–8; as champions of change, 5–8; convergence stage for, 265; dysfunctional stage for, 265–266; and environmental scans, 113–115; as intuitive, 125; leadership by, 268–288; learning principles for, 289–309; life cycle of, 264–266; as obstacle to sustaining change, 263–267; and organizational history, 271–272; ouster of, 68–69; and realities of change, 1–20; and recognition of change imperative, 76–77; senior team for, 132–137; and shared direction, 78–79; and succession planning, 266–267
Choice. *See* Strategic choice
Chrysler: and change realities, 19; and discontinuous change, 73; and leadership, 270; overhauling change at, 58; and strategic choice, 156, 167, 170
Citibank: and change realities, 5; and change responses, 55–58, 66; leadership of, 270, 277, 282, 287; strategic recognition at, 118; strategic selection at, 246, 247; transition state at, 107
Citicorp, 166, 219
Clinton, W. J., 68
Coalition building, for shared direction, 146–150

Codification, in Success Syndrome, 69
Columbia University, 27, 45, 264
Communication: in consolidation, 253–254, 255–256, 260; and culture change, 224; of integrated change agenda, 143–146, 149; by managers, 292, 294, 296; with senior team, 285; in transition state, 105–106
Compaq, 68–69
Competitive advantage: bases of, 156, 184; and change, 16–19
Competitive basis: scanning, 112; and strategy, 30
Complacence, in Success Syndrome, 71
Complexity, in Success Syndrome, 71
Conference Board, 114
Congruence model: aspects of, 26–43; components of, 28–32; and culture, 209; history of, 27–28; horizontal and vertical axes of, 41–43; and organizational fit, 26, 37–43; principles of, 38–42; at recognition stage, 75–77, 122–123, 129; and transition state, 91, 106
Consensus building: and participation, 102; and shared direction, 137
Conservatism, in Success Syndrome, 71
Consolidation: aspects of, 250–260; and baking in change, 255–260; in change cycle, 80; concept of, 249–250
Consultants: information from, 117; at recognition stage, 122, 128–130; and strategic design, 177. See also Delta Consulting Group
Continental Bank, 10, 73
Control, in transition state, 90–92, 105–107
Control Data Corporation, 10

Corning Clinical Laboratories, 98
Corning Inc.: and change realities, 5, 19; culture at, 210, 214–215, 221–222, 224, 225, 226; and leadership, 273–274, 276, 280, 281, 282, 283–284, 285–286; outside experts at, 117; and shared direction, 78, 133, 137, 139–140, 141, 142, 143, 144, 146, 148; strategic design at, 175, 176; strategic selection at, 242; sustaining change at, 262, 266–267; transition state at, 83–84, 98, 103–104
Costs: increased, 72; as symptom, 123
Counterdependence, and mythic leaders, 279
Covance, 175
Cross-unit groups, for linking, 186
Culture. See Operating environment
Cummins Engine Company, 9, 271
Customer focus: and complaint desk, 101; decreased, 71–72; for grouping, 183–184; scanning for, 113, 114–115; and strategic choice, 156

D

Data collection: for consolidation, 251–252; for environmental scan, 111–113; methods of, 121–122; and organizational model, 25–26
Data interpretation, for diagnosis, 122–124
Death spiral, in Success Syndrome, 73–74
Decision making: informed, 306–307; one-off, 159–160; in strategic selection, 238–240, 243–245
Dell, 156
Delta Consulting Group: and change cycle, 76; and change realities, 3, 5; and charting change, 46; and culture change, 209, 214, 220; and leadership, 268; and

organizational model, 22, 24; and recognition stage, 109, 124, 128–130

Design. *See* Strategic design

Destabilizing event, and discontinuous change, 68

Diagnosis: organizational, 119–124; in strategic design, 189

Digital Equipment Company (DEC), 68–69, 163, 167, 246

Dilbert, 252

Direction. *See* Shared direction

Disaster scenario, for current state, 100–101

Disconfirmation, of current state, 99–100

Discontinuous change: aspects of, 63–82; background on, 63–64; dimensions of, 49–52, 59; elements of, 64–67; stages of, 74–82; and Success Syndrome, 67–74, 82

Dissatisfaction, and transition state, 99–101

Dissent, and mythic leaders, 279

Dominant response, in Success Syndrome, 72–73

Dow Jones and Company, 33, 274

Dynacorp case study, 22–26, 40, 43, 308

E

Eastern Airlines, 73

Eastman Kodak, 10, 68–69, 270

Eaton, B., 270

Elevator speech, 294

Eli Lilly and Company: and change realities, 2, 4, 10; culture at, 205, 212; discontinuous change at, 65–66, 68–69, 71; and leadership, 271, 281; and learning, 298; shared direction at, 136; strategic choice at, 154; strategic selection at, 247; transition state at, 85–86, 101

Employees: and culture, 202, 220, 226; frontline, 120–121; as organizational component, 12, 35; and output, 32; recently hired, 116–117, 247; for shared direction, 148–149; strategic selection of, 229–248; ventilating, 96

Empowerment, visible, 283

Enabling, by mythic leaders, 278

Energizing, by mythic leaders, 277–278

Engaging, by managers, 296

Environment: for business, 14–16; and discontinuous change, 67–68, 82; as input, 28–29; and strategy, 40. *See also* Operating environment

Environmental Protection Agency, 210

Environmental scans: aspects of, 110–119; data collection for, 111–113; executive role in, 113–115; information sources for, 115–118; strategic, 118–119

Envisioning, by mythic leaders, 276–277

Expectations: and managers, 295; and mythic leaders, 279

Extroversion, of mythic leaders, 273–275

F

Feedback: for culture change, 223, 225; in transition state, 107

Financial analysts: information from, 115–116; and shared direction, 149

Fischer, G., 270

Fit: concept of, 37–39; and congruence model, 26, 37–43; and discontinuous change, 65; in strategic selection, 242–243

Ford Motor Company: consolidation at, 252–253; culture at, 203, 225; and environment, 29; and overhauling change, 58; and shared direction, 78, 139; strategic design at, 182–183

Forum Corporation, 287
France, competition from, 11, 15, 16
Freeman, K., 98, 224
French, J.R.P., 272
Fukutomi, G. D., 264–265
Funeral, in transition state, 104–105

G

Galbraith, J. R., 28, 185, 188
Gateway, 156
General Electric (GE): consolidation at, 257; culture at, 210, 224; and discontinuous change, 67; and history, 30; and strategic selection, 246
General Foods, 57
General Motors (GM): and change realities, 10; and leadership, 270, 272; and shared direction, 136, 139; and strategic design, 177; and strategic selection, 247; and Success Syndrome, 68–69
Germany: bureaucracy in, 307; competition from, 11, 15
Gerstein, M., 236, 237, 241
Gerstner, L., 65, 105, 135–136, 210–211, 270
Glavin, B., 170
Globalization, in business environment, 15
Golden thread, 295
Goodrich, B. F., 10
Greystone, C., 23–24, 25
Grouping, and strategic design, 181–185, 190
GTE, 98
Guided discovery: and culture change, 224; for managers, 294; at recognition stage, 126–127, 129

H

Haloid Corporation, 29
Hambrick, D. C., 264–265
Harley-Davidson, 59
Harris, R., 86

Harte-Hanks, 146
Harvard University, 25, 27, 118
Heilpern, J., 264
Heskett, J. L., 208, 270
Hewlett-Packard, 210
High-concept principles, in shared direction, 139
History, as input, 29–30
Houghton, J., 83–84, 103, 133, 136–137, 139–140, 142, 143, 144, 175, 205, 266–267, 270–271, 276, 280, 281, 282, 284, 285, 286
Howard, R., 64, 232, 240–242
Human resource practices, and consolidation, 256–260
Hutton, C., 69

I

Iacocca, L., 58, 274, 279
IBM: and change realities, 10; culture at, 210–211; and history, 30; and leadership, 270, 272; magnitude of change at, 65; shared direction at, 135–136; and strategic choice, 163, 167; strategic selection at, 246; and Success Syndrome, 68–69, 73; transition state at, 90, 105
Implementation: aspects of, 151–248; in change cycle, 79–80; operating environment in, 197–228; strategic choice in, 151–172; strategic design in, 173–196; strategic selection for, 229–248
Incentives. See Rewards
Industries, evolution of, 45–49
Inertia, managerial, 298
Information: for diagnosis, 120–121; for environmental scans, 115–118; and strategic design, 180, 181, 194–195; valid, 306
Innovation: less, 72; technological, 15, 112. See also Change
Input: collaborative, for strategic choice, 161, 164; in congruence model, 28–30

Instability, in transition state, 86–87

Insularity, in Success Syndrome, 71

Integrated change agenda: characteristics of, 138–140; communication of, 143–146, 149; constructing, 307–308; critical themes in, 140–143; and realities, 12–14, 20

Integrator roles, for linking, 186

Intellectual capital, for competitive advantage, 17–18

Internal data, for diagnosis, 120

Internal focus, in Success Syndrome, 69, 71

Isolation, in transition state, 95

J

Japan: competition from, 11, 15, 16, 29, 44–45, 58, 73, 77, 100, 168; culture of, 198; learning in, 303; and product differentiation, 156; soldiers of, 291

Jobs, rating, 237–238, 243

Johnson & Johnson, 224

Jordan, M. H., 136

K

Kahn, R., 27–28

Kaiser Foundation Health Plan and Hospitals (Kaiser Permanente): and change realities, 4; consolidation at, 255; culture of, 199–200, 223; intellectual capital of, 17; internal focus at, 69, 71; and leadership, 271; reactive change at, 53; shared direction at, 137, 142, 148, 150; sustaining change at, 263; transition state at, 88, 92, 94, 100

Kaizen, and incremental change, 50

Katz, D., 27–28

Kearns, D. T., 44–45, 63, 64, 66, 77, 86, 115, 133, 152, 163–164, 165, 170–172, 173, 187, 194, 264, 266–267, 270, 273–274, 277, 279, 281

Keller, M., 177

Kennedy, J. F., 273

Kirkpatrick, D., 247

Knight-Ridder, 197–198

Knowledge and skills: for managers, 297–298; for work, 33

Kodak, 10, 68–69, 270

Kolb, D. A., 299

Koretz, G., 124

Kotter, J. P., 118, 208, 270

KPMG Peat Marwick: and change realities, 2–3; consolidation at, 256, 259; culture of, 200–202, 219–220; discontinuous change at, 51, 65; shared direction at, 135, 147; sustaining change at, 261; transition state at, 87, 88, 101

L

Language: and culture, 204, 206, 211; in transition state, 97–98

Lawler, E., 188

Lawrence, D. M., 4, 53, 69, 71, 92, 94, 96, 99, 100, 121, 137, 150, 199–200, 223, 227, 255, 257, 258, 263, 271

Leadership: aspects of, 268–288; background on, 268–272; committed, 305; for culture change, 212, 217–218, 223; developing, 285–288; for discontinuous change, 67; extended, 282–288; mythic, 270, 272–280; operational, 280–281; from outside, 270–271; and participation, 126; in transition state, 96–97

Learning: aspects of, 289–309; background on, 289–290; cycle for, 299, 302; disabled, 71; importance of, 297–299; for managerial roles, 290–299; organizational, 299–303

Leavitt, H., 28

Lever Brothers, 99, 149

Leverage points, in transition state, 106

Levien, R., 164
Levinson, H., 25
Liaison roles, for linking, 185
Lilly. *See* Eli Lilly and Company
Linking, and strategic design, 185–186, 190–194
Lipp, R., 107, 277–278
Lockheed Martin, 5
Loose, J., 284
Lorsch, J. W., 28
Lucent Technologies: and change realities, 1, 4, 9; culture of, 202–203, 213, 217–218; and discontinuous change, 51, 52, 66–67; and executive visits, 117; and leadership, 271; and organizational model, 21; shared direction at, 142–143, 147–148; and strategic choice, 155

M

Madonna, J., 2–3, 4, 7, 51, 65, 87, 88, 101, 135, 147, 149–150, 200–202, 219, 256, 259, 260, 261, 264
Managers and management: action steps for, 92–108; administrative overload for, 144–146; choices for, 291–292; communication by, 292, 294, 296; competence defined for, 286; and consolidation, 250–260; for culture change, 218–219, 226; disenfranchised, 279–280; emotional ties of, 298; environment for, 290–291; fads of, 13–14; leadership development for, 285–288; learning for, 290–299; modeling by, 292, 295–296; ownership by, 293–294; practices in, 293–297; requirements in, 292–293; transition, 60
Mandl, A., 118, 246–247
Manufacturers Hanover Trust, 99, 207
Market structure: shifts in, 112; and strategy, 30
Martinez, A., 113–114
Marx, B., 158

Massachusetts Institute of Technology (MIT), 28, 57, 86, 203
MasterCard, 136, 247
Matrix structures, for linking, 186
McColough, P., 44
McGinn, R., 66–67, 143, 217–218
McKinsey Consulting, 270
McNealy S., 37–38, 66, 67, 78, 86, 88, 102–103, 105, 109, 111, 203–204, 276
Michigan, economy of, 11
Michigan, University of, 27, 28–29
Microsoft, 17–18, 40, 65, 156, 276
Miller, G. A., 141
Mintzberg, H., 32
Modeling, by managers, 292, 295–296
Moose on the table metaphor, 159
Morris, K., 212, 214
Motivation, for change, 99–105
Motorola, 210, 270
Mountain Bell, 89–90, 104
Mythic leadership: attributes of, 272–280; concept of, 270; enabling and energizing by, 277–278; envisioning by, 276–277; extroversion of, 273–275; sources of power for, 272–273; traps of, 278–280

N

Nadler, D. A., 44–45, 72, 84, 133, 137, 140, 149, 174, 236, 245, 248, 264, 269
National Airlines, 302
NCR, 51, 155
New York City: banking changes in, 55–58; informal organization of, 36
Nordstrom, 33, 35

O

Offerings, and strategy, 30
O'Neill, P., 144
Operating environment: aligned with strategy, 197–228; background

on, 197–199; barriers to changing, 199–203; changing, 210–211, 213–228; collaborative definition of, 221–222; content of change for, 213–216; context of, 209, 219–220; as durable, 210; elements of, 203–213; and enterprise culture, 211–212; implications of, 208–212; interventions for, 220–226; layers of, 203–207; leadership for, 212, 217–218, 223; leverage points in, 216–220; management for, 218–219, 226; as organizational component, 12, 36; and performance, 208–209; sources of, 207–208; and strategic design, 174–175, 177–178; and strategic recognition, 118; tactical choices for, 227–228

O'Reilly, C., 262

Organizations: architecture of, 18–19, 74, 173–196; background on, 21–22; capabilities of, 18; case study of, 22–26; components of, 12–13, 21–43; congruence model of, 26–43; diagnosing, 119–124; dominant response by, 72–73; formal, 12, 35, 40, 173–196; informal, 12, 35–37, 197–228; issues for, 16; learning by, 299–303; multiple concepts held by, 141–142; operating, 32–37; underlying assumptions of, 206

Output: in congruence model, 32; grouping by, 183

Ownership, by managers, 293–294

P

Pacific Rim, competition from, 15

Pan American Airways, 10

Parcells, B., 117

Participation: appropriate, 127, 129, 304–305; in culture change, 224–225; at recognition stage, 124–128; in strategic choice, 157; in strategic design, 186–187, 191–193; in transition state, 95, 101–103

Path dependence, and consolidation, 253

Paul Stuart, 113, 156

Pauley, M., 23

Pearlstine, N., 274–275

PepsiCo: leadership at, 269; shared direction at, 133, 141, 148; strategic design at, 178–179; and strategic selection, 246

Performance: and culture, 208–209; and strategy, 30

Perkins, D.N.T., 159, 307

Personnel. See Strategic selection

Persuasion, in transition state, 95

Planning: scenario, 117–118; succession, 266–267

Pockell, D., 148

Porter, M. E., 156, 184

Power: key groups for, 94–96; sources of, for leaders, 272–273; in transition state, 87–88, 92–99

Primerica, 75

Product differentiation, and strategic choice, 156, 168

Production costs, and strategic choice, 156

Public policy: in business environment, 15–16; scanning, 112

Punctuated equilibrium theory, and change, 46–49

Q

Quaker Oats, 113

Quest Diagnostics, 98, 117, 175, 176, 224

R

Raven, B. H., 272

RCA, 30

Recognizing the change imperative: aspects of, 109–130; background on, 109–110; diagnosis for, 119–124; in discontinuous change, 74, 75–77; environmental scan for, 110–119; example of process for, 128–130; and participation, 124–128; strategic, 118–119

Reebok, 136, 247

Reed, J., 57, 166, 219

Reengineering: failure of, 14, 42; and strategic design, 195–196

Refinement, in consolidation, 252–255

Reflection, in learning, 301–303

Reisman, H., 236, 237, 241

Resources, as input, 29

Rewards: in consolidation, 252, 255, 256; and culture change, 226; by managers, 292–293, 297; for team performance, 283–284; in transition state, 95, 103–104; for work, 33

RJR Nabisco, 270

Rocky Mountain Telephone and Telegraph Company, 104

Roman Catholic Church, 27

Russia, organization of, 307

Russo, P., 213, 261, 263–264

S

Sailboat analogy, 53–54

SAS, 210

Satisficing, 306

Saudia Arabia, and customer units, 184

Scenario planning, information from, 117–118

Schacht, H. B., 1, 4, 9, 20, 21, 66–67, 77, 95, 96, 119, 142–143, 147–148, 202–203, 217–218, 254, 271, 278

Schein, E. H., 203, 206

Sea-Land, 247

Sears, 113–114, 168, 170

Seiler, J. A., 28

Selection. See Strategic selection

Sellers, P., 275

Senior team: assessing, 171–172; broadening, 284–285; and consolidation, 250–251, 253, 257–260; developing, 285–288; and leadership, 268–269, 282–288; leveraging, 283–284; and shared direction, 132–137, 147–148; and strategic choice input, 161, 164–171

Shared direction: aspects of developing, 131–150; background on, 131–132; coalition building for, 146–150; developing, in change cycle, 78–79; and integrated change agenda, 138–146; senior team for, 132–137, 147–148

Shaw, R. B., 72, 84, 133, 137, 140, 149, 245, 248, 269

Sheldon, A., 28

Shell Oil, 117–118

Shipley, W., 84, 99, 207

Simon, H., 306

Socialization, for managers, 287

Southern California, University of, 188

Speed, loss of, 72

Spencer, W., 56–58

Stability, in transition state, 98–99

Staffing. See Strategic selection

Stakeholders: and culture change, 222–223; and shared direction, 147

Stanford University, 28

Stemple, R., 272

Stern, B., 68

Strategic choice: aspects of, 151–172; assessment in, 164–165; assumptions in, 158–159, 161, 163, 164; background on, 151–153; case study of, 163–172; debating alternatives in, 168–172; flawed process for, 157–160; and flexibility, 156–157; integrated alternatives in, 163, 166–168; issues in, 155–156; process for, 160–163; and worldview, 164–166

Strategic design: aspects of, 173–196; background on,

174–178; case study of, 186–194; criteria for, 187–189; elements of, 180–186; and grouping, 181–185, 190; impartiality in, 192–193; and information processing, 180, 181, 194–195; integration of, 177–178; and linking, 185–186, 190–194; and operational design, 190–194; process of, 178–180; and reengineering, 195–196; risks of, 176–177; and systems, 194–195

Strategic selection: analytical view of, 230, 231; aspects of, 229–248; background on, 229–232; case study of, 240–244; criteria and profiles for, 233–235, 241–242, 245; defined, 232; emotional view of, 230–231, 243; factors in, 230–231; fit in, 242–243; from outside, 245–248, 270–271; for perspective shifts, 246–247; political view of, 231; process of, 232–235; purpose of, 235; rating and analyzing in, 236–240; shake-up factor in, 247

Strategy: aligned with culture, 197–228; business and corporate types of, 154–155; in congruence model, 30–32; defined, 153–154; and discontinuous change, 65–66, 74; elements of, 153–157; and fit, 40–42; in strategic design, 188; and work, 33, 35

Stress, in transition state, 87, 90

Structure: and culture change, 225–226; and strategic design, 180, 181

Success Syndrome: and discontinuous change, 67–74, 82; and learning, 302; and sustaining change, 260, 262, 265

Succession planning, 266–267

Sun Microsystems: and change realities, 5; culture of, 203–204, 206, 225, 276; and discontinuous change, 66; and organizational fit, 37–38; and recognition stage, 109, 111; transition state at, 86, 88, 102–103, 105

Support, pockets of, 148

Sustaining change: aspects of, 260–267; in change cycle, 81–82; concept of, 250; obstacles to, 263–267

Symbols, in transition state, 97–98

Systems: and congruence model, 27; and output, 32; and strategic design, 194–195

T

Taurel, S., 281, 298–299

Technological innovation: in business environment, 15; scanning, 112

Teece, D. J., 46

Termination: of CEOs, 68–69; for consolidation, 257–260; of employees, 96; for senior team, 133–137, 147

Thought leaders, and shared direction, 146

3M, 18

Time: for discontinuous change, 67; in transition state, 104–105

Times Mirror Company, 51, 246

Timothy, B., 89, 104

Tobias, R., 2, 4, 71, 85–86, 101, 102, 136, 154, 205, 212, 247, 271, 281

Toyota, 139

Training: for culture change, 225; for managers, 287–288

Transference, and mythic leaders, 279

Transition state: administrative overload in, 144–146; anxiety in, 88–90, 99–105; aspects of, 85–108; background on, 83–86; characteristics of, 86–87; control in, 90–92, 105–107; incomplete, 66; managing, 92–108; paralysis

of, 86–87; power of, 87–88,
92–99; problems in, 87–90; struc-
tures for, 106–107
Travelers Insurance, 74–75
Trotman, A., 78, 182, 252
Tushman, M. L., 27, 45–48, 174, 262

U

Uncertainty: of future, 66–67; in
transition state, 87; for work, 33
Union of Soviet Socialist Republics,
as organizational model, 189
Unions, and shared direction, 149
U.S. Bureau of Labor Statistics, 11
Units, and output, 32

V

Values: and culture, 204–205, 212;
espoused, 205–206; and shared
direction, 139–140
Ventilation. *See* Termination
Vision: and discontinuous change,
65–66; of mythic leaders,
276–277
Visits, information from home and
away, 117
Vojta, G., 118

W

Wal-Mart, 33, 35
Walker, B., 23
Wall Street Journal, 33, 246, 274–275
Walton, A. E., 84, 133, 137, 140, 149,
245, 248, 269
Wang, 246
Watson, T., 30
Weatherup, C., 133, 148, 269
Weber, M., 307
Welch, J., 67, 257, 266
Western Electric, 211

Westinghouse, 68–69, 135–136
Weyerhaeuser, 5
Willes, M., 51
Wolfe, T., 230
Work: as organizational component,
12, 33–35; strategic choice in,
151–172; in strategic design, 188
Workforce, as information source,
121. *See also* Employees
World Economic Forum, 11
Wriston, W., 56–58, 118, 270, 282,
302

X

Xerox Corporation: and change dimensions, 44–45; and change realities, 5, 11, 19; consolidation at,
252, 253, 257; culture at, 207,
210, 211, 217, 224, 225; discontinuous change at, 63–64, 66, 67,
68, 73, 77; and formal organization, 40; history for, 29–30; intellectual capital of, 17; leadership
at, 270, 273–274, 281, 285–286;
and learning, 291–292, 294, 298,
300–301, 302–303; and recognition stage, 112, 115, 117, 118,
127–128; shared direction at,
133, 141, 145, 146, 148, 149;
strategic choice at, 151–153,
156, 163–172; strategic design at,
173–175, 176–177, 178, 182, 184,
186–194; strategic selection at,
232, 240–245, 246; sustaining
change at, 262, 264, 266–267;
transition state at, 86, 90, 94, 100,
101

Z

Zealots, and consolidation, 254–255